Reminiscences of an Old Boy.

Reminiscences of an Old Boy:

BEING

Autobiographic Sketches

OF

SCOTTISH RURAL LIFE

FROM

1832 TO 1856.

BY

WILLIAM J. MILNE.

"*Ill fares the land, to hastening ills a prey,
Where wealth accumulates, and men decay;*
. . . .
*—A bold peasantry, their country's pride,
When once destroyed, can never be supplied.*"
—GOLDSMITH.

FORFAR:
PRINTED BY JOHN MACDONALD, "REVIEW" OFFICE.

1901.

Dedication.

TO THE SONS AND DAUGHTERS OF MY ASSOCIATES

WHEN

I "WHISTLED AT THE PLOUGH!"

I

Dedicate the following pages.

It is sad to think that many of them have gone to swell the numbers of the crowded cities of our nation, and also to our Colonies in quest of the comforts they could not get at home. Should these simple Sketches come into their hands, I hope they will enjoy the picture I have tried to draw of the time when their fathers and mothers were my co-workers, in sunshine and shower, in the fields and homesteads of our Native Land, more than half-a-century ago.

Their Well-wisher,

THE OLD BOY.

CONTENTS.

	PAGES.
CHAPTER I. MY FIRST APPEARANCE ON THE SCENE	17-25
CHAPTER II. MY FIRST SORROW	26-33
CHAPTER III. SCHOOLS AND SCHOOLMASTERS	34-41
CHAPTER IV. DISRUPTION OF THE KIRK	42-51
CHAPTER V. OPENING OF ARBROATH AND FORFAR RAILWAY	52-56
CHAPTER VI. THE SMUGGLING RAID	57-65
CHAPTER VII. COCK FIGHTING AT PUBLIC SCHOOLS	66-70
CHAPTER VIII. FECHTIN' MINISTERS AND DISRUPTION	71-79
CHAPTER IX. WORTHIES OF GREYRIGG	80-84
CHAPTER X. JEAN MCHUGH'S DESOLATE HOME	85-87
CHAPTER XI. "VERY LIKE A WHALE"	88-91
CHAPTER XII. SENT TO HERDING AT HIRPLE HOWE	92-94
CHAPTER XIII. WET HARVEST OF 1840	95-97

CONTENTS.

	PAGES
CHAPTER XIV. THE GREAT SNOW-STORM OF 1838	98-100
CHAPTER XV. JEANNIE JAMESON'S CHARITY	101-104
CHAPTER XVI. I BECOME A SHEPHERD AND CATTLE HERD	105-111
CHAPTER XVII. TERRIFIC THUNDER-STORM, 1845	112-122
CHAPTER XVIII. THE WARNER FAMILY	123-129
CHAPTER XIX. VILLAGE ALE-HOUSES AND WHISKY SHOPS	130-135
CHAPTER XX. REV. MR LOWNIE'S CATECHEESIN'	136-142
CHAPTER XXI. THE BROWN-CLOAKED LADY'S PROPHECY	143-150
CHAPTER XXII. REPEAL OF CORN LAWS	151-159
CHAPTER XXIII. A TERRIBLE TRAGEDY	160-166
CHAPTER XXIV. HARVESTING UNDER NEW CONDITIONS	167-172
CHAPTER XXV. CONSTRUCTION OF ABERDEEN RAILWAY	173-178
CHAPTER XXVI. A PITCHED BATTLE	179-185
CHAPTER XXVII. "ABERDEEN AWA'"	186-189
CHAPTER XXVIII. SEVEN KINDS OF BROSE	190-199

CONTENTS.

	PAGES.
CHAPTER XXIX.	
THE EXHIBITION, 1851	200-206
CHAPTER XXX.	
A HARVEST HOME	207-213
CHAPTER XXXI.	
MY ENLISTMENT IN THE 92d REGIMENT	214-219
CHAPTER XXXII.	
THE CLEANEST HOUSE IN THE KINGDOM	220-223
CHAPTER XXXIII.	
MY FIRST AND ONLY LOVE	224-233
CHAPTER XXXIV.	
A MUTUAL IMPROVEMENT SOCIETY	234-240
CHAPTER XXXV.	
I RETURN TO FORFARSHIRE	241-255
CHAPTER XXXVI.	
I SAIL FROM LEITH TO THE TYNE	256-263
CHAPTER XXXVII.	
"ENGLAND, THY BEAUTIES ARE TAME AND DOMESTIC"	264-278
CHAPTER XXXVIII.	
I RETURN TO OLD SCOTLAND	279-286

Index to Poems and Lyrics.

GRIGG'S STUDDY; OR THE TAILOR'S DREAM	289
THE CHILD'S WARNING	295
IN MEMORIAM—LORD AIRLIE	296
SANDY MACSLEEK, THE AULD CLOCK DOCTOR	297
LINES COMPOSED IN FITZ PARK, KESWICK	299
THAT FOUR-LEGGED STULE	301

VIII.   CONTENTS.

	PAGES.
THE BARBER'S OPINION	302
TIBBIE—AN OLD VILLAGE WORTHY	304
THE COMMERCIAL TRAVELLER OF ALL AGES	305
FLOWING YEARS, AND WHITHER	306
A SUMMER MORNING	307
SUMMER EVENING BY LOCH RYAN	308
AN EASTER SONG,	309
A SUMMER EVENING BY THE ALMOND	310
ENGLISH LAKELAND	311
AMONG THE HILLS AND ISLES	313
CISSIE V.R.—A BANFFSHIRE POST MESSENGER	314
THANKSGIVING	315
GLOSSARY OF SCOTCH WORDS AND PHRASES	316-317-318

Index to Illustrations.

FRONTISPIECE—(AUTHOR)	
GREYRIGGS VILLAGE	17
THE RUINS OF RED CASTLE	36
FORFAR FROM THE NORTH	53
FORFAR PARISH CHURCH AND STEEPLE	59
MARKET DAY IN FORFAR	84
FORFAR AND THE LOCH	107
RESCOBIE CHURCH AND LOCH	113
RESTENNETH PRIORY	242
OSNABURG PEND, FORFAR	246
EDZELL CASTLE	252
GEOMETRY, FIGURE OF	254
MUSIC, FIGURE OF	255
AIRLIE MEMORIAL	296

INTRODUCTION.

The writer of the following pages has done good work in giving to the world, in such a lucid and familiar style,—sometimes sparkling with humour and fun,—so full an account of his joys and sorrows—as a schoolboy, as a herd, as a haflin', as a full-fledged ploughman, and as a railway navvy. Some of his readers may think that the author is now and then, just a little self-opinionated, but it is rather the candid expression of strong convictions taught him by the hard taskmaster, experience. His descriptions of bothy life still hold good at the present time. This is certainly a sad blot on our boasted progress in the path of civilisation.

If this little work should be the means of calling the attention of those responsible for the bad conditions in which the stalwart sons of rural life are housed, and make them "tak' a thocht and men'," and erect more comfortable quarters for the men who "whistle at the plough," then these sketches will not have been written in vain.

The history of an individual is to a great extent analogous to the history of the class to which he belongs, and if narrated in the simple manner in which these reminiscences are told, without any gloss or embellishment, they cannot but be of great value to all who wish to have a true estimate of the real facts of human life, as lived by a great number of our fellow-countrymen. Our author has lifted the veil, and given us a peep into the bedrooms and dining apartments of our farm servants, and this cannot fail to be instructive, and perhaps profitable.

The lowliness of the subject matter may be objected to by those who have been bred in cities, yet Gray has sung in his great poem:—

> "Let not Ambition mock their useful toil,
>   Their homely joys, and destiny obscure;
> Nor Grandeur hear with a disdainful smile
>   The short and simple annals of the Poor.
>
> —Knowledge to their eyes her ample page,
>   Rich with the spoils of time, did ne'er unroll;
> Chill Penury repressed their noble rage,
>   And froze the genial current of the soul."

The life-story of any strongly individualised and energetic man, such as our author has proved himself to be, has always in it an inherent and salutary lesson. In these sketches his pluck as a schoolboy, his bitter experiences as a boy-herd, his firm determination to master the mysteries of, and become a first-rate worker of a pair of horses, either on lea or stubble land, and above all, his earnest desire for intellectual improvement, pursuit of knowledge under difficulties, as it were, is a lesson in practical existence which ought to be taken to heart by the youthful reader, whatever his station in life may be, and should teach him to go and do likewise.

From the glimpses we get of our author's nature and disposition as here and there disclosed in the course of his life's story, we can see that he has a keen religious fervour, a fine humour, and a strong will; in fact, he may be set down as a typical Scotsman of the old school. It would be all the better for society that we had many more like him than we have. It may be that in these later days of School Boards, and popular elections, we are not getting among mankind the strong self-possessed minds we got under the old plan. It would seem that our present method is more and more making us all alike, all on the same platform, each man as like his neighbour as one brick is like another brick. This system is crushing out our individuality, and making us commonplace, or may it not be that the advent of railways, and electric telegraphs, and all the many modes of making the transference of our thoughts a matter of ease and expedition, has rubbed off the angularities of our nature, and made us all very much alike? Will we say that what we have gained on the one hand we have lost on the other?

George Elliot, the great philosophical novelist of the nineteenth century, somewhere in her works, says:—"Autobiography saves a man from the publication of a string of mistakes called 'Memoirs.'" If this is true, and there is much truth in it, it is a good reason in itself why a person, about whom the world is likely to be curious, should take care to tell the story of his life in his own way. It does seem passing strange when you come to think of it, that some publisher has not thought of giving to his patrons a collection of the famous autobiographies of the world. Would it be the magnitude of the undertaking that deters him; for such a collection (it would run into many hundreds of volumes) would prove vastly amusing and instructive. Let us cull a few names that might be included in the series. Of the philosophers who have favoured us with their autobiographies are Hume, Voltaire, Gibbon, Mill, and Goethe. Of the poets Byron, Gilfillan, and Hogg. Of the mystics Paracelsus, Liley, and Doctor Dee. Of the showmen, a perfect host, with Barnum, the prince of humbugs at their head.

The Ettrick Shepherd begins his autobiography thus:—" I like to write about myself; in fact there are few things I like better; it is so delightful to call up old reminiscences."

Goethe begins his autobiography in these words:—" On the 29th of August, 1749, at mid-day, as the clock struck twelve, I came into the world at Frankfort-on-the-Main. My horoscope was propitious; the sun stood in the sign of the Virgin, and had culminated for the day; Jupiter and Venus looked on me with a friendly eye, and Mercury not adversely, while Saturn and Mars kept themselves indifferent; the moon alone, just full, exerted the power of her reflection all the more as she had then reached her planetary hour; she opposed herself to my birth, which could not be accomplished until this hour was passed. These good aspects which the astrologers managed subsequently to reckon very auspicious for me, may have been the cause of my preservation; for, through the unskilfulness of the midwife I came into this world as dead, and only after various efforts was I enabled to see the light."

But, perhaps, the greatest autobiography ever given to the

world was that of the French philosopher, Jean Jacques Rousseau, who introduces himself to his readers thus:—" I know my heart, and have studied mankind; I am not made like anyone I have been acquainted with, perhaps with no one in existence; if not better, I at least claim originality, and whether nature did wisely in breaking the mould with which she formed me, can only be determined after reading this work. Whenever the last trumpet shall sound I will present myself before the Sovereign Judge with this book in my hand, and loudly proclaim, thus have I acted; these were my thoughts; such was I. With equal freedom and veracity have I related what was laudable or wicked; I have concealed no crimes, added no virtues; and if I have sometimes introduced superfluous ornament, it was merely to occupy a void occasioned by defective memory. I may have supposed that certain, which I only know to be probable, but have never inserted as truth a conscious falsehood. Such as I was, I have declared myself, sometimes vile and despicable, at others, virtuous, generous, and sublime; even as Thou hast read my soul, Power Eternal! Assemble around Thy throne the innumerable throng of my fellow-mortals; let them listen to my confessions; let them blush at my depravity; let them tremble at my sufferings; let each in his turn expose with equal sincerity his failings, the wanderings of his heart, and if he dare, aver, I was better than that man."

Enough has been said to prove that a complete collection of the best autobiographies of the world would be a great fountain of amusement, delight, and instruction to the general reader. At present many of these bright gems are scattered here and there over our literature, not easily accessible, and in fact comparatively unknown, unless to that individual, the omnivorous devourer of books, sometimes irreverently designated by the non-studious, a book-worm.

For the benefit of his English readers the Author has appended a Glossary of the unusual Scotch words used in the Sketches and Poems. In a few instances it may be objected that the Scotch is not quite pure. If this be so, then it may be answered that it is correct so far as the Forfarshire dialect is concerned, and that this dialect is held to be the purest "doric" in Scotland.

Oh! how some of us love "our guid auld mither tongue." The Scottish language is a precious inheritance, and we should therefore try to keep it pure. What triumphs in description, delineation, and pathos have the giants of Scottish literature achieved in the Scottish language! If you wish for proof search the pages of Allan Ramsay, Robert Ferguson, Robert Burns, Walter Scott, Professor Wilson, John Galt, David Moir, and a host of others. About the real "doric," an accomplished writer says:—"Time was within living memory when the upper classes prided themselves on their native "doric," when Judges on the bench delivered their judgments in the broadest Scotch, and would have thought themselves guilty of puerile and unworthy affectation if they had preferred English words or English accents to the language of their boyhood; when advocates pleaded in the same homely and forcible tongue; when ministers of religion found their best way to the hearts and to the understandings of their congregations in the use of the language most familiar to themselves, as well as to those whom they addressed; and when ladies of the highest rank, celebrated alike for their wit and beauty, sang the tenderest, archest, and most affecting songs, and directed their bravest thrusts and parries in the sparkling encounters of conversation in the familiar speech of their own country."

The Poems appended at the end of the Sketches do not require to be apologised for. " Grigg's Studdy " is a witty, well-told, weird story of a drunkard's dream, which might with profit be taken up by our advanced temperance leaders. Were the story declaimed in their lodges it would not only amuse, but at the same time teach a much-needed salutary lesson of the danger of whisky and the safety of tea; for we may be sure that what his Satanic Majesty so strongly condemns in the way of a drinkable, must be good both for soul and body. The character sketches depict with a masterly hand some fine specimens of a type of Scottish individuality fast disappearing from our midst, and many of the lyrics are simple, sweet, and musical.

Should a few words be said in order to propitiate the critics to give a favourable comment on the book? Perhaps better not so, for in the history of literature no amount of praise or blame ever made or marred a book; its ultimate destiny is altogether independent of contemporary criticism. When you think of the host of incompetents who profess to lead the opinions of the world in matters literary, and the venom they spue on all and sundry (always unless you are within the charmed circle of the log-rollers), the thought brings to mind the bitter words of William Hazlett, who spoke from dire experience of these cattle when he said:—"Every one in a crowd has the power to throw dirt, and nine out of ten have the inclination." Alas! that saying is as true to-day as it was when written a hundred years ago.

The sociologist, the philosopher, and the historian, should thank the author for the valuable material he has afforded them in these sketches of lowly Scottish life.

ALEXANDER LOWSON.

FORFAR, *March*, 1901.

LAIGH TOON END, GREYRIGG (MYRE STANE).

Reminiscences of an Old Boy:

AUTOBIOGRAPHIC SKETCHES

of Scottish Village Rural Life from 1832 to 1856.

Chapter I.

"I remember, I remember the fir-trees, dark and high,
I used to think their tiny tops were close against the sky;
It was a childish ignorance, but now 'tis little joy
To know I'm farther off from heaven than when I was a boy."

—T. HOOD.

My arrival in Greyrigg.—Description of the Village.—Watty Wabblestraught, Victualler and Vintner, and his dog Spottie. — Johnnie, my first Playmate, and Bob his cat.

The first incident in my rather changeful, and eventful career, or at least the first one of which I have any mental memorial, is being handed down from the top-seat of a stage coach in the midst of a country village, on what I have since learned was a fine spring day. But my retrospect of that circumstance is somewhat hazy and indistinct, as no daily coach or other public conveyance was a visitor in that hamlet, which then became my home, and that I should have been landed there per hired vehicle was out of the question, for various reasons, chiefly of a financial nature. So far as I am able to reckon, my arrival would be about the year 1832-33, and I would be some four years old when landed in Greyrigg. This was not the real name of the place, but for my purpose it will do as well as any other.

Where I had been, or how I had fared, from my entrance on this sublunary sphere, to this time, has always been to me an unsolved mystery of the days before my perceptions were awakened to the environment of my earthly lot. I was told afterwards that during the mysterious period here alluded to, I had been knocked about from one home to another—that in fact, small as I was, it had for sometime appeared as if room was not to be found for me on this rather expansive scene, and it was often related as proof of this little difficulty, that in one instance, when one of my rather luke-warm guardians called to see how I was getting on in the habitation last provided for me, I was found sitting tied to a little broken chair, dressed in dirty old rags, and ravenously eating a piece of dry oaten bread, or Scotch bannock, which had been hastily thrust into my hand when the visitor was announced. At the same time it is said to have been observed by my visitor, that the hired nurse's own son was arrayed in the good and suitable clothes which had been provided for my wear only.

I never knew the nature of the interview which ensued between the high contracting parties when the afore-mentioned ugly discovery took place, but I understand my quarters were shifted there and then, and that soon after I was sent to Greyrigg, and there a few infant and boyish years (happy or otherwise) were passed. The place which now became my home was a type of many small clusters of houses then to be met with in Scotland, more frequently than now, and although the location of Greyrigg was in the very centre of the soft pavement, thick-rock, and grey-slate quarries, there was only one slated roof in the whole place. The architecture and habiliments of those quaint cottages would now be considered decidedly unique, and more picturesque than comfortable, one of the chief primitive features being that the houses were not thatched with straw or heather, or reeds of any kind, but with broom! Aye, broom! cut on the hills, fells, and moorlands of the Greyrigg estate, where it grew in great profusion. And the remembrance of the light shining on that "bonnie broom" is with me still, and I think I see the glow from Nature's lovely lamps when it hung them out in moon, or sunshine. That added colour to the golden blossom on the whins, made up a rare spectacle of brilliant beauty, teeming with light, and filled with the loves and industries of bird and bee.

Then when the long summer days were closing, and the sun sinking afar beyond the Athole mountains, sometimes his evening beams fell on a soft rain-shower descending in the south-east. Each level ray made millions of water prisms; then a rainbow spanned our valley, and below that gorgeous arch the floral adornment of the far hill-sides, and the out-spread moors and fields were bespangled as with jewels of silver and gold. And when the centre of that glorious bow reached such an altitude that in my boyish fancy I thought it touched the heavenly gates, it took no great addition of fancy for me to imagine how the angels might step out from yon dark cloud behind, and by that majestic bridge descend on visits to this beautiful world.

The inhabitants of my boyhood's home were quaint, simple-minded, happy folk, as yet unspoiled by modern or mechanical devices, as for years after the date I am writing, the sound of a locomotive, or steam or air-propelled machine, had not been heard in that land, nor had that terror of the worthy housewife, who had heard it rumoured that "a far waur set a' craturs than the Irish were coming," to wit, the railway navvy, had not as yet arrived.

The population of our village, like the place itself, was small, but now recalling their histories and appearances as they plodded on in the even current of their quiet lives, they look to me as having been very select. First, there was Watty Wabblestraught, the vintner and victualler, whose sign over his door in red-white-and-blue, told of reaming bickers of the harmless and wholesome ale of the time. It also spoke of whangs o' hame-made cheese, and ait-meal farles, baken wi' butter; also mentioning spirits, good or otherwise; aye, and fell draps of that same liquor which had never seen the Exciseman, or ever paid toll to King William. The iron rings fastened in the house walls at each side of the door told of hungry and thirsty steeds being fed and watered there. The range of broom-thatched byres and stables, with square enclosure on your right, told of sheep and cattle being lodged there.

Then Watty himself was a hamely, happy, and assuring sight for the weary eyes of the wayfarers, as from the red top-knot of his Kilmarnock bonnet to the siller buckles on his shoon, all bespoke a man o' wecht—a man o' wecht, mind ye.

Oh! his welcome was grand to see, and the hearty shake of his comfortable hand was better, far better than any patent plaster to an aching back. Then Watty's hearty guffaw of laughter as he ushered his guests and patrons to the comforts of his long snow-white deal table, and the big kitchen fire, with its over-hanging canopy, up through whose wide chimney on clear nights could be seen the pole star and Peter's plough, those everlasting celestial lights, the watchers on the hills of time! Then, even when the same great kitchen, as one would have thought, was full, Watty's laugh could still be heard welcoming others from as far as the Laigh Toon-end. Truly that great laugh had a melody which made the wayworn traveller glad.

"Wat" was a most free-and-easy landlord, who never scrupled to drink his guests' health, all unbidden, even at the customer's or guest's expense, and although a jolly, kind, and courteous host, he kept a very clear look-out on the interest of number one; for had you inquired as the evening wore on, as to how he was getting on, "Wat" would very likely answer, "Oh! jist a gryte heap o' muckle wirds but little siller."

Then Watty's brown-and-white dog "Spottie" was a celebrated canine institution, and it was a very unruly flock or herd that Spottie could not keep in order. For Spottie was monarch of dog-land as far as he could survey it, and no single, or for that matter no couple of dogs dared to dispute his authority on any dog question of the day. Spottie's general demeanour proved that he was a dog of decision, and when he spoke in dog Latin, the air of his conversation said plainly

"When I speak let no other dog bark."

But I think that dog spoke French. Of course I am not sure, as I never got beyond English, and not much of that.

Such was Watty Wabblestraught and his dog Spottie, vintners, victuallers, and innkeepers in the ancient hamlet of Greyrigg, of which not a vestige is now to be found but the croft and cottage of the Laigh Toon-end, and the original slated cottage is now empty and forlorn.

There are a few more erstwhile denizens of that old spot very dear to memory still. I have mentioned Watty first as the one I remember as the first and only public man of the village. The Laigh Toon-end folk deserve more than a passing notice. Their name was Jameson, one brother and two sisters, also their mother. When I made my appearance in the hamlet the family were near middle-age, but the youngest of the three only died four years ago in her 90th year. Their mother was a sister to the vintner's wife; Annie Gow being Watty's wife, and Jenny Gow the Jamesons' mother. There were no mistresses then among the common folks. Such titles were reserved for the laird's, the dominie's, and the parish minister's wives. The Parish, or Auld Kirk, now so called, was the only theological institution then acknowledged by the majority. But there were ominous signs in the Kirk's atmosphere that vast changes were approaching, but of that more anon.

It would be too tedious to tell the characteristic of each individual in that curious old community (for each had his or her's), but all had the same kind, helpful, sympathetic, and neighbourly manner, both in word and deed, a charm potent in the day of distress, the evening of old age, or when sickness, and the last grim messenger's shadow hovered o'er the broom-thatched roofs. It was then that one family's sorrow was shared by each and all, and as I stand gazing through the vista of sixty-two byegone years, and think of sacrifices made there by one neighbour for another, and of the unmurmuring unselfishness practised by these simple unassuming cottagers, I conclude it must have been from examples like those that Motherwell, or some other brother of the Muse, got the idea which he puts on the dying lips of our national bard, where in the fancied address to Jessie Lewars (the kind attendant and never-to-be-forgotten good angel who tried to soothe the last moments of that gifted soul, Burns), exclaims—

"O, did the poor not help the poor ?
Each in their humble way,
With simple gift and kindly deed,
God pity them, I say."

I may here be permitted to mention, that I found in coming years, and before I left the dear old spot, that many of those old people were intelligent and well read in the history of our common country, as also well up in the political history of the time. Although there were no daily penny or halfpenny newspapers, and the weekly broad-sheets issuing from the press of Montrose or Arbroath (and which cost either 4½d, or 7½d each), were the only mediums of public news, yet many, I may say all, could have told you correctly who was the coming statesman, Churchman, or celebrated scientist of that day.

Returning to the family of Laigh Toon-end, viz., the Jamesons, and their mother. I have mentioned that she was a sister of Annie Gow, Watty Wabblestraught's wife. Annie was a complete opposite of her husband, as also of her sister in all respects, except in the goodness of disposition, being rather diminutive in body, while her sister was of most ample physical proportions. So marked was the difference that the two were known to us as muckle Granny and little Granny.

Both the sisters, however, bore on all outward lineaments, on face, dress, and manner, the stamp of that divinity which is the glory of and adds beauty to the fading cheek and grey hairs of grandmother, mother, or maiden aunt.

Dear reader, if you have never seen this stamp of feminine age, I pity you. It is certainly to be met with yet, though I cannot describe it; but, under the clear starched and spotless white mutch, bound with black silk ribbon, which was the characteristic head dress of the Scotch lowland female cottager when she had passed the meridian of life's firmament about sixty-two years ago, there often rested that indescribable something which had a most heart-warming influence on all that came within its radius; and when, as was not seldom the case, the face was lighted up by that glow which was kindled at the lamp of God's love.

> "Such faces seen in life's young morn
> Bide with us till life's eve."

The Jamesons' grand old grandmother had a grandson, a splendid little fellow, my first playmate! and each of us were under the care of old folk, where no other children lived, and both were of the same age. Although the society of the hamlet was severely Republican, and caste almost unknown, yet there being several families of boys, older and much rougher and boisterous in their manner, Johnny and I were brothers in all events, and inseparable companions in arms, along with a beautiful light-coloured tiger-striped cat named "Bob." Therefore, through sunshine and shadow, we two, with Bob, the cat, were together; and when our morning prayers had been repeated, each at his faithful guardian's knee, and the alphabetical exercises—"muckle A," "little a," with "long s," and "short s," and the whole thing laboriously gone over, then, oh! glory and sunshine! daisy-chains, and rushwoven caps! cornel whips and sauchen whistles! and the rolling about on the green braes! I now believe that we were then about as happy as it is possible for sentient beings to be in this imperfect state.

But a change, dire and sorrowful, my first sorrow, was coming, the sad record of which I must reserve for another chapter.

CHAPTER II.

*"The tear down childhood's cheeks that flows
Is like the dewdrop on the rose."*
—SCOTT.

Johnnie's Death.—Fortitude of the Jamesons under the loss of Johnnie.—Death of Johnnie's Cat.—Johnnie still unforgotten—proved at the death-bed of his mother, fifty-four years after.—Alex. Hardwird, my next playmate.—His eleven Sisters.—Mrs Hardwird (the Mother).—Sandy Hardwird, farmer o' Hirple Howe.

Our previous chapter closed with a reference to a circumstance which, in its sudden sadness, changed the current of my childhood's happy companionship into very genuine sorrow. This was caused by the death of my first dear playmate, Johnny. He fell a victim to that cruel child-destroyer, then known in our district as "rush," or scarlet fever, a pestilence yet walking in darkness, decimating household ranks, and blighting the fond and loving hopes of affectionate fathers and mothers. This fever did its deadly work on Johnny in a very few days, and I never saw my beloved companion after the night I saw him on his mother's knee, telling her his "heid was awfu' sair," while his beautiful cat walked around, purring and rubbing himself against Johnny, and looking up in the boy's face as if sympathising, and seeming to say, "I am sorry for you, Johnny." I stood by sad and perplexed, but more perplexed and sad was I when next morning I was forbidden to go to the Laigh Toon-end, as Johnny Ramage had "rush" fever. Yes, I had seen the last of Johnny, but when about a year after I was taken across the hill for the first time to the auld kirk of Rescobie, I saw a little grave in the sweet God's-acre there, and on that small green mound the daisies and dandelions of the early spring were brightly blooming, their eyes of gold and silver directed, as they ever are, and as the eye of faith ever is directed, upward and outward to that pure source

> "From whence all true comfort flows,
> Which heals all life's sorrows,
> While we calmly bear life's woes."

Young as I was then, and although nearly sixty years have carried their sunshine and shadows over that hallowed spot, I have never forgotten the memory of Johnny. Looking on his little green grave, I had no doubt then, nor have I the least doubt now, that that small hillock only contained the little clay shell from which the pure and happy spirit of my dear comrade had winged its way to fairer worlds beyond.

The Jamesons were not a loud-mouthed demonstrative folk. You would have heard no weeping and wailing, and seen very few tears, although you had met them around that saddened hearth at this time.

But there was one individual, a very notable exception, among these mourners, who could not keep silent, and who in his own inarticulate expression told his grief in a most pathetic manner. That was "Bob," the cat. For days that affectionate animal wandered out and in, and up and down, searching for, and calling on our departed playmate in that mournful yet musical note peculiar to the feline race. At length, never finding him he sought, "Bob" broke down in his grief, refused food, and died in less than six months. This is no fiction, as "Bob's" heartbreaking sorrow, and his death following so soon, was well known and much commented on all over the place. I remember very well hearing the animal calling and searching high and low many days after Johnny's death, and in a short time I saw that cat sitting at the fireside, all faded and crushed up, a complete wreck, and after this I saw him no more.

In this and other well-authenticated instances of strong attachment to humanity, pervaded by something akin to human reason and calculation on the part of the equine, canine, and feline examples, let the advanced student of psychology tell us from his scientific researches in the mysteries of domestic animal life, whether a horse, a dog, or a cat, do or do not reason.

I have already told with what brave and silent fortitude the Jamesons took up and sustained the burden of this great sorrow, in the sudden bereavement which befel them at this time. Thoughtless neighbours, or mere casual visitors, might have concluded that the bright little boy was very soon forgotten, but what I am now to relate will, I think, prove that such was not, and never could have been, the case.

My young friend's death took place in 1836, and fifty-four years thereafter, in 1890, the last of the Laigh Toon-end family lay dying, in the 90th year of her age, and under the roof of the same house in which she was born. This was Betty Jameson, who was Johnny Ramage's mother. Betty was a handloom weaver in her youth, and on the last day she lived, when the faithful minister of Christ from Rescobie manse was in attendance, it was observed she was working her hands as if winding something on to a spool or pirn, and when the good man asked her how she she felt in the near view of the change about to pass on her soon, Betty replied that she now had hold of a thread by one end, and her long lost boy was holding the other end. By that thread, she said, she was warping herself home to where Johnny Ramage had lived so long, and where they were now soon to meet after all those years of faithful waiting, to be parted no more for ever! The history of this beautiful and soul-stirring idea was repeated to me by the attendant who was with Betty at her demise, and who had been with her for many years.

My next special companion and playmate was Alec Hardwird, the only son of the farmer of Hirple Howe, a farm lying on the north side of the Lemno Burn, in the parish of Aberlemno, bounding the parish of Rescobie on the north and east, and part of which was situated in the then existing hamlet of Greyrigg. My new companion had eleven sisters, who each grew to nearly six feet in height, and his mother weighed fifteen stone imperial. Sandy, the father, or "Hirple," as he was known best by the short name of his farm, was a complete denial to the name of Hardwird, he being one of the very quietest and most soft-spoken of men, and incapable of doing or saying anything hard to anyone.

In these days of hurry-scurry, bustle or burst, when the strong tread down the weak, I believe Sandy would be voted slow. Even with a farm rented on the old moderate terms, and not overburdened with restrictions, Sandy, with his dozen of a family, consisting of eleven daughters, each standing five feet ten inches in their stockings, and a son likely to stretch to six feet, and adding to all that their mother weighing fifteen stones imperial in her boots, this poor man found his generation overstretched, and himself overweighted, so after securing a small grassum, or goodwill fee, from a successor, Sandy gave up farming, and betook himself to another pursuit in the ancient and royal burgh of Forfar, the nearest market town, and the capital of the county.

So noted was Mrs Hardwird in her day, it is only just that a special paragraph in this sketch should be devoted to her memory. This ponderous female had earned the title of mistress—rare in those days—by the advantage which a phenomenal weight in more ways than one gave her.

This will be better understood when I tell you that this woman could dictate secular orders at the rate of sixty to the minute, and quote Scripture by the yard, at same time interlarding her conversation with all the extra news which five parishes round could have contained. Were she now in the flesh she would give points to the most industrious daily news-sheet of our time. I can yet in retrospect see the flush and flutter of excitement which overspread the faces of the younger members, especially of the female portion, of our village, whenever it was announced that the huge form of this celebrated visitor was bearing down on Greyrigg. Oh! then there was a complete clearance of idlers, and by the intent earnestness and speed at which the looms and pirn-wheels were driven, a stranger might have fancied they were all racing against time. At same time each had an eye in her neck to note where the stupendous hull would come to anchor. I have seen "the mistress" in fine weather, alongside little Granny on the stone seat by that gracious old lady's door. Little Granny by that time was the retired widow of Watty, the late village publican, who, after suffering a great deal in a short time, died of cancer of the throat, and was gathered to his native dust in the quiet kirkyard of Aberlemno. Mrs Hardwird, I have no doubt, believed she was fulfilling Scripture in patronising the village, and in specially letting the little old widow shelter under her ample shadow, while she (Mrs. H.) made a general redd-up of personal character far and near, from the laird and the minister downwards. I never heard how her quiet, aged neighbour appreciated such patronage and visits, but I have heard the younger members of the female persuasion there wishing that Mrs Hardwird would be "reisted" where she sat. I did not know the meaning of the wish when I heard it first, but, being always of an inquiring mind, I learned that it expressed their wish that she might never rise from where she sat down! Such was the goodwill and esteem this estimable woman had earned in the practice of her moral and Christian efforts to inform, guide, and teach the benighted people of Greyrigg.

How often, in like manner, does moral and Christian zeal go unrewarded and unrecognised. I "guess" (as Jonathan says) there are not a few Mrs Hardwirds about yet, who find themselves in the same plight as regards the estimation in which their self-sufficiency lands them with those they so gratuitously pretend to benefit. But I seriously question if any woman could be found now so capable, or of such capacity, outside a showman's wagon, as the wonderful female I have here tried to immortalise. Certainly the mother who could rule and train eleven daughters, five feet ten inches in their stockings, and a son who grew beyond six feet, take care of a husband, and keep a personal record of the characters of the most prominent inhabitants of five parishes, yet still retain her own weight at fifteen stones imperial, was no ordinary woman!

My intimate association with the young male Hardwird, and the growing members of Hirple Howe's tall family, was cut short in a very abrupt manner, and as follows.

Alec had a small four-wheeled coach, a rather primitive sample of the modern perambulator, without springs or cushions, and in this chariot we dragged each other along by turns. One fine summer evening I was at Hirple Howe, and the two of us were busily engaged at our exhilerating pastime, while Mrs Hardwird at the farmhouse door was seated in the midst of her tall daughters and had a full view of the chariot course, which was along the edge of a deep grassy dry ditch. It was Alec's turn of the coach, and I was the fiery steed dragging him along, but as bad luck had it, I had gone too near the edge of the ditch. The result was a coach catastrophe, for the vehicle and passenger disappeared in an instant, and with such a bang as knocked the pole out of my hand, and that then remained about the only signal of where the coach and passenger might be found. Then in the midst of my fright and confusion Mrs Hardwird bore down on me, but although both coach and passenger were extricated unhurt, my lady of ample dimensions poured the vials of her wrath with characteristic energy on my unfortunate head, and after calling me some choice names, prophesied my future in rather lurid colours, declaring that hanging would be much too good for me! She actually insinuated that I had tumbled her "Alecky" into the ditch wilfully. I, fearing she might throw me in too, and jump on me (which would have extinguished me), took to my heels, and did not halt until I gained the shelter of my home in Greyrigg; and I never courted young Hardwird's acquaintance again.

How I was sent to school some time previous to this, together with a sketch of my schools and schoolmasters, behold! is it not written in the next chapter?

Chapter III.

*"Beside yon straggling fence that skirts the way
With blossom'ng furze, unprofitably gay,
There in his noisy mansion, skilled to rule,
The village master taught his little school."*
—GOLDSMITH.

Sent to School.—Description of my Schoolmasters:— 1st, the Barefit Minister; 2nd, Mr Easypen.— Remarks on Parish, Voluntary, and Dame Schools of the District at that time.

Nearly two miles from Greyrigg, and between that village and the town of Forfar, straggling along the north side of the road, was, and still is, a row of houses named "The Barracks." Those small grey-slated houses were built during the twenty years of war between this country and France. They were erected for the accommodation of the sergeants and other members of a corps of volunteers which was raised, equipped, and trained to arms by the public-spirited and martial-minded Laird of Carsegray, the proprietor of the beautiful and compact estate which lies east and west along the road referred to. It was said the expenses of the erection, and whole upkeep of the corps, were borne by the proprietor mentioned; but to the everlasting discredit of the Government of the time, the Laird was allowed to live and die unrewarded or reimbursed for his outlay, to the extent of a single coin. This outlay exhausted all his means, except his entailed estate, which he had to mortgage deeply, during the time of the threatened danger of invasion, and so rudely did the creditors of this gentleman use him, that he left them to their own devices, and to save his person from imprisonment, he took a debtor's sanctuary, and there ended his days, the victim of an ungrateful country, hunted down by the myrmidons of the law of the land he had robbed himself to serve and defend!

On the south side of the road referred to lies the estate of Dunnichen, the property then of another public-spirited and popular landlord. Several houses had been built there about 1829, and now (in 1835) their number was being added to on the perpetual and other feuing systems. A considerable number of children lived there; the sons and daughters of weavers, quarry-workers, and others. That side of the road with its inhabitants is known as Lunanhead, as the waters of the beautiful streamlet Lunan rise there, and flow eastwards through Restenneth moss, and Rescoble Loch, and thence through the Loch of Balgavies. On its devious onward way the Lunan meanders by field and farm, receiving aqueous tribute as it flows, until after a course of about thirty-two miles, near an ancient stronghold which belonged to a famous clan of the olden time, the little streamlet, now grown to a fair and rushing river, takes its final plunge, and is lost in the restless tidal waters of Lunan Bay, over whose waves the Castle ruins have for ages past kept watch and ward.

It is now a small seminary at Lunanhead we have to do with. That little school was got up by the joint efforts and subscriptions of the inhabitants and surrounding lairds, and had been opened but a short time before I was sent to it. The first teacher there was the "Barefit minister." What was the origin of that chill-

THE RUINS OF REDCASTLE.

looking title I never learned, and his name even I do not recollect. His term of office was brief after I made my debut, and I never knew whence he came, nor whither he went, but I remember that his likeness, caricatured in charcoal, and barefooted, adorned the walls of the precious little school-house. One day the big boys stole the key of the outer door, and locked the minister in all by himself, and we (the small fry) were locked out. I saw the whole band of conspirators running round the building, and making faces at their prisoner through the windows. The outcome of this rebellion was the dismissal of the " Barefit minister."

His successor was Mr Easypen, a rather remarkable man, who, I have been told, had never been a half year at any day-school when a boy. He was a great friend and admirer of my grandfather, with whom I lived in Greyrigg. The rebellious boys who defied Mr Easypen's predecessor soon found that in the new teacher they had a different subject to deal with.

Mr Easypen was young, and I thought him such a big handsome man. I often wished I would grow to be such a braw big man as he was, and when one day big Andra Thrawnsnoot, the farmer's son of Soorick-Brae, answered the new teacher with, "No, a' winna," we got a specimen of what Mr E. was made of, for on hearing that defiant answer, the teacher made one bound on Andra like a tiger, and before he knew what had happened Andra was prostrate on the floor, and a leather tawse about three-and-a-half feet in length, with nine tags cut on one end, and a slit cut for the hand in the other end.

This formidable "leather" was now in Mr Easypen's hand, while the boy Andra lay on the floor. I was much alarmed, yet I saw how beautifully the new master wielded the tawse round the ears and across the shoulders, and other unmentionable but prominent parts of that rebel's anatomy.

However, when the flogging ceased, the rebel did not yield, nor pledge better behaviour for the future, so after a short exchange of views between the opposing forces, the master ordered the school doors to be opened, and to the still obdurate and defiant boy was given the choice of yielding obedience, promising better conduct in the future, or taking himself off by the open door immediately. Andra accepted the latter alternative, went out, and never came back.

This drastic but needful example struck terror to the hearts of the other would-be mutineers, and Mr Easypen, notwithstanding his lack of formal school training, proved a model teacher, keeping fine order, and having the happy knack of imparting what he knew himself in a form which charmed and opened the young mind most successfully.

The emoluments for these teachers were small, and in a number of cases in such communities the fees were not well paid, although they were the only source of income.

Only the Parish Schoolmasters had fixed salaries, as well as fees, in pre-Disruption days, and adventure schools, subscription, and other unendowed teaching-houses could only exist where pupils were numerous and parents had that fine Scotch desire that their children should at least be blessed with fair elementary education. There were very few families utterly neglected in that respect. The exceptions who did totally neglect this were considered very ungodly and disreputable.

At the same time, there were many parents willing, nay, even anxious, that their children should be educated, who by their unthrifty and dissolute habits were never able to pay fees; but even their children, as well as those of the very poor or unfortunate, got the benefits of either parochial or adventure school teaching. The want of being able to master the three R's (especially the first) was looked on, where I was brought up, as nothing short of a calamity for any child that might be so neglected.

Probably a different view of the need for education prevailed where population increased and became concentrated, owing to the advance of mechanical invention, and consequent crowding into towns. This crowding into towns took place first because the Conservative tendencies of the old landed proprietors refused scope or opportunity for building houses or manufacturing premises, save in some more enlightened examples, where whatever was the proprietor's politics, he moved with the times.

But returning to my schools and schoolmasters, I may mention that being found possessed of a very retentive memory and "raither clever i' the uptak'," as it was expressed, I got on well with Mr Easypen, and that good gentleman was foolish enough, or partial enough, when I had done some rather extra mental feat, to clap me on the head and say, "Man, that's fine! What a grand scholar you could be made if you had some one to take you by the hand and help you on." That "if" was never supplied, but in a very meagre degree. Yet the praise, so foolishly though innocently bestowed, filled me with emulation, at the same time loading me with vain conceit. I do think such praise foolish, if given in the hearing of children, as in nine cases out of ten it really gives them such a notion of their own superiority that boys and girls are apt to become insufferable juvenile Solomons.

Before such adventure schools as the one at Lunanhead was

constituted there were various "Dame" schools, where tuition of a kind was imparted, but the erudition of their classes would not pass the Government inspection of the time we are living in now. There was a decent villager of Greyrigg, who I have heard mentioned as having taught a number of girls to sew and knit, as also to read the Old and New Testaments. The schoolroom was in her cottage, and she also took a number of boys into her reading class, but she had evidently not "passed" in any training college, for I have heard some of her old pupils tell how when a more than ordinary long word staggered them she would say, "Spell it, my laddie," and when that sweet, guileless urchin would spell two or three short words as one, old Maggie would look over her specs. and declare, "Oh, laddie, that's surely Jeroosalem! juist go on, like a guid bairn," and the guid, if not a very godly bairn, would go on rejoicing, as Maggie's mastery of English printed matter drew the line at the word "Jeroosalem!"

There was another, a male teacher, in the parish of Dunnichen, at the village of Bowriefauld, who, it was said, had even an easier way of disposing of pronouncing difficulties, for when a deadlock occurred, as it often did, when a "lang-nebbit" word was reached, this dominie lifted the young hopeful and himself over the difficulty by simply marking "P.S." over the word, which being interpreted meant "pass this over," and this master of learning would say to the boy, "P.S., Cockie; that's the name of a gentleman's house in the north!"

There was another school, the first of its kind in the district, started by the ruling elder of the parish of Rescobie, a king of men, who tried to do and accomplish much good in his day and generation. The record of his praiseworthy efforts and the history of the Sunday School which he taught in his own parlour at Gate End of Pitandrew, I must reserve to next chapter.

Chapter IV.

"Faith lights us through the dark to Deity."
—SIR W. DAVENANT.

*"Howe'er it be it seems to me,
'Tis only noble to be good;
Kind hearts are more than coronets
And simple faith than Norman blood."*
—TENNYSON.

John Endever, first Sunday School Teacher in Greyrigg Valley.—Death of my Foster-Mother and Jenny Jamieson.—A Double Funeral in that District Sixty years ago.—John Endever and the Kirk of the Disruption.—My Grandfather's Predictions regarding the coming change, seven years before the event.—I and my Mother driven from my Grandfather's house. — Death of the old man, and his character.

His name was John Endever. He lived at Gate-End, a small hamlet about half a mile from Greyrigg; and in John's ben-end or parlour were gathered on Sunday evenings all the boys and girls, or as many as were sent by their parents from both hamlets, and there we were duly "tairged," as Burns calls it, on the questions contained in the Catechisms of the Auld Kirk.

John was great in scripture and theology, and he was a fond admirer of the poetry of the Sacred Book, and had the ear to hear, and the taste to appreciate the talent of any pupil who read well, or repeated correctly, and with the proper inflection, any of the glorious descriptions of God's wonderful works as pourtrayed in the grand word-pictures, by inspired Shepherd Kings and Prophets of Israel. He was a true and living type of the uncompromising and steadfast believer in the doctrines of Knox and the Reformation and Covenanting times; one of these heroic men who would have walked up to a loaded cannon's mouth, or braved peril and sword for what he believed to be true Church government, and pure and spiritual worship of the true God.

He was also the district joiner, and for many years was the only one in the district employed in the manufacture of household furniture for respectable working people about to marry. Indeed, most worthy couples would not have considered their plenishing complete unless they had been put in possession of one at least of John Endever's box-beds, and a combination chest of drawers of the same handicraft. Then, when many of the same employer's friends had laid down life's burdens, at the close of a longer or shorter tenure of mortal clay tabernacles, many would have thought it unco-like if such friend's coffins were not furnished at Gate-End. The religious service conducted by John at "the kistin'," or coffining of the corpse, and the prayer offered up by that gifted man on such occasions, was a most striking and heart-stirring appeal, and contained earnest supplications for the living. His strong but simple faith breathed forth from his tall figure as he stood erect, with bent head and eyes closed, with his finger-tips resting on the table where lay the Book from which he had been reading those ever living words of consolation—"Let not your hearts be troubled, ye believe in God, believe also in Me," and also speaking of "a house of many mansions." Then he would at such times also cheer the company by reading from the same volume the grand assurance that though the "Earthly house of this tabernacle be dissolved, we have a building of God, an house not made with hands."

Such times and scenes are well remembered yet by many living who had the privilege of being present. I can yet recall the awe with which I, a small but very sorrowful boy, looked on that man, and heard his prayer that cold March morning, when the remains of my dear old guardian, the first mother I knew, were laid in her coffin.

John had the same sad duty to perform twice that day, for Mrs Jameson ("Muckle Granny,") of the Laigh Toon-end died the same day as my friend. They were both conveyed to their narrow homes in the auld Kirkyaird in one funeral procession. The conveyances were two open-bodied carts, there being no hearse available nearer than Forfar, and the hire of such a conveyance was not to be thought of, so, with each coffin covered with a black "mortcloth," or pall, and made fast to the carts, as the road was long, and in some places very rough, everyone on foot wound his way up the avenue, and past the house and hill of Pitandrew, that being the name of the manor and the adjoining hill-ridge which formed the south-western boundary of the Carsegray valley. Before starting, all the males over seventeen or eighteen years of age attending such funerals were offered a glass of wine or other liquor, and whatever may have been the practice at funerals generally in other districts around, the excesses, of which much has been made by some exceedingly veracious chroniclers, were not existent. I never saw excess at any funeral I have attended for the last fifty-six years. Certainly all made the semblance of lifting the glass to their lips, but I question if one of every ten really imbibed any of the contents, for the glasses were seldom replenished.

But to continue my short memoir of the worthy elder who conducted the funerals I have here described, I may note that at the time I am now speaking of, that great controversy which rent the Church of Scotland in twain was only three years old. Seven years later saw the breach completed, and John Endever had entered the same breach with the joy of a high-spirited warrior, who, even at midnight, may be called on to lead a forlorn hope against any deadly enemy of either his faith or his country. I am not certain that he, or very many equally zealous for what they called religious freedom and purity of worship, really saw what had to be the inevitable result, except one party or the other (the Church on one side or the State on the other) gave way. I heard my revered grandfather often say to fireside inquirers that he might not live to see what took place in '43, but, he said, that one of three things would certainly happen. First—The Government would give way; or second, the Church party must betray their faith and prove false to the position they had taken up; or third, if the Government did not concede what the Churchmen demanded, and if the latter were as he believed, they would be true and determined. The whole of the Established Church ministers would have to leave their homes and livings and go forth as the Seceders had done years before. At this time the old man predicted what came to be an accomplished fact, that was, that if the third alternative had to be taken, then would ensue such an exodus as had not been in this country, not even in the days of prelacy and persecution.

My old relation did not live to see his prediction accomplished. But John Endever, with some others of the Kirk Session, left the elder's office of Rescobie parish, and many of the communicants left at the same time. The worthy pastor of their parish died a few weeks before the Disruption took place, then John cast in his theological lot with the pastors who had resigned the loaves and fishes of State emolument, and State patronage, and freed themselves (as they thought) of State obligation. John became an elder in the First Free Kirk of Forfar, and took part in the ministrations there, until he was nearly eighty-five years old, a consistent and zealous supporter of liberty of conscience, one who would not veer about with every wind of doctrine, or any new-fangled fad, from pure and spiritual worship.

My grandfather's relations, almost to the last man and woman, took the non-intrusion side, and for a number of years nons and moderates were a divided people so far as it was possible to separate, both at Kirk and market, yet there were not wanting many notable examples of tolerance and fair-mindedness, where both agreed to differ, and where the words "I am of Paul and you are of Apollos" were never heard.

Some time before the death of my grandfather's wife, a stranger appeared in Greyrigg, and took up her abode in the same house, and learned the handloom weaving from one of the Jamesons. I was then about seven years old, and the old lady who had been for more than four years my kind and faithful guardian, and who I had always looked on as my mither, and always addressed by that loving title, now told me that the newcomer was my mother, and that I was to address her as such. But I refused point blank to do anything of the kind, and persisted in my refusal so long as Elsie Lovington, the dear old friend referred to, lived. But she died and was buried as already related, and on the evening of the funeral, immediately on our return from the Kirkyaird, although a heavy fall of snow had come down, my grandfather's oldest son (I believe), with the concurrence of his three sisters who were present, ordered my mother out of the house, and also to take me with her.

Here was a change with a vengeance uncalled for, as my mother was a most respectable and industrious Christian woman, whose only fault had been in her faith in that uncle's brother, who had quarrelled with her when almost within sight of the sacred edifice where they were to be made one, and each went, therefore, their own way.

I never saw my father to my knowledge till I was eight years of age, and I saw him only as he called on his father while on his way to embark for England from some Scotch port, passage by sea being the means of conveyance then for those who did not care to afford the expense of stage coach travelling. I saw my male parent again when about twelve years old, and not till I was twenty-seven did we meet again; then it was in a crowd within the old station at Birmingham, the mark of my identity as previously arranged, being a beautiful bouquet of white daisies which I wore in my coat, the surroundings and all circumstances attending this meeting being a happy contrast of the cold night twenty years before this, when the woman he had deserted, and his boy sat homeless by the wind-swept clay-cottages in the old Scotch village, while that spoiled but precocious little rascal, who had defiantly ignored the lonely woman, even now in her and his own helplessness, would hardly yet acknowledge her. But there we were, and the memory of that helpless hour brings to my mind the saying that "only they have conquered fate, who fate hath nobly borne!"

It is in such a crisis as we in our humble lot had now reached that fortitude inherent in natures schooled in misfortune come out, whether their estate has been lofty or lowly. That fortitude gives a grandeur to frail humanity. On such occasions so also comes forth the beauty of that sympathy which is the inalienable heritage of generous souls, for as I and my mother were thus suddenly sent adrift, and she had neither father, mother, nor any relation to take her in, we were then to all intents helpless. It was then our good angels appeared in the persons of the Jamesons of the Laigh Toon-end. They came to the rescue, and their brother John soon made ready a small house for us, while one and another of the neighbours assisted. In the course of twenty-four hours, they had a little tenement ready next door to the house from which we had been cast out.

My grandfather's family all left him after his wife's funeral, for although his son put us out, he put no one in to attend to the domestic affairs of the old man. But my mother, notwithstanding the unjust and harsh usage she had received, did what she could to make him comfortable. Though nearly 80 years af age, the old man yet climbed the Greyrigg hill every morning before six o'clock, and wrought light quarry-work, returning in the evening. His employer, for whom he had wrought many years, had guaranteed to give him work so long as he had it, but then modern improvements in modes of quarrying and dressing pavement, or slates, and other materials both for roofing and paving, coming into builders' markets, and an unprofitable "post" (as sections of such quarries are called), drove this employer, as well as many other quarry-masters from the field at this time, and all hands were paid off.

In the case of old men without means, or friends with whom they could live, such failures of a staple industry were nothing short of a local calamity. The younger hands could and did leave the district, and found plenty of employment, as railway lines connecting the great towns in the southern parts of the Kingdom were being constructed, employing unlimited numbers. Old men could not leave the district nor find employment at home, and where their life's vicissitudes had prevented them from making provision for the inevitable period of enforced idleness, their plight was pitiable indeed.

The law for the relief of the poor was not then as now, and although private charity was much more in vogue, yet the true-blue spirit of self-support, and honest independence, was also stronger and more common then than now, and I believe that many cases of actual starvation occurred before the victims of such dire necessity would let their condition be known.

In the case of my grandfather, when he fell out of employment he seemed to have no more interest in life, and appeared to have seen an end of all perfection. Then it was arranged that his household effects should be sold off, and he be removed to the nearest town to live with a married daughter. When this arrangement was made known to the old man he said, "Weel, if they wad let me alane for anither twa-three 'ooks (weeks), I wadna bather ony o' them langer." This prediction proved true, for the life-long ties that had bound him to this quiet valley were strong, and with their severance the old man's heart-strings broke. So, with no apparent illness, in the short space of about two weeks after his removal to the town he laid him down, and in a few days yielded up the blameless life's burden he had carried so long.

Thus ended the simple life histories of my old foster mother and grandfather. Both were types of Scotland's old unspoiled peasantry, and both did their duty faithfully to God and man during their generation, and according to their lights, without fuss, pretension, or noise. My grandfather was a lover of our country's history, the most delightful of fireside companions. His amply-stored mind was like a well-arranged book, and the inquirer had only to indicate the name or nature of any great public event which had occurred at almost any recorded date, and there it was, as the old student had read of it, or gathered it from authentic or reliable sources of information. He was great in the history of feats of arms performed by flood and field, against the enemies of his faith or his country, and when other people would repeat legends and tell hair-raising ghost-stories, he would describe French and British battles, and sieges of the twenty-years' war, and repeat with glorious ardour the deeds of great commanders. Besides, he was very clear in the history of old aristocratic families, and he could tell who were the ancestors, and founders of patrician and noble houses. He could also relate what national or other benefit such and such a man accounted great had conferred on his country or his kind.

In politics he would now be numbered among Liberals of the Cobden, Peel, and John Bright stamp, and in forecasting political, industrial, and social changes his predictions seem to me to have been truly prophetic, for many, and especially the triumphs of mechanical genius he foretold, have been more than accomplished. He would have had no sympathy with the fads of Collectivism, nor the freaks of municipal aggrandizement, which seems (if not checked) likely to turn our over-crowded towns and cities into intolerable police-ridden magisterial tyrannies.

Yet civic freaks and fads seem to be encouraged by the unthinking mob of electors who now find their way to the municipal polling-booths. But a truce to fault-finding, and peace to the grand old man's memory! I have never met another of his class like him!

Chapter V.

No poetry in railways—foolish thought.
. . . .
The young improvement ripening to her prime,
Prepares the way of Liberty and Truth,
And breaks the barriers that since earth began
Have made mankind the enemy of man.
—CHARLES MACKAY.

Opening of the Railway between Arbroath and Forfar, and also between Dundee and Arbroath. — The interest and curiosity of the Public regarding the new mode of conveyance.—My Schoolmaster No. 3, Mr Roostycrank.

Mr Easypen continued master of Lunanhead School with much acceptance to parents and children, until the opening of the Forfar and Arbroath Railway in 1839, when he became the first agent for goods and passengers at Forfar. This was the first railway terminus at a town of any importance in the Strathmore valley, while at the same time another line was opened along the north side of the estuary of the River Tay, and connected Arbroath with what is now the city of Dundee, but curiously enough the two termini in Arbroath did not run into each other, and passengers to Dundee or vice-versa had to find their own way from the one station to the other as best they could, until the broad-guage single lines were doubled on the narrow guage as at present, and the great main line to Aberdeen was constructed.

FORFAR FROM THE NORTH.

Mr Easypen, from stationmaster at Forfar advanced to emolument, place, and power, steadily and successfully, until he reached the chief seat of officialism, and for a number of years he had the management of the whole system of railways running from the city of Aberdeen in the north-east to Dundee in the south, and extending to the city of Perth in the west. These lines each now form part of the great Caledonian and North British systems. The first company has its headquarters in the big black city of Glasgow, and the latter's seat of government is in the grand old grey Metropolis of Scotland.

Mr Easypen's successor was Mr Roostycrank, an M.A., not a barefit, not a sticket, but a stopped minister, who lost the only kirk he was ever offered through his love for a bonnie lass. He was a well-educated man, who wrecked a life which might have adorned any rank. During his time the school was very much neglected, as only those who could ask for attention in the branches they wished to learn were taught, and the others were just left where they were. Among the latter number was your humble servant, who was left behind in the arithmetic, which he had only commenced when the change of teachers was made. Mr Roostycrank looked after his fees, although he certainly did not work for them. He was the only teacher I ever saw there who made or tried to make all pay up. However, carelessness in his work reached a stage beyond the bounds of toleration, and he was dismissed. A short time after his appointment the railway between Arbroath and Forfar was opened.

Of all the company who from Laigh Toon-end at Greyrigg on that fine Saturday in April, 1839, who beheld the first "'loco-engine" returning from Forfar, I find I am the only survivor, all the others having passed on and reached that "unknown land from whose bourne no traveller returns." We thought that first train came along very slowly, as we did not then know of the preliminaries required before opening and running at speed on railways, and of course we were not aware that the occupants of that first train were only testing the fitness of the road before being used by the public.

On the following Monday my idea of slow running was dispelled very completely, for when we were leaving school at Lunanhead at mid-day by the door facing the railway, an engine passed along at such a rate that although we had the line in full view for a mile and a half, the boys who came last got only a slight glimpse of the novel and wonderful sight.

The present generation, who never saw the world without trains, can have little idea of the interest and enjoyment there was in the sight for the first time of a long train of carriages or wagons going at even twenty-five miles an hour. Why, at both ends, and all along this line, when first opened, hundreds turned out, especially at the meal-hours, and some walked a mile and more day after day, for some time to look on the extraordinary spectacle, and it was difficult to believe that people spoke truth who declared that railway trains would yet be so common that the horses or cattle grazing in fields alongside railways would not even lift their heads to look at them. At the same time many old, and some not very old people, were unconvinced of their utility, and especially sceptical as to their safety, in fact, declared " that it was naething bit a temptin' o' Providence that folk sid mak sic machines, an' flee frae toon tae toon on sic a bease " (hurry).

Many a dire calamity was predicted as to what might happen

in the way of accidents, and when a farther-seeing wise-acre than his neighbours one day declared that he "widna winder though he saw the hale concern o' a train blawn up i' the air like peelins o' ingins (onions) and comin' doon in targets like raw skate," with some more timorous of his audience that settled and confirmed the resolution that they at least " wad ne'er risk their lives on nae sic dangerous, sheenwhirrs as a railway train."

Neither my folks nor myself had any fears of the foregoing sort, for on a Friday, some weeks after the opening, Mrs Easypen called me out of one of our games on the school green, and there gave me an invitation to go to Forfar station the next afternoon. The late master was to give me a trip on a train as far as the nearest station eastwards, from whence I could cross the hill northwards to Greyrigg.

This was the first trip I had on a railway, and was certainly a red-letter day in my life, and did I not crow over my school companions when I, about the most solitary chap there, was thus preferred! The distance was only three miles. I was then about ten years old, and looking back through the fifty-six years that have come and gone since then, and having travelled safely any journeys over every line in Scotland and England, and a good part of the Irish railways, and only been in one instance on a train which left the metals (through the breaking of an axle) I am justified in looking with true gratitude and thankfulness to

"That Divinity which shapes our ends,
Rough hew them as we will."

and also think that Mr Easypen's kindness in giving a free ticket for my first little journey has had good luck, and has been a presage of many pleasant journeys.

Chapter VI.

*Some books are lees frae end to end,
And some great lees were never penn'd;*

*We'll mak' oor maut, we'll brew oor drink,
We'll dance, and sing, and rejoice man.*
—BURNS.

Leein' Jamie Langbow.—Tam Fanklerigg and the Whisky-smuggling Raid. — The Ghaist o' the Knowe. — The Gauger's Coach.—Gunner Grigg.--Rob Linkinsteel and the miller o' Steenyrigg. — A night of terror in Greyrigg.

About this date a change in the occupancy of the hostelry in Greyrigg took place, and it was the second since the days of Watty Wabblestraught. The place now became the tenancy of a man from Forfar. His name was Langbow, or "Leein' Langbow," as he was called, he being one of the most accomplished liars ever seen or rather heard of in that region. It was said that the imaginations he gave forth hurt no one but himself, but they did him irreparable damage, as no one who had once been taken in with his very long bow-shots, would ever come within range again, or believe one word he said.

"Leein' Jamie" would soon have made his fortune in some of our large towns now, as a concocter of those dreadful whoppers, which some enterprising but unscrupulous shop-keepers send out in print from day to day. This advertising literature has become one of the branches of College learning in America (I hear). This man and his wife, Jean McHugh, were now master and mistress of the Greyrigg Tavern and Hotel.

The farm of Hirple Howe, of which this house was a pendicle, had changed hands also, and the young farmer, Tam Fanklerigg being in charge for his father, who was the tacksman, and successor of Sandy Hardwird (already mentioned). Now, "Leein' Jamie," not finding the public-house anything like what it was in byegone days, doubtless thought, like the heather besom dealer we have heard of, if he could steal the manufactured article, he would manage to keep house profitably.

He therefore got young Fanklerigg induced to try his hand at the manufacture of raw grain whisky, but "Leein' Jamie" disappeared about the time the following event took place, which broke up the whisky distilling scheme and nearly ruined the elder Fanklerigg. Indeed, it was believed that Langbow doubled on young Tam, and went and informed the Board of Excise. So one quiet but very dark night in the early part of the year my mother and Jenny Jameson were working late on their looms to get their webs finished by a certain time. There was a small window at the right hand, where my mother worked, from which we had a full view of Forfar Parish Church and Steeple, three miles off, and also of the public road thereto. About eleven o'clock my mother happened to look through this window, when lo, a light shone out; it seemed half a mile to the west, and as if stationary on the high road. Calling to her neighbour, "Come here, Jeannie, and see this licht aboot the knowe o' the road," a general name the apparent location of the light had. Jeannie, stepping off her seat, came and looked out through the window, and exclaims, "Oh, that licht is mony, mony a time there. They say it's a ghaist. It

FORFAR PARISH CHURCH AND STEEPLE.

stravaigs aboot there, and sometimes daunders doon the Sclate Steen Park, aye, and whiles ventures up north through the parks as far as East Bar Bank."

"Keeps a'," says my mither, "what can be the meanin' o' that?" "The lord only kens," says Jeannie; "but they say it's often seen there, and looks juist like a bare burnin' caunle kerried in somebody's haund." "Gie me anither luik," quo' my mither; "I'm shuir yer welcome," says Jeannie, for I'm a' trimlin. I wiss

John (referring to her brother) wad come up and ging doon the road wi' me this nicht." My mother took anither guid look, and in a wee cries oot, "Oh! Jeannie Jameson, somebody maun hae been stuffin' yer heid wi' something safter nor tow aboot the Knoweheid ghaist, for I'll tak' ma aith yon licht is frae neither ghaist nor deil, aye an' there's a pair o' lichts, and there's nane o' them kerried in onybody's or bogle's hand, for they are movin' alang quite cannily, and the lichts baith lowin' clear, an' gin they haud on they'll sune be here, for they are wearin' nearer and nearer."

And nearer they did come sure enough. The most of the older villagers were now awake, for the sound of wheels was very unusual there at midnight. The cause of the disturbance turned out to be a carriage, drawn by a pair of pure thorough-bred, black, well-trained horses, who came round in fine style, and four men in long grey greatcoats, with something like military caps and long-legged boots protecting their upper and lower extremities, stepped out of the vehicle. The horses were unyoked and the carriage left on the public-house green; the horses were then led to a stable to which the coachman with his beautiful steeds were lighted by the landlady, who carried a great horn-glazed lanthorn. The four men who alighted meantime had walked into the kitchen, where they partook of some sort of liquor, for which the leader paid. Then each took from his under garments something which shone like steel, which, after being carefully examined, was returned to where it was taken from; then, at a word from the leader, they left the tavern, and forming in files two abreast they crossed the green and turned eastward, marching with steady martial step until they reached the gate on the left at the end of the road leading north to Hirple Howe.

They were followed at a considerable distance by a watcher from Greyrigg, more curious than the rest, who went on until he knew they had reached the front door of the farm-house. The watcher then concealing himself behind the wall of the garden, which lay in front of the house, heard the leader of the four muffled men he had followed, after knocking loudly at the farm-house door, demanding admission in the Queen's name. The door was soon opened, and the housekeeper and women servants, with young Fanklerigg in their midst, were seen in the hall or passage, and all looking very terror-stricken.

The officer in charge then ordered one of his followers to go to the kitchen or back way, and another to guard the stair entrance which led to the upper part of the house. This the two men, pistol in hand, proceeded to do instantly, then bolting the door by which he and his men entered the chief officer opened his warrant and read his authority for the arrest and secure keeping of one Thomas Fanklerigg, jun., farmer, or farmer's son, residing at Hirple Howe, parish of Aberlemno, county of Forfar, on a charge of defrauding her Majesty's Board of Excise by distilling or attempted to distil proof spirit or low wines from barley, or some other grain malt to the prosecutor unknown, the approximate dates and place where the offences were committed being told. The warrant further ordered that the said Thomas Fanklerigg be kept in safe and close custody until a guarantee or legal bond be given for the payment of a money penalty to Her Majesty's Board of Excise of five hundred pounds, failing which the said Thomas Fanklerigg be committed to Her Majesty's County Prison at Forfar, until the law is vindicated.

Further, the same warrant authorised the seizing and destruction of all and every utensil, article, or tool used in the foresaid illegal offence.

After some short parley with the young man thus charged, the housekeeper (who was his aunt), knowing he was his father, the tacksman's proxy, advised her nephew to sign the bond for the payment of the penalty, and show the officers where the distilling apparatus was. The charge and knowledge of the attempted smuggling took her and the house servants completely by surprise, so closely had the two confederates kept the nefarious secret, that when one of the men-servants was aroused and ordered to yoke a cart to go to Forfar with the seizure, the man scarcely understood the meaning of the untimeous order, but in those days for a servant to hear his master's order was to obey. So Shoosie, the fine old trusty dun mare was seen in the dusk of the morning passing with her long steady step through Greyrigg about four o'clock, and those who had watched, or who had not slept after the previous night's alarm, declared "there was something covered up in the cart, aye, an' it made a sound like a dog wurrin'." When this was first told at dawn, it increased the sensation, and the village was more mystified than ever, especially as it was declared that shortly after "the cart gaed wast the road, the stately black horses were re-yoked to the carriage, and went off after the cart at full speed, an' a' that the beasts cud lay doon."

To crown the awful secret, although four men "cam' wi' the coach," as they in Greyrigg vernacular named the vehicle, only three men went back. This was the climax of mystery now. But at length daylight came, and the wintry sunbeams once more lighted up the edges of the northern range of Carsegray fells, and men and maids hied them forth to their usual and varied tasks.

But the events of the past night sat big on their minds, and many surmises, each wilder and more improbable than the other, were made.

At last old Gunner Grigg, who had served on board a privateer, and had been a member of the hated press-gang at Arbroath in the times of the French wars, swore by his buttons "that it must have been a chase after a deserter, who, on being overhauled, had refused to lie-to, and had then been brought up by a round shot; and the sound which had been heard as Shoosie's cart passed through the toon must have been the groans of the wounded lubber."

"O, Grigg," quo Rob Linkinsteel, the tailor, "yer a' oot like the fut o' a pot; did I not follow the chase to Hirple Howe, an' I am verra shuir there wisna a shot fired, nor a nieve lifted, by ony ane there, for I crap up near close to the front door, fan it was steekit, an' I'm shuir there was nae fechtin', or I wad hae seen it, aye an' maybe haen a haun' in't. Tho' I cudna mak' oot what the heid billie wis sayin', I'm certain there wis nae fechtin'. Fan the door wis opened again I crept back a bit faurer oot o' sicht, an' the men and Tam cam' oot. He stoiter't roon near tae whaur I wis hodin' (hiding); he gied a bit jump fan he got a glisk o' me, but he had presence o' mind eneuch tae keep quate, an' hearkening inta ma lug, he says, 'Ye micht rin doon the Winkleburn side and tell the miller o' Steenyrigg tae see at his kil' beddin' is clean sweepit at ance,' and tell him at the same time tae look oot for squalls. He'll ken fine what ye mean.'

"He'll need," quo I, "for I'm fair ramfoozled, an' disna ken."

"Never mind, tyler," says Tam, "rin noo, if ever you ran i' your life."

"An' I wat I ran, an' the miller said, 'Juist let them squall awa', I hae naething here but fat's a' ma ain, an' little eneuch.'"

This demolished the old gunner's theory, but did not clear up the awful secret. Then Jean McHugh was thought to be the only one who could throw some light on the dark subject.

Jean, some short time before this, seeing that the public-house was not to earn bread for her and Langbow, and an adopted boy about my own age, had betaken her to her original occupation of weaving, and occupied a loom in the same shop where my relation, Jeannie Jameson worked, and on her appearance about ten o'clock on this morning, so full of anxious and stark-staring inquiry, my mother put the question—

"Fat wis a' that ado aboot the'streen (yestreen), Jean, and fat earant wis yon four men on at cam' i' the coach, flegin' a'body hauf oot o' their wit, at sic an oonholy oor?"

Jean at first rather hedged the question, but her questioner continued, "Oh, ye needna seek tae smort up; it'll hae to come oot some time, an' gin ye tell noo fat ye ken, it may keep lees frae bein' telt aboot the frigac."*

"Weel," says Jean, "they've been tryin' to mak' smuggled whisky at Hirple Howe, the gaugers got wind o' it, an' yon wis them. They hae lifted the hale concern, an' I think they hae young Hirple confined i' the farm-house, an' a man wi' a loaded pistol is keepin' gaird owre 'im."

"Fat's that for?" says my mother.

"Oh," says Jean, "they say the guagers didna like tae tak him to the prison, an' they are keepin' 'im a prisoner at hame till they get anither name pit on some paper, ca'd a bond, for the duty, or

---

* A local term for any curious incident.

the fine, an' they say its five hunner pound."

"Guidsake," said the questioner, "that'll ruin them a', but faur's Jeemes Langbow a' this time?"

"O," says Jean, "I dinna ken whaur he is, an' I wiss I cud say I dinna care."

This closed the inquiry so far as Jean was concerned, and also as to the whereabouts of leein' Jamie, who, however, turned up and lived in his own likeness in this same spot for some years after the smuggling episode was forgotten, and still he was "Leein' Jamie" to the end of the chapter.

The sequel to his and Jean McHugh's career, and the close of my schooldays, will duly appear in my next chapter. Those days were all too few and unimproved, when I had all too soon to cross their boundary, and join the ranks of toil, in the same kind of occupation which fell to the sin-laden lot of man's primordial ancestor.

Chapter VII.

"*A school-boy with his noise and fun,
The veriest mystery under the sun;
As brimful of mischief and wit and glee,
As even a human frame can be.*"
—M. A. KIDDER.

Mr Plaintext and his famous Bible Class. — My First Christmas Tree—Cock Fighting at Public Schools. Scholars' Pitched Battles —I refuse to Fecht; am Bullied.—Banton Bricklug, and how I fought him at last.

After Mr Roostycrank's dismissal from the school at Lunanhead, the place was occupied by a very good little man from about Dundee. His name was Andrew Plaintext, and he tried to make it all plain to us, so far as his abilities and his own scholastic attainments went.

He was not very learned, but what he did know he made the most of, and could teach it to others. He gathered a large attendance around him, and the schoolroom becoming over-crowded, a new one was built by the same means as was the old one, and a grant of £10 per annum was got on the opening from Government. That was the first time I ever heard of an educational Government grant being obtained for a small undenominational school.

There was also a female teacher's room for sewing and knitting. The first lady teacher became engaged to Mr Plaintext, and they were married, and after a short time gave up the school for a larger one near Dundee. Mr Plaintext was locally famous in his Lunanhead appointment for conducting the largest Bible class on the Sunday evenings ever seen in that district. We met in the new schoolroom, and numbers of grown-up men and women attended. The exercises were not merely repeating passages by rote from Bible or Psalm-book. Oh, no; it was the best exegesis of Bible history, Bible lands, Bible geography, and general Scripture information that I have ever known.

Parents and the general public were admitted to hear and see at those meetings, and the place was often full and sometimes crowded. Question and answer was one of this teacher's methods, and there was always a number of rounds of that form for arriving at hidden meanings, and expounding the sacred texts, and very often when a stiff question went the round of the class, or some geographical question as to Eastern holy places had to make the same journey unanswered, I would at last be called on by name to answer, or point out the place on the map of Palestine. I generally came off with flying colours.

In this schoolmaster's time here he abolished the Christmas or Yule gratitudes which all his predecessors were wont to look for and accept on such festive occasions, and instead he let each contribute one penny, in the case of the junior classes, and threepence for seniors, and the collections being handed to him, he provided what is now known as a Christmas tree, and the whole school partook of the fruit.

Cock-fighting used to be a feature of the Yule-tide entertainments, but I never saw a main fought, although the barbarous pastime had not then been prohibited by law, but even after it became unlawful to pit game cocks against each other at public schools, numbers of men in the Barracks, Lunanhead, and Forfar yet bred, reared, and trained the pure game fowl for these cruel matches, and there was cock-fighting, although not at public schools, but secretly, at Yule-times, as well as at other seasons, and such mains were fought between the pugnacious and savage birds, armed with steel spurs, specimens of which I have seen in the hands of big boys, with whose pursuits and amusements I never had any sympathy.

I now believe it must have been from cock-fighting that the pitched battles between boys at those schools had originated, for both at Lunanhead Adventure and the Rescobie Parochial Schools, every new boy had to prove in the boxing ring and on the school-green battle-ground whether he was made of true Scotch material, and able to give and take in a stand-up fight. "Aye, an' ony ane 'at widna or cudna fecht" was either relegated to oblivion, or set down on the school-green as an oddity if he did not accept as a challenge and respond at once in proper style, should anyone dare to stroke down his breast-buttons with a wet forefinger, or venture further and give "the cowardie blow."

When I was sent first to Lunanhead School, having no brothers or male friends to fight for me, if challenged to an unfair match, and not being a very robust Christian, my female trustee was much concerned for my safety. The school was three miles off, and she, knowing the invariable ordeal which all the new-comers had to pass through, hired a big boy who attended from Greyrigg, and accompanied us morning and evening. This lad for a small gift undertook to see that I was not urged to fight, nor bullied by boys bigger and stronger than myself.

The way this hired protector fulfilled his part of the bargain was characteristic of the inborn love for fighting, and seeing fights permeating schoolboy nature. The very first evening on our way home, he got a boy smaller than I, but about two years older, viz., Banton Bricklug, the miller's son o' Steenyrigg Mill, to challenge me in true orthodox style. I did not take it as a challenge, and when my unfaithful schoolmate explained that it meant an invitation to fecht, I refused to fecht, as I had been warned by my mither (as I called her) against fechtin', for she telt me it was only ruffians and bad laddies that focht.

My companions made great fun of my scruples, and the smaller bruiser who had challenged me grew so crouse that he ventured to hit me, but I did not retaliate on this occasion. The same sort of thing was repeated several nights following on our way home, and duly reported to Elsie on my arrival. I did not tell grandfather, neither did she, because that old-time school pupil would have despised me if he ever heard that I would take a blow from any boy without returning the same, as one time when one of the village boys much bigger and older had hit me, the old man hearing me complaining to his partner lifted his eyes from the book he was reading, and burst out quite indignant with, "Ugh! min, yer father wid hae thrashed a pair o'm." But Elsie took up my defence at once, and said, "Deed, Peter, a' winder tae hear ye. Ye surely ken there's no' ony comparison 'atween the laddie an' his father at the yeild confeerin' in buik, or beens, an' tae think this laddie cud staun up afore a lump o' a ruffian like Clinker is juist onrizenable."

This settled the old man's question for the time being, but did not prevent him from giving me lessons in the art of self-defence, and as I expected I had not yet got quite rid of the annoyance of my little bully, I secretly resolved that if he ever hit me again I would try if I could not strike back.

I very soon got a chance, for on our way home the very next night after, when he commenced to smite as before, I considerably surprised the Banton, as also myself, by landing him a right-hander on the mouth which drew blood from his teeth, and left a mark on his chin. Bricklug broke down and cried, and I was the exultant victor on that field of blood, and was left in peace ever after!

But it got abroad at school that I was dead set against fighting, and I have no doubt I was despised accordingly.

Mr Plaintext did his best to put down the ring fights and pitched battles, and for that purpose used to superintend and take part in the big boys' games, and played often at shinty with them on the road which lay east and west behind the school, till one day a player was struck on the face by the flying nacket—a piece of square hard wood they used instead of a ball. This being a rather severe wound the master gave up taking any part in that game, but he encouraged all safe and innocent amusements. He was much beloved by all who came in contact with him, and when the new school was built he put £20 into the building fund (a large sum then), yet when he left, it was said the unpaid fees were about the same amount.

There were no official examinations of such schools, nor was this one ever examined in my time. We had therefore no stimulus of anticipated reward to lead us on, and many who had no thirst for knowledge did not get on, but this teacher did not fail to keep us in mind of the essential use and advantage to be gained by having our minds stored with useful knowledge, and he showed us how education was the key wherewith we could unlock wisdom's stores.

Chapter VIII.

" Train up a child in the way he should go ; and when he is old he will not depart from it."
—SOLOMON'S PROVERBS.

Dave and Will's speculations on my antipathy to fechtin' and swearin'.—A Dialogue on Things in General.—relating to Fechtin' ministers and the impending Disruption.—Mr Problem, my 5th and last Schoolmaster, a learned man and strict disciplinarian.

I have recorded my antipathy to fighting set fights, and swearing, as proving the sound home-training received at the faithful hands of one who, though no blood relation, yet left her teaching ever fresh in my recollection as an imperishable legacy, which time cannot wither or decay.

This priceless possession through life has ever had a powerful influence with me, because it instilled in me the idea that although none in his innocence may trust, yet the pure in heart, word, and deed, alone can see God. I mean seeing Him and understanding Him in his works, both of Nature and of Grace.

The following dialogue between two boys, one of them a schoolmate, and the other a stranger, brings out my meaning. This conversation was overheard by a person passing from Forfar one day, and repeated to my real mother, who I afterwards heard telling it to one of her neighbours, she being also on the road.

One boy, Dave by name, says to another named Will—" Fa's that fleet strappin' lass 'at passed enoo, Dave?"

Dave: "Ou, that's so and so's mither," naming me, "The guid scholar at Lunanhead?"

Will: "That's her, is't. An' is he that guid as to be ca'd guid specially?"

Dave: "Weel, I dinna ken, he's alloed to be the best English scholar there."

Will: "Is there onything but English there, an' his he elocution? I doot they canna gi'e that at Lunanhead."

Dave: "I dinna think they can elocute 'im there, but they say Plaintext canna tak' 'im ony faurer, an' he's to be sent twa quarters ower the hill tae Rescobie, tae Mr Problem."

Will: "He maun be a kind o' a problem himsel'."

Dave: "Maybe, but he's licket a' at learnin' things quick 'at ever cam' there. They say he'll read a thing ower ance or twice, and minds the hail jing-bang, kittle words an' a', in a jiffey. But there's some queer things aboot him too; he winna fecht, an' a'e day fan Jeem Dryster an' him war playin' at the peery-ring, Jeem loot a wee swear, an' he turned on him like winkin' an' wi' a face as white's his mither's mutch, he says, 'Jeem, that was an ill wird, an' ye sudna swear.' Jeem says, 'Tell me, dae ye ne'er swear yersel?' 'No,' says he, wi' sic a force, 'there's no real gentleman swears.' 'But,' says Jeem, ' ye are no' a man yet, ne'er speakin' o' a gentleman.' 'But,' says he, 'I mean to be baith yet, if I'm spared.' Syne Jeem he says, 'Aye; an' fat are ye thinkin' to be to your trade gin yer spaired?' says he. 'I want to be a minister.' 'Weel,' says Jeem, 'it's michty onlikely ye'll ever win the length o' bein' a minister, but ye'll hae to fecht, aye, an' swear too, afore ye dee, or ye'll no' live lang.'"

How true! Jeem's words became in a short time, and how their utterance came back to my mind as a prophecy being actually fulfilled in future events will be seen hereafter.

However, Will and Dave finished their speculation on my peculiarities, and also my aspirations, by Will exclaiming—

"Weel, that dings a' thing, did onybody ever hear o' the like. He'll no' fecht, rages at folk 'at lats a little swear, an' wants to be a minister."

Dave adds, "Puir sinner, he has a sair job afore him, but gin his folk hivna siller I canna see, except they war kinda rich an' him wad fecht, hoo he has the least chance o' bein' a minister."

Then Will returning to the subject, said, "I dinna exactly see faur the fechtin' comes into the makin' o' a minister."

Dave replies: "I dinna fairly ken aither, but I ken a' the ministers fecht."

Then Will says: "Ye'll hae noticed a heip o' things awful queer i' this warl'. Do you no' think the hale hesp's gane ravelled, like Tammy Timmerfit's hank o' threid?"

"Aye," says Dave; "I aften think that, an' I hear the auld folk sayin' there'll be bonnets on the green; aye, an' tufts o' hair in them afore this rook amon' the ministers is settled." (It was shortly before the Disruption.)

It will have been observed that at one part of Will and Dave's interview, a reference is made to me being sent ower the hill to the Parish School at Rescobie. This was to make up for time lost under Mr Roostycrank. As Mr Plaintext could not take me further in English reading, and as his arithmetical knowledge was not very extensive, it was believed one half-year in Mr Problem's classes would equip me completely for business, if I ever required figures extensively in my life's pursuits.

The teacher at Rescobie was a famed arithmetician and mathematical scholar, and it was very often a perplexing mystery to me how he could keep body and soul together, and bring up a family as he did, on the very small salary which that school gave.

The harvest was not quite finished in 1839 when I went there, and for about a month after there were only the farmer of Mains o' Templeheid's son, and I in attendance. Even when the full number of pupils came forward, they did not exceed forty all told, nearly all males.

Mr Problem was a very learned man, but except for advanced pupils, not much of a success as a teacher. He was a dark stern-looking man, tall and thin, great in figures and calculation, which he drove into our heads through our palms, with plenty of leather. He was a very strict disciplinarian, indeed. Woe betide the unfortunate youth whom he found disobeying rules, or inattentive to his lessons. He never lifted his tawse to me, but he once hit me a box on the ear for bad writing, and declared I was the best reader and the worst penman he had ever encountered. He was an artist in penmanship himself, and no matter how good a pupil might be at mental work, if he did not write like copperplate he had no real merit in Mr Problem's eyes.

At another time he exclaimed, in his impatience, that "it was just like my father," who had attended there too when a boy. I was not able then to find out the resemblance Mr Problem spoke of, as up till then I had only seen my prototype once, but after many years, and when the model spoken of was ending his days under my roof, except a personal resemblance there was not the shadow of a similarity between us. I have heard my father say in his old age that he never had any love for the school, and had a very bad memory. Moreover, as his mother died when he was only about six years old, and there were several children younger, and only a sister about sixteen years old to look after the household, he sometimes played truant day after day, and was thrashed by his father at home when it became known. Then he was again punished when he ventured back to school.

A good story was often told in the district as to how an aunt of my father's discovered how the boy was being abused and mismanaged as regarded his school truancy.

This aunt lived near the schoolhouse, on a small croft of land, and was waited on one day by two rather stout-looking boys, the oldest of whom asked for the loan of a box-barrow. Being questioned as to the purpose for which the Christian cart was required, he said it was to " tak' a laddie to the schule."

His aunt says, " What's the matter wi' the laddie, has he broken his leg ?"

" Na," says the spokesman, " he winna ging."

" Lat me see him; faur is he noo? Lat me see," quo she.

The barrow borrowers did not seem very much inclined to show the delinquent, but reluctantly led the way along a private cross road, near by, when lo! they came on her hopeful nephew lying in a ditch, with his hands and feet tied, and bleeding from wounds in the face and head, inflicted by the two compulsory officers.

Before they had overpowered my awful dad, they had torn up his cravat and made manacles of it, and bound him as his aunt found him.

" Mercy me, Bob," she says, when she saw him in such a plight, " fat are you lying there for?"

"Because I canna get up," says Bob. "The beggars grippit me and kicket me wi' their feet, or I wad hae lickit them baith, and I'll dae it yet if ye'll no' lat them grip me."

"Na, na, Bob," says his aunt, "we're for nae mair lickin' nor fechtin'," and she began to untie his bonds.

The biggest boy now tried to prevent that, and attempted to shove her aside, but the other lad whispered to him, "Lat her alane, min, that's his auntie."

So poor Bob's hands and feet were untied, his torn cravat adjusted, his bonnet replaced, and his wounded face and head washed in a clear road-side burn. Bob agreed to be taken to face Mr Problem along with his auntie, of course expecting the usual dose of leather. His auntie was clever, and a well-educated woman for her situation in life, a managing and prudent woman, who was in her day a credit and ornament to that station.

The two boys who had made this memorable capture meantime hied to the school to report, and at length Bob and his aunt reached the schoolhouse. On being announced Mr Problem came to the door and put forth his hand to drag Bob in, but his aunt held the boy back, and said:

"No, no, Mr Problem, we're no' quite the length o' lattin' Bob in ower your schule door again, till we see if he is to be better used for the time to come." This relative used to say she would never forget the rage that Mr Problem got into. The veins on his forehead seemed to swell, and he grew as red in the neck as a turkey cock.

But she kept her hold of Bob, and continued her advocacy, saying, "We micht as weel brak the laddie's neck an hae dune wi' him as aloo you, Mr Problem, here at the schule, and his father at hame to thrash and abuse him as ye've been daein' a while back, and syne sendin' oot twa big, strong geeskins like yon 'at cam' for the len o' my barrow to bring him here to be half-killed, after they struggled wi' him, kickit him wi' their feet, and torn his cravat, an' bits o' duds near aff his back. He hisna a mither to tak' his pairt and be kind till him at hame. I hae a family o' my ain, an' have eneuch to do, but rather than see a brave high-spirited manly laddie wasted as Bob is bein' wasted I'll tak' him hame wi' me, and fin' anither schule for him, except ye undertak' here an' noo, that you winna lick him for bein' absent this mornin', an' Bob here promises if you winna lick him this time, he'll no' play truant again."

So, on these conditions Bob was taken inside, and was not punished for this time, and never played truant again, and was less harshly dealt with, as although Mr Problem was very strict and hot-tempered, he did not mean to be cruel.

But to resume the record of my experiences at this rather select school. Being the solitary exception who came across the hill from Greyrigg, and the way being only a path through moors and woods, it was arranged during the short days in the dead of winter that I was let off in time to get through the woods with daylight.

This was looked on by the big farmers' sons and the minister's family as a very great partiality shown to me, although they knew I had no companion to go with me over the dreary and rather dangerous road after dark. Their jealousy showed itself in many little spiteful acts and petty abuses when they got outside, and yet where English readings or composition were concerned inside, I held my own and more, with the best of them. There was a lesson book of readings, where the sentences were left void of many of the more important words. It was an afternoon lesson, and the teacher always read it once over in the class, and each member was understood to be able (after a short study of it in his seat) to read any sentence correctly when the class was again called up.

I never had any difficulty in reading any sentence, or the whole lesson for that matter, when it came to my turn, but it was interesting to see how the others exchanged seats with each other on the sly, to get me to tell the missing words. Forgiving, if not forgetting, their out-door unkindness and jealousies, I never refused to help them.

But the short winter days passed on and came to an end, and so did my arithmetical school-days.

> And when the emerald tassels hung
>   Frae the larch tree,
> Those beloved school lessons
>   Were ended for me.

Mr Problem pleaded hard for me to be left on his hands for another six months, promising if left at his classes for that further time, he would undertake to turn me out a first-rate arithmetician, and he insisted I should learn mathematics also. But no; fees were high, and my mother was unable, unaided as she was, to continue me longer idle (as she called it). So on finishing my eleventh year I joined the ranks of labour, first as a farm-servant, and cattle-herd on the moors and fells and green rolling braes I have tried to describe in the first chapter of these sketches. As the next year and a half closed my connection with Greyrigg as my home, and as there are one or two more of its rare old villagers whose memories I would like to give a place among the momentoes of my boyhood-days, a few lines will be devoted to them in my next chapter.

Chapter IX.

*"Still o'er the grave that holds the dear remains,
  The mouldering urn her spirit left below;
Fond fancy dwells, and pours funereal strains,
  The soul-dissolving melody of woe."*

—SCOTT OF AMWELL.

Some worthies of Greyrigg — Tibbie of the slated house—Tibbie's Death and Funeral — after the Funeral — Her nephew from Montrose addresses the mourners—His generosity.

I have mentioned in the first chapter of these sketches that in 1833 there was only one slated roof in the hamlet of Greyrigg. This had been occupied as a feu in her own right, given for life (some years previous to the date of my arrival there) to a widow named Tibbie Tytler, who was a true specimen of sturdy old Scotch independence and thrift, who earned her living for many years by working out-door work in summer, and in-door and barn-room work in winter on the home farm of Pitandrew. She was a bit of a character in her way, had a sharp tongue, and could give a very ready answer, but at the same time a most upright and God-fearing woman.

I remember well, after I had come under my real mother's management, when she had set up house for herself and me, she used to take me across the green, by invitation, to Tibbie's biggin' on the Sunday evenings, and on those occasions, at the little end-window of her kitchen in summer, or at the rush-lit "cruisie" in the winter, with my blue worsted bonnet laid reverently aside, I had to read over the favourite passages from the Old or New Testaments, in which my two hearers delighted. How delightful it is to me now, remembering how those two women (the old and the young) seemed to enjoy such readings, and with what assurance they spoke of Bible promises, and how they were wont to expatiate on the love of God, of His justice and judgment, speaking often of the believer's waiting heritage in the hereafter. There were no doubts; no vain questionings seemed ever to cross their minds, for, like Cowper's "Cottager,"

"They both just knew, and knew no more,
Their Bible true."

Although the rather long spells of Bible reading were sometimes felt by me rather irksome, yet I thought I was well rewarded on seeing the pleasure which beamed in my mother's face, when, on my being let off I would hear Tibbie say, "Eh, but he's a winderfu' fine reader. Be sure an' keep guid buiks in his haun', Mary, for ye may lippen (depend) fatever that laddie reads or hears it'll stick tae 'im."

Tibbie's end was (as all such ends are) a consistent finish to a faithful and consistent life. She took ill when nearing her eightieth year, and when my mother called and found Tibbie not up as usual one morning, on asking her what she thought was the matter, Tibbie replied, "Ah, Mary, there's no' muckle the maitter wi' me, but this is death noo, lass."

My mother was much moved, but said she hoped it was not so serious as that, and would it not be well to send to Forfar for a doctor. Tibbie said, "Bring nae doctors here, Mary, the last and only doctor for me will be here sune and sure. Dinna grieve," she added, "it's a' richt, and I'll sune join my ain guidman. I ken Wha I hae believed, and the promises you an' me hae sae aften spoken o' will be all fulfilled for me; aye, an' for you too, gin ye haud on tae Him 'at gies the promise."

And so in about a fortnight's time Tibbie laid down the brave life she had adorned so long, and left a record behind her untarnished by a single stain. I attended her funeral as the representative of my mother, being then in my tenth year. Tibbie left no family, and only one relative was found to lay her head in the grave, yet there were many very sincere mourners, both friends and neighbours who had known her worth, and enjoyed association with her for many years.

The relative who attended her funeral was a nephew, a fine gentlemanly man about middle age. He came from Montrose, and on our return from Aberlemno Kirkyaird, he had to make his way across the hill at once to join a stage-coach to return to his home that night. The whole company had been invited back to the house of the deceased, where he addressed them as follows: "Dear friends," he said, "you have all been kind and Christian-hearted neighbours to my deceased aunt. She served her day and generation well, and has, I doubt not, now reaped the reward of her faith and patience. She has left no children, or near kin, to mourn her demise, and we need not mourn, but we may all follow her track in the sure and certain faith, that through the same grace we may all reach the same goal and reap the same reward." He then paused and said, "I have been put in possession of over five pounds of money, a surplus left after all funeral expenses are paid. From that money I wish you all to have your tea, and if you drink a glass of toddy in moderation, and to the memory of my aunt I shall be gratified."

He then handed the money to the elder who had furnished the coffin, even our old friend John Endever, saying, "Whatever balance is left over please give it for behoof of the poor of the parish," closing with the words, "I do not require any of this money, as the Lord has blessed me with plenty."

He then made over the household furniture and all the house contained to "leein' Jamie Langbow" and his wife, Jean McHugh, who, along with an adopted boy, occupied one end of Tibbie's house, the adopted boy and his foster-mother having lodged there a year and a half, or since about a fortnight after the raid on the illicit distillery seized at Hirple Howe. Langbow's wife is the Jean McHugh whom we left at her loom on that memorable morning when she declared that Langbow had betaken himself to parts unknown.

The lodgment of Jean and her boy with Tibbie was sufficiently pathetic to warrant special record in a new chapter.

MARKET-DAY IN FORFAR.

Chapter X.

*" The fate o' our neebour may sune be our fa',
An' neebours are near us when kindred's awa'."*
—ALEXANDER LAING.

Jean McHugh's home made desolate—Little Alec takes it sore to heart. — The two befriended by good Tibbie Tytler—Return of Langbow to his deserted wife Jean.

About the second day after young Fanklerigg's arrest a Sheriff Officer and his concurrent arrived in Greyrigg and poinded the whole furniture and every article movable found within the village tavern, and ten days after the same functionary returned, but this time accompanied by men, horses, and carts, and removed the complete lot for public sale at the Market Cross of Forfar. I remember seeing the officer who had charge of the removal take up two dinner plates, and handing them to Jean, he said, " Here, these may be some use to you." Jean took the delf and sent them into a thousand pieces against a wall, saying as the pieces fell around, " If they are of no use to you they are of as little use to me." She then crossed the road to the weaving shop, and took her seat with the air of a princess, and no one ever saw a tear in her eye. She commenced work at her loom as calmly as if she had but returned from dinner, although it is doubtful if she had any dinner that day, and one thing is certain, she was left with nothing now wherein to cook a dinner. My mother and Jeannie

Jameson were at work, but none of them ventured to question Jean as to where she was to sleep that night.

There was something in that stern, set face, and the unnatural calm of that now homeless woman, which kept them silent. But night came, as it always comes on those who have home and on the homeless alike, whether its shadows hide joy or grief! Alec McHugh and I, who had been almost the only and sorely astonished witnesses of the hasty removal of his kind foster parents' whole household goods, were still at our play, when Jean McHugh appeared at the weaving shop door and called out to Alec to "Come awa' hame." Thought I "Where is yer hame this nicht?" However, the two crossed the road, Jean leading Alec by the hand. They entered the long low empty house, and in a few minutes the reflection of a light from the big kitchen fireplace was seen at the window, and Jean then came forth again, and gathering up an armful of straw from the heap left by the men who emptied the house in the forenoon. She returned inside, evidently bent on bed-making. My playmate, Alec, was seated in a corner of the kitchen fireplace, weeping as if his heart would break, his mother trying to comfort him by telling him that God saw both him and her, and saying it would "a' come richt by an' bye."

Meantime a figure was seen through the gathering gloom crossing the road from the south, which turned out to be Tibbie Tytler from the slated cottage, and next was heard Tibbie saying:

"Preserve me, Jean McHugh, fat are ye tryin' tae dae?"

"Jean replied "I'm tryin' tae mak' a bed for Alec an' me."

"The Lord help ye," says Tibbie, reverently, "is that puckle strae a' the bed ye hae?"

"Aye," says Jean, quite cheerfully, "an' dae ye no' think its a brawer and better bed than mony better fowk nor me hiv ha'en?"

"Aye," says Tibbie, "that's true, but if ye'll only come wi' me I'll gie ye a better bed this nicht yet."

"O, Tibbie," says Jean, "I'm no' able tae pey ye for a bed. I hinna a saxpence i' the world till I get oot ma wob (web). I gied Alec ma hin'most coin this mornin' an' sent him tae the merchant for something tae live on for this day onywye."

"Never mind," says Tibbie, "come yer wa's upbye wi' me, and ye can pey me fan I seek payment for yer lodgin's an' the use o' sic things as my hoose affords, an' mind, if ye come an' lodge wi' me, gin ye ever offer me payment afore I seek it it'll be yer term-day. And Langbow, wha sud a' been here tae help ye through this awfu' day, if he ever comes back ye maun tak' him in an' mak' him welcome, an' he maybe winna rin awa' again, for disna the buik say 'whom the Lord has joined, lat nought pit them sindry.' I ken ye fear God, Jean, an' I hiv nae fear o' you."

Did not the benefactor, and the person benefited, in this case both reap the meed of their simple and certain faith? and whether Jean and Langbow ever paid lodgings to Tibbie there is nothing to show, nor has anyone a call to inquire.

As already mentioned, on the evening of Tibbie's funeral, those lodgers were put in possession of a well-appointed house and furniture, and Langbow never deserted Jean again.

Chapter XI.

"Very like a whale."
—SHAKESPERE.

Leein' Jamie's Story.—John Endever and Gunner Grigg—John put down the gunner.—1840.—I am put out to the world to earn my bread.

I have already hinted at Langbow's talent for telling wonderful tales of his own imaginative and marvellous invention.

He was wont to frequent the streams and lochs of the neighbourhood on fishing excursions, duly accoutred in all the panoply of an angler, prepared for raids on the fresh-water finny tribes of the crystal pools and limpid streams of the beautiful strath. One of his gigantic fabrications was a record of a fishing incident in Jamie's best style. He used to tell it, as if he seriously believed it himself, its frequent repetition, I suppose, had made it appear to him as if it had actually occurred.

He said, "A'e day I wis tryin' Watter Esk for saumon, near where the Goudie Burn fa's in, jist a wee bit abune the Beardie Brig, an' nine mile frae the watter mou', an', by gosh," he said, "I saw a sicht 'at gied me the mirligoes i' ma e'en! The Goudie pule (pool) was in flood, an' the Esk rinnin' fu' 'tween bank and brae. I saw plenty o' fish a' roond the edges o' the pule, but nane gaed swimmin' in or oot o' it. Syne," quo' Jamie, "I laid doon ma wand, and ran doon the bank tae see fat ailed them at the pule, an' eh, man! it was nae winder they cudna gae in, for the place was filled wi' the biggest fish I ever saw except a whale I ance saw at Dindee herbour, an' hoo the fish i' the Goudie pule ever got in there is a mystery, except it had juist grown up frae a troot there. Thinks I, ma lad, I'll hook ye, an' I sets aboot it, an' baits twa o' ma best saumon huiks on twa double-ply gut ends, an' fixin' anither reel on my rod wi' dooble thick lines I then made a cast i' the pule. The beauty seemed sleepin', for the gut-ends juist scuffed his nose an' he never moved. Syne I dropped a pebble in the pule, an' up he started at ance grabbed the double bait, an' seemingly fan' the huiks at ance, as he cam' to the surface in a jiffey, an' finever he saw me, he jaloosed 'at I wis in some wye the cause o' his toothache, for he made a'e fearfu' breenge richt at me. I started back, an' ran up the brae, lattin' line oot a' the time, an' fan I turned roond tae see if the monster wis efter me, I declare he sprang richt aff the bank an' played lick i' the watter an' barkit like a doug, an' syne ma wark only began in earnest, an' for seevin lang hoors I chased that fish and keepit 'im fast up an' doon the Esk, an' i' the lang length I landit him at the watter-mou', below the pillar brig, nine mile frae the place whaur I huikit 'im!"

One man who heard this big fish story ventured to ask what size the troot was when it was landed, to whom Jamie replied, "Weel, ye wad hae been little bookit aside it." This inquirer stood six feet in height, and was stout in proportion.

Another party who listened to the same narrative, at second-hand, asked the re-teller:

"An' did ye speir hoo Langbow got the big troot hame?"

"No," said the man, "I didna wis' the cratur tae sin his sowl ony mair by ekein' oot sic an awfu' lee. He wad hae juist sworn 'at he hired a cairt an' a pair o' horse tae haul the great brute tae Greyrigg, thirteen mile o' road!"

This legend, long known as the Watter-mou' fresh-water whale story, like the inventor thereof, has long passed to the limbo of the forgotten, but leein' Jamie and his consort got a much better catch on the evening of their kind benefactor's funeral.

They were two of the company at tea when the obsequies were over. If ever any tea-party on such an occasion were happy without hilarity, and enjoyed themselves without unseemly mirth, I think it was that party. John Endever presided, and had on his right John Jameson, a host of geniality in himself. Gunner Grigg was there, not much of a man anyway, but a sort of "retired R.N.," about as intelligent as an ordinary old mule. He had been rather a handsome and vigorous man in his prime, but had lost the sight of one of his eyes in some unrecorded scrimmage. A number more of the rustic fathers of the village were also present, and one round of a glass each of whisky-toddy was drunk by the men only, it not being customary for boys or females to be offered anything on such occasions in the shape of strong drink.

I remember very well there were many queer stories told of the times long gone, as, except I and another, there were no very young persons present. Many reminiscences of the departed owner of the house (old Tibbie) were told, and some of her smart answers were repeated.

Gunner Grigg upset the gravity of the company when he was asked if he was ever in Asia?

"Oh, yes," he declared with much pomp, "I was through the Bay of Biscie, by jingo," and when he leaned his head across the table and said to the chairman, "John, do you no' think this has been a godsend, to let us puir craturs get some refreshment?"

"Aye," says John, "aboot as providential as that mornin' you met the laird o' Reekit Wa's, an' he gied you a shillin' tae help ye on the road tae Arbroath, where the press-gang nabbed ye, an' you had either tae march aboard a privateer, or be a member o' the gang and help tae nab ither fowk!"

After this time, and when the hawthorn of 1840 was in blossom, I was sent to Hirple Howe to tend cattle on the moors and fells described in the first chapter of these sketches. At this point commences the story of my days of toil and endeavour to earn my own living, and will treat generally of a description of country farm service, and of rural life at homesteads in three of the best farms in the most important counties of Scotland and England.

Chapter XII.

> —"When lust
> Lets in defilements to the inward parts,
> The soul grows clotted by contagion,
> Inbodies and imbrutes, till she quite lose
> The divine property of her first being."
> —MILTON.

I am sent to the herdin' at Hirple Howe.—The Fankleriggs.—Their wicked career and complete disappearance from the District.

The first occupation I was set to as a means of helping to earn my own living, was tending young cattle on the moors of Hirple Howe, then rented to the Fankleriggs. In the year 1839 the Fankleriggs came from the south-west border of the county, where the head of the family rented a mill and large farm, lying about eight miles north of Dundee.

Their new holding previous to this, and under the old system of slow-going and ease-taking, had been found a very unproductive farm, although the farms on either side produced abundantly and gave good returns of all kinds. But Hirple Howe, under new management and new methods of many kinds, was brought in a few years to give better returns, and had the lives and characters of the five or six stalwart sons (who each had the management in turn) been as good as their farming was, there would have been nothing but the most unqualified praise to bestow in the recital of their lives.

Their conduct became a hissing and bye-word to the district, and the detestable example which they gave did much to degrade the social life of farm service, and in many mournful cases almost, if not entirely extinguish the light and glory which ever surrounds that shield of modesty and virtue which is the bulwark of woman's honour and woman's worth, and while it is true, as Longfellow sings:—

> "Lives of good men all remind us,
> We may make our lives sublime,
> And departing leave behind us,
> Footprints on the sands of time."

So as true and dismally sad it is, as Shakespeare says:— "Men's evil manners live in brass." Evil men's examples are copied and followed by the weak, the vicious, and the unprincipled. So the evil conduct and unspeakable depravity of the Fankleriggs of Hirple Howe leave a memorial there which defiles the name of the class to which they belonged, and as at the first, marks the record of man's primeval occupation, with the trail of the serpent.

However, there is cause for thankfulness, for they seem to have disappeared as completely from the district as if the earth had swallowed them. The farm-house in which they lived has also disappeared, and another has been erected, but not where the old one stood, which I think is another change to be thankful for, as their name, with their house and habitation ought to have no place on God's fair earth; and yet when I review my recollections of several of this family, whom I knew in their guileless happy childhood, and when in after years I have heard of their manhood's awful degeneracy, I have been almost ready to question if it really can have been the same individuals.

Two of the boys, the one six and the other seven years of age, often accompanied me at the herding, and their innocent gambols and the unanswerable questions they would sometimes put, were a continual source of amusement and interest to me, especially where these infant searchers after truth, with their question, " How is that?" It often set me a thinking, and made me endeavour to learn and know more of the unsolvable entities which surround this marvellous existence.

For instance, one fine evening in early autumn, when on our way home with the herd, the harvest moon was shedding her half-phased silver light on town and tower, the youngest boy, fixing his look on that orb, cried out in his childish treble, and calling me by name, said, " Oh, look,, look! de side of de moon is broken off and away, away altogether! Oh! how is that?" he repeated in great distress. I said I supposed the side broken off had been sent to the joiner's for repairs. The child being of a mechanical turn understood at once and quite believed that half a moon could be repaired, or a whole new moon made by the same great Joiner, who I tried to explain to him, made both me and him. Yet, notwithstanding the heavenly halo which lies all about us in our days of innocence and childhood, as one poet of my own native strath exclaims:—

"How soon we slide from Richt's blessed realm,
When ance that auld Satan gets poo'er o' the helm."

Thus the wondering curiosity of these beautiful children appears not to have borne fruit, for the after life of these individuals was polluted and immoral, as I have tried but faintly to describe, yet wholly to denounce.

Chapter XIII.

" When that I was a little tiny boy,
With hey, ho, the wind and the rain,
A foolish thing was but a joy,
For the rain it raineth every day."
—SHAKESPERE.

The wet Harvest of 1840.—That Disaster and its effects on working People contrasted with the present time 1890.

But to continue my own simple story. I was at the end of eighteen months taken from the service of Hirple Howe, having finished my engagement at the winter term of 1841. This winter followed the wettest and most disastrous harvest ever known in the district.

A very fine summer had just ended, and the heavy laden fields were waving wide with their golden burdens. On early farms a good deal had been done to the shearing.

Up to this year the harvests in Scotland were all reaped by the hand hook or sickle. The reapers went from towns and villages all round, and nearly all who could bore a hand at the harvest, but the weather broke suddenly (I think after a great storm), and for seven successive weeks there was not one whole dry day. I have the best of reasons for remembering this, as I was on the moors every day, and was never dry at the skin for even a few hours at a time, except when in bed. My mother's cottage in Greyrigg stood close by one side of the pasture where my herd grazed, and I lodged at home all the while I was employed there. During this time of almost incessant rain, I have had my clothes changed sometimes more than twice in a day. Waterproofs had not appeared at Greyrigg up to this time, at anyrate they were not one of the articles in my wardrobe, and the "herd's plaidie," though "a guid grey," was but a poor protection against the pluvial outpour, which came down from day to day.

My mother used to say sometimes as she assisted me to change my wet soaked raiment for the other dry suit (I had but two), "Oh, laddie, gin ye live to be an auld man ye'll tell them a' aboot this, for ye'll never forget it."

I have never forgotten that time, nor its damp discomforts, and I mind of seeing large portions of the beautiful crops of that harvest standing in stooks in the fields among snow, and before the snow came the sheaves in many instances were closely stuck together, for the grain had sprouted, and the young roots interlaced, while the green briard appeared all over the outsides; but the frost following the snow killed the growth, and the whole then became a total loss. There was one feature accompanying this agricultural disaster, which contrasts that time with the results of weather wrecks now, much to the apparent discredit of present times. That was, there was no special loud-mouthed wailing, or starving workman's cry heard, nor no very special complaint of high prices of food, although a heavy import duty was leviable on foreign corn, etc.; neither was seen gaunt-limbed and red-eyed hunger crowding relief halls and soup kitchens, as is the case now, although wages were at least a third lower then than the average to-day.

Prices of bread stuffs were certainly dear, and wages were too low, while the hours of labour in their daily number made the worker's life a dismal dreary round of almost incessant toil. Such a disaster as happened to this harvest intensified the efforts being put forth for the repeal of the duties leviable on foreign grain imports. These efforts were strongest in the manufacturing centres, but in no county of Scotland, nor in any town, was the cause of free trade in corn, etc., more strongly advocated than in the county of Angus, and especially among all classes in its capital, viz., the burgh of Forfar. Why, the People's Charter, in its adoption by the masses, had as almost its first demand, open ports and free trade.

At length, with the assistance of the heroic, self-denying, and talented men, the iniquitous imposts were removed, and their repeal accomplished after five years of Parliamentary conflict.

Chapter XIV.

*"Beautiful snow, beautiful snow,
Falling so lightly—daily and nightly,
All round the dwellings of the lofty and low.
Children exult though the winds fiercely blow,
Hailing the snowflakes—falling as day breaks—
Joyful they welcome the beautiful snow.
Decking the window-panes softly and slow;
Forest and city—figure so pretty,
Left by the magical fingers of snow."*
—W. A. SIGOURNEY.

The great Snow-Storm of 1838.

In writing from memory only, I find I have omitted a reminiscence of my experience of the great snow-storm of 1838, as it affected Greyrigg and the district. This was three years before the wet harvest described above. We have heard a great deal, and read a great deal more about the severity and duration of the storms and frost of the year 1895, but the storm of February 1838, with the intense and prolonged frost, which continued till well into May following, exceeded everything of the kind yet witnessed in my time.

The year 1837 closed with a heavy snow storm, which blocked the roads so that they had to be cleared by manual labour before the thaw came. January was uncommonly mild and genial, and it continued so up till the end of that month, and until the 13th of February. This was old Candlemas Day, the date on which the Fiars' prices were being struck in the county towns. The ground was then quite free from frost, and the young grass looked fresh and green.

Snow began to fall on the morning of the 13th February, thick and heavy, and it seemed as if the whole air was filled with a great snow wave, for it fell without intermission all day. It was unaccompanied with wind for the first twelve hours, and during that time it was computed that about twenty inches remained all over, but towards evening the wind rose, and snow came with it, continuing a full gale and dry drifting snow all Friday night, and rather increasing towards Saturday morning.

The last twenty-four hours' drift was thus blown into the hollows, and piled up against all standing obstacles, while the heavy snow which fell the first twelve hours lay upblown in the fields and all level surfaces to a depth averaging two feet.

The gale, with drifting powdery snow, continued all Saturday and all Saturday night, and by Sunday morning the range of broom-thatched cottages facing east north-east in Greyrigg were all banked up, and the only light visible was from the wide overhanging vent-canopies or the small windows on the western walls of those clay-built domiciles, the snow being as fine as the finest sand, penetrating every crevice, crack, or chink, however narrow. Through a shrunk seam in the outer door of our dwelling it had been blown in a pile as high as the bar on the inside. This pile had a rim along the top which appeared as fine as the edge of a knife, and the sides sloped on to the floor, making such a beautiful figure that I implored my mother not to disturb it till I got a right look at it.

However, the lovely pile had to be moved before the door could be opened; by this time it was nine o'clock on Sunday morning. One villager whose house faced north-west, and whose door the wind had not blocked, dug paths to the banked-up doors, and the sides of the cuttings made were (next the houses) more than seven feet deep; in fact, higher than the walls of the houses.

When we did get out, the spectacle presented to our wondering eyes was the most bewildering. yet the most entrancingly beautiful I have ever beheld—a sight which can never be effaced from my recollection so long as life and memory remains.

There was no mark of roads left, and in nearly all directions the outlines of the stone-fenced fields were lost, while the innumerable and varied forms of the tremendous snow-wreaths no mortal mind has ever conceived. Then the dazzling white purity of this beautiful mantle, as I think of it now in all its resplendent outspread Sunday morning glory, appears to me as the grandest earthly emblem of God's infinite power and purity, at the same time a type of the sublimity of death, as that wonderful sheet wound over and around every object, even in its unspeakable beauty spoke not of life of any kind.

Chapter XV.

>—"*Charity ever
Finds in the act reward, and needs no trumpet
In the receiver.*"
>
>—BEAUMONT AND FLETCHER.

Great suffering for want of food and fuel.—Jeannie Jameson's noble charity—Reflections on same—the killing and also the protecting power of the snow-storm.

In the preceding chapter I have described the pictorial or poetical side of this memorable phenomenon. Life is not all poetry, for the daily wants of the elders of the hamlet brought home the practical side; even the meal, the milk, the oil, and fuel side of the picture stood in strong relief, as only two, or at the most three of the householders of Greyrigg were provided with a stock of life's necessaries, enabling them to withstand a snow and frost siege like this sudden and unheralded visitation.

One man was "the Edomite," as he was called, his name corresponding to that of an old king of Edom. This Edomite, although he it was who dug the snowed-up cottagers out, had an ample stock of food and fuel, from which he was asked to lend or sell to those in need. Strangely, and contrary to all precedent there, he refused to do either the one or the other. The roads and paths to the woods and to the town being all blocked with light powdery snow, on which the intense frost that had set in had not yet hardened a crust, completely stopped communication, and a day came when those not provided with stocks of food and fuel reached the last bit of coal or fire-wood, poured their last drop of oil into the cruisie, and heard the ominous sound of the bottom of the meal barrel, and on a clear and frosty afternoon I remember of seeing my mother getting over the back yard (or garden) fence, trying to make her way up a field to the woods whose fallen or withered branches were free to the villagers for fire-wood.

In her attempt she was sinking sometimes to the waist, but had not proceeded far when I heard the click of a back-window opening, and Jeannie Jameson's voice calling out—

"Hoy, Mary, faur are ye gaen?"

"I'm tryin' tae ging tae the auld wid," says Mary. "My firein's dune, an' I canna hae that laddie sittin' at an oot fire."

The laddie referred to was this individual "sittin' at an oot fire, and naething mair to re-licht it," except the handful reserved wherewith to cook the next meal, but I was deep in a fine old copy of the "Pilgrim's Progress," bound in leather, and printed in old English type, kindly lent to me by Tibbie Tytler, and which I read, and re-read three times during my enforced absence from school, for all schools were empty for more than two months, and subscriptions against the loss of fees for adventure schools were raised after this storm.

But resuming the story, and giving the sequel to my mother's attempted fuel-foraging expedition, Jeannie Jameson called again,

"Oh, ye'll never mak' the wid. Come awa back, for ony guid I can dae ye, an' I'll see fat we can dae fan I ging to my four oors. Afternoon teas were not fashionable then and there, the cheapest tea being about six shillings per pound, and sugar cost ninepence for the same weight.

However, Jeannie kept her word, and on her return from the Laigh Toon-end, brought, with some assistance, an ample supply of coals and firewood, etc., which served us till the woods were reached and the roads to Lunanhead and Forfar were again opened.

Ours was not the only case of the kind relieved from the Laigh Toon-end during this trying time. Oh, no; the Jamesons' character for brotherly kindness, with their practice of humble and unostentatious Christian duty resembled that so finely pictured in Alexander Laing's "Archie Allan."

> "When a friend or a neebor gaed speirin' their weel,
> They had meal i' the bannock and maut i' the yill;
> Wi' herts that cud pairt an' haunds that were free,
> An' looks that bade welcome, an' warm as cud be;
> Gaed ye in, com' ye oot, they were aye, aye the same,
> There's few noo-a-days 'mang oor neebors like them."

Before concluding this record of the great storm and long continued frost of 1838, I may mention that I saw the farmers breaking up the great frozen snow-wreaths on the shaded side of the field fences, and sending their horses and harrows over it to let the sun's rays reach it at the end of May, and where in some cases of early-sown beans which had been put in about the 1st of February, when the snow was cleared off it was seen those seeds had sprung and briared below the snow, and were well above the mould when the heavy mantle of winter was doffed by warm winds from some far summer zone; so that the dazzling but deathly white covering described as not bearing the semblance of life, on the morning of the 15th February, when stripped from Nature's face at 27th May of the same year really proved that it had, under Providence, protected the germs of life in many kinds of seeds, but all young and tender plants of many kinds of trees and bushes died where exposed to the north, especially young larch plantations, and even broom, on exposed situations.

These all died, and the mortality among wild birds was deplorable. In the old woods, where there were colonies of field rooks, many of those unfortunate birds might be seen hanging dead in rows, with their feet frozen to the branches.

This is no exaggeration, for among the woods surrounding an old priory near Arbroath such sights were seen and attested to by many who went out in the clear and continued frosty days which followed each other in regular order for more than twelve weeks, and during the time of the day lengthening which makes it more memorable than if this had been the character of the weather at the dead of winter and onward.

Chapter XVI.

*"At service oot amang the farmers roun'.
Some ca' the pleugh, some herd, some tentie rin
A cannie errand to a ncebor toon."*

—BURNS.

Last months of 1841.—Rescobie Parish Library.—Some account of the Popular Books of the time—1842. I became a Shepherd and a Cattle-herd.—Lochbank. — Mrs Muggywig and her two Nephews (Jamie and Geordie Littledune).—Bell, the servant.—The Twa Collie Dogs. — I despair and run home.—My reception there. — Induced to return and Serve out my Engagement.

I lived at home doing little during the last months of 1841, except that I employed my time mostly reading. I may mention here that although the tax on paper, and the drawback of a Government impost yet rested on literature, and the best books were accessible only to those who possessed means wherewith to buy them, yet in retrospect I now believe the books such as I had access to then were of a more substantial and useful nature than at least two-thirds of the literary pabulum now daily served out in almost every popular publication.

Chambers' " Miscellany of useful and entertaining Tracts " had been for some time in circulation, previous to 1841, and they were soon followed by the same firm's " Information for the People," while " Chambers' Journal " had been issued monthly for some time also. Standard English works were not much within my reach, but many excellent biographical and historical works were available for me, and all others connected with the Parish of Rescobie.

The Parish Church Library there contained over a thousand volumes, and it was under the charge of Mr Problem, my old teacher, who knew just what books would interest me, and who handed such to my mother at the close of the church services, and I got them on my visits about once a month. I used to carry the precious volumes sometimes twenty miles to the place where I happened to be serving, and what little I do know of ancient history I got from such books as were to be found in that library.

My mother was a hearer of the Word at Rescobie Church so long as she lived at Merlin Brae, and sometimes, after she removed to Forfar she walked out the three miles along that fine road which leads to the quiet, sweet lochside scene, amid whose umbrageous surroundings stands the beautiful little church, where my fathers worshipped! and within the sound of whose Sabbath bell my mother's dust rests! after life's fitful fever past and gone!

In April of 1842 I had to resume the herd's staff and plaid. This time beheld me a young shepherd, as well as cattle-herd, on the green banks of St Margaret's Loch, and the adjoining morasses, over which the waters of the same lake had flowed, but from which tradition says, the waters were lowered, before the days of the Romans, who here left vestiges of their paved roads, which the same tradition says traversed the whole length of this lake, and led from a Roman stronghold still to be seen in Forfar or its neighbourhood, this road is connected with the famed old Castle of Glamis. This castle is said to be the most entire, and part of it the oldest in Scotland.

RESCOBIE LOCH, KIRK, AND KIRKYAIRD, FORFARSHIRE.

(SEE PAGE 106.)

FORFAR AND THE LOCH.

Lochbank was the name of the small farm where my services were now to be rendered, and in April, while that month's aspect still wore a wintry frown, I commenced duty there. The mixed multitude I had in charge, especially some Highland ewes (or crossbreds) with their lambs, and the cattle, did not consort well, in fact sometimes would not consort at all. And although there were two collies, those dogs had not been trained to obey any orders but those of their respective owners, two half-idle brothers, nephews of the old widow.

This old lady wore a blue mutch, and used a pair of crutches. She was the tenant of the small holding, which only employed a pair of horses, but which afforded a living to the tenant, Mrs Muggywig. Her two nephews, Geordie and Jamie Littledune, Bell, the maid of all-work, and your humble servant, as sheep and cattle herd, did all the work of the farm.

The weather was stormy, with alternate showers and sunshine. When I went there pasture was not plentiful, and between the Halyracket and hill-run flock of sheep, and the restless half-starved cattle, my job was not a sinecure. In fact I was about run off my feet (being only in my fourteenth year). Besides, there were many things so uncongenial and distasteful to me in the household society of the place, that I got quite into despair with it.

Mrs Muggywig swore, her two nephews swore, Bell, the servant swore, even the two dogs seemed to swear too, but they sat on their tails and swore up in the air, and, I thought, winked to each other, seeming to say, "Lat 'im rin himsel' after his sheep and nowt; he's no' oor maister!"

Seriously reviewing the situation after one of these swearing bouts, I resolved to cut and run for it! So on the third Saturday morning after I had gone to the place, I took "leg-bail," and made for home. My mother had left Greyrigg before this, and was now domiciled in a better house, a mile nearer Forfar, and about a quarter of a mile from Lunanhead. The place was called Merlin Brae, near Gate end of Pitandrew. The fine farm of Merlin Brae, with its neat and cosy-looking farmhouse and garden were close alongside my mother's garden. In any weather, or at any season, this spot had a beautiful, rich, and comfortable appearance. Although our cottage has long disappeared,

> "And corn grows green where our garden hedge stude,
> And the siller birks gane wi' the storm and the flude,
> Yet the strae-theeckit biggin' in fancy I see,
> And the dwallin' where ance woun'd my mither and me."

Continuing the history of my flight from Lochbank, and the reception accorded me on my arrival at Merlin Brae that blustering April morning, my welcome was "a caution," or ought to be, to all discontented boys of thirteen, and my mother's face was a study!

Stepping off her loom, she fired her first question at me, "Fat are ye daein' here?"

I said I was come hame "cause I canna bide yonder."

"Ay, an' faur are ye thinkin' tae bide na? Mind, ye canna be here, be faur ye like," came as quick as lightning.

I said "I wisna seekin' to bide here, an' I would get some ither place."

"Ay," quo' she, wi' fine sifted sarcasm, "it's very likely; but fat ails ye at the place? Dae ye get eneuch to eat, an' a guid clean bed to rest ye?"

I could not deny but that I got both.

"Weel," says she, bringing her closed fist down on a table wi' a thump, "it's there ye'll bide, and at nae ither place," adding, "in the meantime, cut yer stick back again, faster than ye cam' awa', for I'se herbour nae ither body's servant aboot my hoose."

My next answer was, "No, I winna ging back, an' ye can dae what ye like."

Oh, most unfortunate of answers! My mother let out at me with a big stick, but missed, and I seized the business end of the weapon, and stayed operations with that instrument, but before I could escape, I was seized and laid across my mother's knee! Though by strategy she thus placed me, as it appeared, in the limbo for punishment, she had not science enough to keep me on her knee. Then commenced such a struggle on both sides, just like the fox when in the power of its enemies.

I fought for more than liberty, but did not cry for mercy, and my opponent had to give up, completely baffled in her effort for my corporeal chastisement in the old orthodox style, which fathers and mothers of bad boys sometimes adopted, when such boys rebelled or refused to do as they were bidden.

My mother then seeing that force of the kind she had attempted was a failure, did what she should have tried at first. She appealed to my honour, and said what a disgrace it would bring on her and me, if it were known (as it was bound to be) that I had run away from my place, besides showing me she was not able to provide for herself and me, if I were to be idle on her hands. So a compromise was effected.

This was that she would go back with me, and see what was the grievance on either side, and it was agreed therefore that the order of return should be that in passing Lunanhead my escort should go a considerable distance ahead, for I could not bear the idea of meeting any of my late school-fellows, as they might think I had run away from my place, and " here was the fule wi' his mither takin' him back." So after about an hour's walk we reached Lochbank, where my mother got a fairly good reception.

They had nothing to say against me, and could not understand what made me run off. They allowed the herding was difficult, and they promised to give me some assistance till the grass was more plentiful, but little did they or my mother ken' that hame-sickness, and the society of the strange, rough, and uncongenial house had most to do with my aversion to the place. I had really never been from home before. However, I served out my time, but never took kindly to the manners and ways of those rough though kindly folks, and was allowed to leave at the end of my engagement.

Chapter XVII.

*"Curs'd be the man, the poorest wretch in life,
The crouching vassal to the tyrant wife."*

*"The wind blew as 'twad blawn its last,
The rattling show'rs rose on the blast,
The speedy gleams the darkness swallow'd,
Loud, deep, and lang the thunder bellow'd.
That night a child might understand,
The de'il had business on his hand."*

—BURNS.

1843.—The Hiring Fair at Letham.—I get hired to Davie Blackbang of Drookit Furs. — Am learned to work and Live on Short Rations. — Mrs Blackbang, a lady dark by name and nature. — Lowrie, my Predecessor, and how he made Mrs B. sit up.— The terrific Thunder-storm of the Summer.—The Autumn Rain-storm and my full share of the same.—The flittin' of the Colt and his antics.— A precocious young Horse.

After spending most of the winter of 1842 and 1843 at home, at my beloved reading, and earning a few shillings working at Pitandrew home farm, Whitsunday, 1843, found me at the feeing or servant, hiring fair, held in the bright little village of Letham, where a noted half-yearly gathering of masters and servants was held. This market is still kept up, and very one-sided engagements were and are made, and where are still to be seen, alongside of our boasted freedom and civilisation, many practices which appear to me only the badges of Satan's bondage, exhibiting constituent elements of that potentate's empire in its very essentials.

A hiring market for males is bad enough, but for females it always seemed to me a degradation, both for employers and employees. The first-named appeared as a free agent, the latter seemed very much in the position of a bondsman, and especially grievously bound, when as often happens in both yearly and half-yearly engagements, masters and servants are found unsuited to each other.

I intend to return to this subject again when relating my own farm life history, when a hired man. Meantime I was at the fair mentioned accompanied by my mother, and waiting to be hired, and did get hired to a stout, square-set, middle-sized man with a red beard, named David Blackbang. The farm he occupied was named Drookit Furs, three miles from Arbroath, and close on the side of the road to Forfar. This man (a complete stranger to us), if taken at his own estimate, was certainly the best master by a long way to be found in Letham fair that day.

He described his farm as a model, and promised to learn me farm-work in such a style that I might become a farm steward before my mother knew. I do not know if the poor woman believed all he said, but I think I shall be able to prove from my account of my next half-year's life, that Blackbang and his whole concern turned out for me about as black a bargain as any poor friendless lad in his fourteenth year could have met with. But he fulfilled one part of his promise. He learned me to work, and no mistake.

Mrs Blackbang, this farmer's wife, looked black, and had numerous habits which, if not positively dark, made her conduct to me look very shady. The spring of this, the year 1843, had been very wet and backward, especially the latter end, and on the East Coast some of the spring seeds had not been put under ground till after Whitsunday, while on the farm of Drookit Furs the potatoes were not planted till the week after the term.

Often when the rain drove us from the fields, Blackbang and his family took shelter at home, and I would be sent to tend the cows, etc., which his own son herded so long as the weather was fine, and while I was at work. They kept no other hired hand, and it was quite common for me to work the regular hours all day, and be ordered to tend the cattle from 6.30 till about 9 o'clock at night, and again to tend them on the unfenced pasture all Sunday.

But the way my work and working hours were arranged was not the worst part of life's fulfilment there for me. Mrs Blackbang was one of those niggards who took on herself to settle, and practised the undertaking most religiously—that a young, growing, hard-working boy should not eat what he required, but only what she thought he required, and the Lord knows, and I knew to my cost afterwards, she might have canonised for her devotion to that tenet of her daily religion. It is no exaggeration, and I speak only the truth, when I declare I never got a full meal during the whole course of my engagement, except twice or thrice when the only relation I then knew, came, bringing me a change of clothing, and again for a few days in harvest, when they had extra assistants.

On such occasions they sent their oldest son to dine with me at a side table. At all other times I dined or supped in solitary state, at that side board, while Mr and Mrs Blackbang and family surrounded their family table, over the food on which I do not remember hearing a blessing invoked. There might have been grace before meat, but if there was I think I would have remembered of it.

I thought nothing of my own isolation at those meal times, but I thought a good deal, and with a very heavy heart too, when rising after such scanty fare nearly as hungry as when I sat down, the worst of the circumstance being, I could never summon up courage to ask for more, and was never offered a second helping of anything.

These are facts, and had I not realised them in my own experience, I could not have believed that such hard unthinking greed could have been practised by professing Christians, for withal, they all made professions of Christianity, though they undoubtedly did half starve their hired boy.

I saw one of my predecessors one day as he passed along the public road, and on introducing himself, almost the first thing he asked was how I got on in the victualling line. This lad was older than me when he served there, and on us comparing notes, I found his experience tallied with mine exactly, only that he said that after a short continuation of such short commons, he saw that the result would be in his case the destruction of a fine property, and he at last asked " for more!"

But as in the boy's case, recorded by Dickens, Mrs Blackbang, although she did not knock this lad down with an iron ladle, she floored him in a metaphor, by declaring her belief that this wicked boy "had a guts like a sawin' sheet." However, Lourie, as they named him, said he stuck in, and made the mistress sit-up in the victualling line.

This woman and her husband were an ill-assorted pair, but he was much the best of the two, although he did go on the spree when he went to Arbroath, and once or twice did not turn up for about twenty-four hours after he was due. At another time he fell among thieves, and was robbed of the price of a cow, yet he was of the two the most worthy of respect. I do not wonder that the man took to the village ale-house seeking more agreeable company, seeing the way his wife nagged and scolded, and taunted him in anyone's presence, and even encouraged his own family to do the same.

I think he did not observe, or dared not take notice, how I was treated in the matter of my food, or if he had seen it I think he would have bettered my lot in that respect, as I remember one forenoon as he was sending me away to do something at a distance, he happened to remark that of course I had got breakfast, and I replied that I had not heard of breakfast yet. He looked his watch, and seeing it was past eleven o'clock—oh! don't mention the row which then ensued between that enraged man and his unlovely spouse! He swore like a trooper at her, and demanded what she meant by keeping me without food for such a length of time? She did not seem the least concerned; said she had forgotten all about me. Then he told her he believed it was a willing forget, and further, that he also believed she would starve me, or any other man or beast with as little concern. Then he turned on me and blew me up for not asking for breakfast, a thing I could not have done at that age if it had been to save my life.

When I went first to Drookit Furs I slept in the farm-house, but Mrs Blackbang, determined to make money by any means, let my attic bed-room to two road keepers, and a bed was hastily knocked up for me in a corner of the stable, made of stout rough posts, and undressed boards. This bed took up the breadth of a stall, and was placed cross-wise at the wall, behind where the horse stood, if the stall had been occupied.

It was set pretty high, and an old wooden harrow, minus the teeth, was my ladder whereon to mount and get into this gloomy couch, for it was dark there even in the day-time, as the only light reaching this not downy, but oaten-chaff, and oaten-straw couch, came by the stable door, and only showed the foot of the bed. The roof was tiled, and although that did admit a little light, there was not sufficient of that sweet boon for me to see to read. However, I got no time, nor no books to read there. I was allowed plenty of bed-clothes, and except when I turned in more hungry than usual I slept as soundly, all alone in that dark corner, as I have ever done in the most superbly-furnished bed-room I have ever occupied, and I have had the run of quite a variety of bed-rooms since then.

One night a dreadful thunderstorm passed over the land. It burst out just at the time of turning in. My master's son, already mentioned, sometimes on very warm nights came and slept with me, as it was cooler than his couch in the house. On the night of the great storm I got him coaxed to bear me company, as I was terrified at the awful peals of thunder.

He was very much afraid too. I remember some of the crashes seemed like opening the earth, and gleams of terrific lightning were coming through the chinks of the roof and lighting up the whole interior, showing the two horses and the pony trembling in their stalls. I proposed that we should pray to God to keep us safe and free from fear, and this we did.

The sceptic who may read this may scoff, may even laugh, but let him laugh only who wins. We won that time, as true prayer always wins. For even in the midst of that dread tempest, and encircled by the sounds and sights of the lashing rain, hail, fire, and thunder, while the poor dumb horses were whining to each other in their terror, we fell asleep, and we slept the sound blissful slumber of unquestioning boyhood, until called next morning.

Dawn shone forth in all the beauty summer bears, when leaf and flower have been refreshed, and bathed in the morning light, making such a new day (after such a night) a joyful morning indeed!

In case of wearying my reader I must hurry on. Yet at the risk of being tedious I must mention one other incident in this weary half-year's bondage. I give it as an example of man's unreflecting inhumanity to man, which often causes much needless suffering, and in many cases endangers and shortens life.

This farmer had sent a young colt to graze at a distance at the beginning of the harvest, to have it weaned from its mother, and now towards the end of October, when the harvest sheaves were all gathered in, a heavy rain-storm broke out, accompanied and driven before a great gale of wind from the south-west. The foal had to be brought home. The field was distant about four miles. So with Blackbang mounted on the pony, and I on the foal's dam, to be a decoy for the young one, we set out about three o'clock in the afternoon, and as the tornado continued without intermission all the way going and returning, and beating into us on the left side going, and on the right coming, I having no overcoat then, nor for several years after this, and no protection but my ordinary clothes, by the time we got back I was completely drenched, and the wet gushed from my boots when I dismounted.

After we put up the horses, and had the young colt tied up, and got into the house I did not get near the fire, and had no dry clothing to exchange for my now-thoroughly soaked garments, I occupied my usual seat at the family's backs, where I " discussed " my scanty supper, which now invariably consisted of early American potatoes in their jackets, and salt, with about a quarter of an imperial pint of weak over-skimmed milk, and the usual small piece of oaten bread. When I had finished this sumptuous repast, I sat shivering with my teeth chattering on each other, while Blackbang called attention to me, declaring that during the journey I seemed to stand the storm better than he did. No room was made for me, and no invitation given to me to approach the fire.

Now, I think, in their utter disregard for my condition, in not giving me a seat by the fire (although, no thanks to them) had lain my immunity from after illness, for if I had got to the fire, and remained there with my wet clothes steaming on me, I would have most certainly been laid up after. I thought it very hard selfish treatment at the time. But I crept to my dark chamber in the stable, not being allowed any light to illumine that unique bed-room when alone. When I began to undress, all my clothes were so wet, and I was so benumbed, I only got out of them with the greatest difficulty, and minding I had no dry underclothing for next morning, I stript off every stitch, and turned down the bed clothes, of which there was quite an ample supply. This was the only supply which was ample. I first placed my shirt and stockings between a fold or two of the blankets, and lay down nude as I came to this world. I soon got warm, and to this proceeding, under Providence, I attribute my complete freedom from any after effect of such a soaking, as I was never a bit the worse. During this night I had one of the most startling adventures of my boyhood.

The colt had never been tied up before, and being fully aware of each other's presence under the same roof, he and his mother kept up a conversation at intervals, and I think, like some foolish mothers of mankind, this foal's mother, in her mistaken kindness, was encouraging her son to break the restraint put upon him, burst his bonds, and get beside her, and she would cuddle him. This conversation between the equine pair was carried on for some time, and I heard the young one making strong efforts to burst the rope that bound him.

I was very comfortable by this time, and as I could not think of anything I could get in the dark to strengthen Tom, the foal's binding, I lay still, till at length, with one mighty jerk, he broke loose, and in his eagerness to reach his mother's side, he rushed up beside the other mare. This "lady" never had any children of her own, and was not fond of baby horses. She therefore expressed her displeasure in unmistakable "horsey" language, screaming and kicking, and a ruction took place in the dungeon-dark stalls which defies description.

So by the light of sparks of fire, sent from the stones of the stalls by the enraged animals, I had to rise and try to quell the disturbance, having the same amount of clothes on that Adam had when he gave names to all the lower animals, including the horse. I think I would not venture on such a job now, for it was both difficult and dangerous. However, I went up between the enraged beast and the terrified colt. Poor fellow, he was in a great state of fear. Nanse (the mare) had not managed to get hold with her teeth, and had also missed him with her feet. By shouting I quieted them, and by canny handling I got Tom (the young one) rescued, and sent into the same stall with his beloved mother. I took some credit to myself, as having made two loving, though only equine hearts, happy once again, and restored peace in my stable bed-room.

This was not my last adventure with that fine young horse (he was a very nice one too). It was seen after this first night how dangerous it was to tie him up, so a little gate was hung from the lower left-hand corner of my bed, and opening on hinges attached to the division post of the stall next, and Tom's stall was turned into a loose box wherein the young rogue could enjoy himself until he should reach the years of discretion, when, like douce grown horses, and grown men too, he would submit to the restraint of the halter.

This was all very well, and the fore-mentioned unteethed harrow, my bed-room stair, and at the same time my bed-room chair, was brought round to the end of my bed, and outside the gate which shut in Tom. It will be seen that my bed now formed one side of Tom's bed-room, which was also his parlour and dining-room, and the antics which that very lively four-legged gentleman played there are really worth mentioning.

He used to come to my bedside in the mornings, inquiring in his own way as to my health, and how I had slept, and offering to help me to dress, and often at the time of me climbing the old harrow and lying down, he would come and lay one of his forefeet on the coverlet, letting me understand he was bidding me good-night. I did not always reciprocate, and sometimes responded in a different way than this very kind neighbour expected, as the limb meant for the right-hand shake was not often very sweetly clean, after a gambol round his bedroom.

I had a worsted-woven night-cap, one of the stiff kind which sticks up straight when placed on the head. I used to place it on one of the corner posts in the same way as I wore it. Tom discovered it there one morning, and being of a very inquiring mind, he commenced investigations by taking it in his teeth, to prove, I suppose, if it was good to eat. At last, I think, he concluded that it was one of a set of baby horse gloves, for my cap was lost for several days, and, it is a fact, I found it on one of that foal's fore-feet, neatly fitted like a glove! I could only think that he had used it as a glove by not putting that foot heavily down, as after being scoured it was none the worse, and I have therefore imagined, if there had been a pair of caps the same, that foal would have ornamented both fore-feet like a pair of hands, and gone strutting about erect on his hind legs, with all the airs, and with as much grace, as some uncouth "city dudes" do, who have about as correct a taste, and even less sense than any young horse.

At last, thank God, at last! the weary half-year's bondage ended, and I got my release. But was it much of a release? for I thought whatever comes now, it cannot be worse than Drookit Furs. The after effects of that house of bondage came next, for on getting sufficient food at home, I took ill, and it could not be found out for some time what was wrong, until the tale of last half-year's privations came out bit by bit, when it was found that some of my organs of digestion had been damaged. Thanks to a sound constitution and plenty of vital energy, I got better before the daisies decked the lea in the spring of 1844.

Chapter XVIII.

"*O God! that men should put an enemy in their mouths to steal away their brains.*"
—SHAKESPERE.

"*The noble dog! in life the firmest friend,
The first to welcome, foremost to defend,
Whose honest heart is still his master's own,
Who labours, fights, lives, breathes for him alone.*"
—BYRON.

1844. — Service at Dryriggs. — Merlin Brae. — Andrew Warner, the farmer there.—Mrs Warner and their family.—The plot to burn down the Farm Buildings.—The history of two famous watch dogs.

After recovery from the evil effects of my sojourn at Drookit Furs, and seeing it was not possible for me to get the opportunity of learning any of the mechanical trades, or business professions, which, owing to my antipathy to the social life of farm service, I was at this time anxious to do, I got hired, without attending any hiring fair, this time to a farmer occupying that steep-set, but rather prettily-situated holding overlooking Forfar from the south.

The place may be appropriately named Dryriggs, for from its position, with its fields sloping so steep to the north, and its thin soil resting on rock, it does not retain moisture, and in very dry seasons the scanty rains and dews pass from its verdure with characteristic speed, and the brown and scorched appearance of its fields sometimes even at mid-summer gives the grass an autumn hue long before the general landscape is pensive in yellow and grey.

My occupation here was chiefly that of milk messenger, the place being wrought as a milk farm in 1843-44, and is so still. I went to the town once, and sometimes twice a-day, wheeling the lacteal and precious fluid on a big barrow of strong but light construction, and found by the conformation of the steep Hung Road, that returning with the emptied vessels and barrow was much harder work than conveying the load to the town. The farmer bore a clan name, and both he and his worthy partner were very kind and considerate to their servants. We had to work hard, but were well fed and well lodged, our master and mistress occupying the head of the table along with their servants and family.

There was no stinting of food, nor no waste. My wages were 30s for the half-year, but many a sixpence and lesser sums the mistress bestowed on me, and she often sent her oldest son in the evenings under my charge to whatever cheap and healthy entertainments were to be found in Forfar. The summer was fine, and quite a host of itinerant showmen with exhibitions visited the town of Forfar, such as Wombwell's menagerie of wild animals, and Ord's circus, then almost in all its pristine vigour, both as to men and horses. A branch of Batty's Royal Circus, from Astley's, London, and also Cook's circus, were visitors that season.

Martinmas came round again, and although offered a substantial advance of wages to stay, the spirit of unrest was on the rolling-stone, and the longing for something better than the job

I had; besides the love of change inherent in me, prevented me from accepting those worthy folks' offer, and I left, and once again got engaged without the medium of the detested hiring markets, this time to attempt to drive a pair of horses on the fine fertile farm of Merlin Brae. This holding, as previously described, was practically at home. The very sad and even tragical history of the farmer and his family who came to occupy that beautiful place in 1829 would fill a volume, and form such an addition to the thousand and one arguments in favour of strict sobriety, and to every thinking mind convey a warning of danger, so that no one should need to give or take any special pledge in favour of total abstinence from strong drink, and all its works.

This farmer's name was Andrew Warner, and he in his prime, full of energy and prosperity, came from a fine district, where he had occupied a remunerative farm, the fields of which are overlooked by the houses of that small but now notable burgh, made famous by the genius of a popular present-day novelist. The same burgh is also celebrated as the birth-place of a gifted doctor of Divinity, of the Free Kirk persuasion. At Whitsunday, 1829, the year in which I was born, Mr Warner, with his handsome and clever wife, and fine young family, consisting of two girls and three boys, came to Merlin Brae. His possessions were a full cover of live stock, and complete sets of all kinds of farm implements of the most approved kind, as used at that date. His bank account, I am told, footed up to £2500, considered a large sum in those days. For a while, and so long as the family were boys and girls, apparent peace, plenty, and contentment blest both him and his partner's lives, but during the period of their children's infancy, it is said were sown the insidious seeds of that which, in the after lives of the three who alone survived, grew a ruinous disease, for all three (one daughter and two sons) became dipsomaniacs. It was often said that Mrs Warner never retired to rest the same day she rose, and while the children were young they were regaled with whisky-punch every night before retiring.

The mother's nocturnal habit, it was said, was acquired before they came to Merlin Brae, in consequence of a foul conspiracy, which had been formed in league with the wicked proprietrix of the estate on which their late farm was situated. This was to burn down the farm buildings. The aim the chief conspirator had to serve in this diabolical scheme was to compel the outgoing tenant to erect a new steading, the terms of his lease binding Warner to leave the buildings only in as good repair as when he began his tenancy.

It was said an armed night watchman was employed for two years, at £30 per annum, with bed and board added, that precaution being adopted after the place had been set on fire on two different occasions. The outbreak was extinguished in one case after one grain stack had been consumed, and the other was put out when but a small part of the stable, roofed with thatch, was burned. The gang employed by the unprincipled woman who owned the farm, although suspected and watched, eluded capture, until Mr Warner and his family moved east to Merlin Brae. But even here they followed them, and endeavoured to burn the new home, but evidently unacquainted with the locality, they set fire to the premises of a crofter alongside, whose tenements were straw-thatched, and these were totally destroyed.

Two of the gang, as it was thought, were arrested, but one got off through an alibi being proved. In the other case, after a long and patient trial, before the Justiciary Court in the Scottish Metropolis, a verdict of " not proven " was returned, as the chief witness (Mrs Warner) could not positively on her oath declare he was the man she saw in the vicinity of her neighbour's premises on the night of the fire, and as fire-raising was a capital offence then, and till that date always expiated by the life of the criminal, Mrs Warner often, in relating her recollection of this famous trial, said that it was the terrible thought of what the fate of this wretched man would be that caused her to hesitate in identifying him; and the clever advocate for the defence, taking advantage of her hesitancy in his cross-examination, got her to admit that she could not swear that the prisoner at the bar was the man she had seen on the spot immediately before the deed was accomplished.

In connection with the watch the Warners had kept to preserve their late as well as the present place they had come to, they had two magnificent mastiffs, which the watchman I have mentioned trained to patrol the steadings by night. Aye, and the animals took sentinel duty in turn; while one slept the other went the round. They were the biggest dogs I ever saw, but both were old and frail when I remember seeing them first. The name of the one was " Cæsar," and the other " Nero." The one had been jet black, and the other grey-and-dark brindled or striped, short-haired, and short-eared, and the manner in which these intelligent animals did their watch duty had been, as their history recorded, like something even superior to human sagacity, as, besides watching during the night, one or other used to mount guard over the premises during the day, when all the servants would be at work on fields distant from the farmhouse and steading.

Either of the dogs had only to hear the word "watch," and be shown by signs given by his master the subject and extent of his charge, then the faithful animal took up his perambulation at once. If he saw anyone approaching by the public road which passed close by the place, he went off at a trot and met them a short distance beyond the farm; then walking on the side next the buildings he conveyed the passenger the same distance on the opposite side, and whether the person (male or female, mounted or on foot) wished to call at the house or steading, he could not do so until the dog got permission from his employers to allow him or her to enter the gates! Neither dog barked, or made a noise, in the performance of his duty; but they had several sounds they made which their owners knew meant inquiry, remonstrance, warning, or defiance, as each case required, and it would not have been healthy for either man or beast to have attempted going on when either of those mighty dogs pronounced in dog language the word "stop," as at the same time either dog always showed such a beautiful set of molars and incisors, the sight of which never failed in arresting the trespasser's progress, or in bringing authority for this watching quadruped to release the quarantine. They were eventually superannuated. When I saw them first one was nearly blind, but both were kindly treated until they died of old age. If ever a memorial was erected to record any master's remembrance of faithful service, rendered without fee or special reward, one to the memory of those noble animals was more than justly due.

The mistress was wont to tell of an incident in the day watch of one of the celebrated canines. While the dog was escorting a rider one afternoon past the place, that foolish or self-confident equestrian, mounted on a short-legged pony, began to irritate Cæsar by cracking his riding-whip at him. Mrs Warner, seeing the danger the man was courting by his bravado, ran out and warned him to let the animal alone, but instead of giving heed to her, the insolent fellow replied with an oath, and made a cut with his whip at either her or the dog. In less than no time (she said), before the man could draw another stroke, the dog leapt in one bound from the ground, seized and dragged him from the saddle, and laid him on his back by the roadside, and had the dog's mistress not been present the man would have been choked, as the enraged animal had him firmly by the throat, and only desisted when his mistress seized his collar and drew him off. This foolish victim, who appeared ten times more a fool as he raised himself from where the dog laid him, when he did get up, spoke not a word, but made off after his pony, which had fled when its rider was floored. A curious feature of this stirring dog fracas was that no part of the man's clothes were torn, nor had the dog's teeth even cut his skin, and in whatever action he might have taken he had nothing to show that the animal had ever laid a mouth on him.

Chapter XIX.

> "*Pass when we may through city or through town,*
> *Village or hamlet of this merry land,*
> *Though lean and beggar'd every twentieth-pace*
> *Conducts the unguarded nose to such a whiff*
> *Of late debauch, forth issuing from the styes*
> *That Law has licensed, as makes temperance reel*
> *Then sit involved and lost by curling clouds*
> *Of Indian fume and guzzling deep the beer,*
> *The lackey, and the groom; the craftsman there*
> *Takes a Lethean leave of all his toil,*
> *Smith, cobbler, joiner, he that plies the shears,*
> *And he that kneads the dough—all loud alike,*
> *All learned, and all drunk."*
>
> —COWPER.

Helen Warner and her Brother. — Their downfall and its cause. — Reclamation of Helen. — Kirkton of Oathlaw and my experiences there. — Village Alehouses and country Whisky-shops before the Sunday Closing Act. — Lazy Tam o' the Kirkton. — Rescue of Vagrant Boy.

By the year 1844, when I joined the service at Merlin Brae, Mrs Warner and the wonderful dogs had gone the way of all things earthly; the clever, kind-hearted mother, the faithful wife, died brokenhearted, through the fate which befel her oldest daughter, who fell a victim and filled an early grave after being for a short time the wife of a detestable villain, who, by his dissolute habits, compassed her death. The two eldest sons died of consumption, each under thirty years of age. There was no one left by the date I went there, but the old and grief-stricken father, and other two survivors—two living sorrows, the youngest son and daughter, who went from bad to worse, till the daughter had to be sent to a home for fallen women in Dundee. The son, who was bred to the drapery trade in London, and afterwards was set up in a business of the same kind in Forfar, had run through that, and involved his father in debts to a large extent. He was now at home, but was a hindrance to his father, instead of a help, and only ruining others by the same wicked means with which he had ruined himself.

This son was eventually sent out of the country, after getting mixed up in a poaching affray, where a gamekeeper lost his life. The half-year, 1844-45, which I spent here was very near the close of the old man's occupation of Merlin Brae, for at the end of 1848 he left the place, with little but his staff in his hand, and his sorrow-stricken grey hair waving in the cold November wind, a sad heart-moving sample of fate's vicissitudes!

My mother saw him as he departed, and invited him into her humble abode, where he partook of a cup of tea, the last he ever shared near the spot where the joys of his early manhood had long been extinguished, in the terrible sorrows of his old age!

He did not survive long, but before his decease he had a blessed gleam of comfort to cheer his latter days. That was his youngest daughter's return a completely reformed and humbly-penitent woman, with all her personal charm, both of body and mind renewed, and she saw the old man gathered to kindred dust in the sweet little cemetery of Rescobie!

"There he sleeps at length, where all troubles cease,
Where the weary rest, and all is peace!"

In a short time after the death of her father, Miss Warner was wooed and won by a respectable man, and, reformed inebriate though she was, they were soon married. They emigrated to America, from where word reached Forfar this past year of her death, in her 72nd year. Hers was the most striking example of a reformed character I have ever been aware of, and gives the strongest proof of the saying—

"That while life's lamp holds on to burn,
The greatest sinner may return."

When the merry month of May of the year 1845 had arrayed itself in its wealth of bud and blossom, I left Merlin Brae, and found employment, once again hired for the half-year to a small farmer, at a place near the Gudie Burn, where, as a local poet sings, "Brae borne Esk rins doon." The place was named Kirkton o' Lemlydale.

The occupier of this small farm lived in a separate house, along with his wife and a young servant girl, and having no family, they kept no other female help. A younger boy and myself lived with the farmer's father and mother in what had been the original farmhouse, and at the same time this house was the village alehouse and tavern. The scenes I saw enacted there on week days, and also on Sundays, are among the least pleasing recollections of my youth.

The Forbes M'Kenzie Act had not up to this time come with its benevolent relief to the aid of licensed victuallers, and vendors of public-house refreshments, who were the bondsmen, and bondwomen of the riotous and the drunken by night and day, while Sunday and Saturday were the same. The public-house, in country places, especially in the vicinity of towns, immediately before the passing of the Act referred to, was simply a scandal and disgrace to civilisation, not to speak of Christianity and religion at all, and had not legislation interfered to regulate the hours, and close such places on Sundays, with the increase of population which was taking place all over, and the growing neglect of education of working-class children, bad as is the condition of what is termed "the lapsed masses" now, the numbers and condition of those masses would have been such by this time as to defy control, and might have hastened a social catastrophe.

During the summer I served at Lemlydale, and lodged in the above-mentioned public-house, the old landlord died, and although he and his female partner fought and snarled at each other continually almost to the last day he lived (for his end came suddenly), the widow made night hideous for more than a week after his death, weeping and wailing over her loss, and from the manner of the two to each other when the man was alive, anyone would have thought they would be better separate.

I could not understand the woman's loud-mouthed grief at all, and in my mind heartily despised it. I have heard a proverb as to "bitin' an' scartin' bein' guid Scotch coortin'," and if that is so, the old couple I have here described never ceased "coortin'."

There were a number of crofts around the Kirkton of Lemlydale then, which have long disappeared, as they have been bound together and made into large farms by land-hiring monopolisers of the last fifty years, who never had any idea of farming, but as merely a means of accumulating money.

The earth money-hunger was really in full swing by 1845, and before it, but yet in some quiet out of the way nooks, like the one I am writing of, the crofter who kept a cow or two, still flourished. There was a specimen of the sort here, a stone dyker (or fence builder), "lazy Tam," he was called. He had a cow, but whether he also had the now proverbial three acres of land I cannot say, but this I know, he excelled the world for downright indolence.

One winter day, and during a heavy snow-drift, Tam's wife said to him, "Dod, min, ye'll hae to ging tae the bauk for neeps to the coo, for they're a' dune."

Tam was sitting doing nought, but keeping himself comfortable by the fire; but on hearing his wife's proposal he gave his shoulders a shake, and disposed of the proposal by saying—

"Dod, 'umman, ye can ca' the coo to the bauk, an' let her tak' neeps till hersel', i' sic a day."

History saith not how the hungry cow got her neeps that day, but it is safe to suppose Tam's hard-wrought wife would have to go for them herself.

At another time Tam was re-building the parish minister's garden wall, and his reverence took occasion to go round and inspect the work. Finding Tam's re-erection off the line, both horizontally and vertically, the minister calls out to him, "See, Thomas, you are building that wall crooked."

"Ou, maybe," says Tam quite calmly, "Watter Esk's cruicket, but it rins brawly!"

It is not recorded what was the minister's further reply.

The only other incident of this half-year, worth mentioning, was the rescue of a boy about eleven years old, a member of the family of an old half-heathenish man-o'-war's man, who, with a rather respectable woman for his wife, went about the country with other two or three children younger than the boy referred to. The mother kept them all fairly tidy and clean. They slept in the barn, but were supplied with proper bedclothes. I do not know who proposed taking Johnnie, the boy, from the wandering life, but I seconded that proposal readily, and it is some satisfaction to me now in recording that our scheme for the boy's improvement turned out highly successful. The other boy (a grandson of the old landlady of the tavern), was not very enthusiastic in his assistance in the poor lad's rescue, and when his folks left, and he was accorded a share of the kitchen bed, where he had to sleep crosswise at our feet, this grandson would have ousted the lad, who was as cleanly in his person and clothes as any of us, if I had not championed the stranger's cause, and not allowed the would-be tyrant to molest him. He was taken in about the end of August, and before I left in November I had taught him to read, and a very apt, willing, and grateful pupil he turned out.

After Martinmas came the boy and I parted, and we have never met since. The spirit of unrest was on me again, with a desire for higher wages, so I had once more to seek other scenes and pastures new.

Chapter XX.

*"I rule them as I ought, discreetly,
And often labour them completely;
And aye on Sundays duly nightly,
I on the question tairge them tightly,
Till faith wee Davie's turn'd sae gleg,
Though scarcely langer than my leg,
He'll screed you aff Effectual Calling
As fast as ony in the dwelling."*

—BURNS.

1845.—The unseemly Feein' Fair again.—A New Master—Samson Bank, the farmer and his sisters. — A mild winter.—Kinnettles Kirk.—Mr Lownie.—Sleepin' i' the Kirk. — The Minister's visit to Samson Bank farm parlour. — Catecheesin' Sandy, the Smith's criticism of a sermon, and his idea of fuel and fires in the world unseen.

With the term time of Martinmas, 1845, came the unlovely hiring fair at Letham, and on a cold clear November morning, when, as is usual at that season, a vaporous frost hangs in the air, and wets the ground below, and the breath of the coming winter seems all around. On such a day I was one in that gathering of semi-slaves, where their owners and would-be owners, met them, and had continued to meet such bondsmen and women for I suppose nearly a century. After standing and waiting about for several hours, I got an offer from a farmer for a year's engagement, to feed his cattle in winter, and work a pair of horses, or do other farm work as required, during the period of my undertaking.

The place was about a mile to the west of Forfar, in the parish of Kinnettles, and on a vast estate which gives a name to an ancient Earldom and a stately old Castle, already referred to in these pages, both famed in old Scottish story.

The name of the farm was Samsonbank, a highly-cultivated, and at that time a richly-productive and lucrative subject. The farmer bore a clan name, and he who has the place yet is of the same name and lineage. The tenant who hired me had been left the management when quite young, owing to his father's death. The father had come to the place from a smaller farm further south, and it was said that all he had to leave to his wife, one son, and three daughters, was the place, and the lease and stock, free of debt, and a silver crown piece to each, which, it was said, he handed to them on his death-bed, enjoining them to work hard, fear God, be just to man, and the reward of well-doing would be theirs!

How well the family, with their brother, had fulfilled their dying parent's injunction, was seen in the order they had the farm in by this time, and the complete system the manager had arranged for the almost scientific working of the whole. He knew to a furrow how much should be done per hour, or per day, of each kind of work, hand, or horse labour. He himself was an excellent worker, while his two sisters wrought all kinds of female out-door work most deftly, and yet remained quite refined, modest, and real ladies all the time. The grown men who worked the three pairs of horses had their allowance of oatmeal and milk, and cooked their meals in the kitchen, but they and I, and a younger boy, slept in the "bothy," as they called it. It was a rather uncomfortable-looking appartment, with but one small window, through which the dim winter light streamed in over the top of a large horse-food boiler, the vapour from which at that season kept the place damp, if not cold.

This sleeping-place was a contrast to the cheerful and beautifully clean-kept kitchen where we took our meals, and spent our evenings or what little leisure time we got, and where the master and his sisters, the young ladies mentioned, often joined us in song or dance. The winter was unusually mild and open, the temperature never falling to frost, and only one slight shower of snow fell in the district, and that scarcely whitened the ground. The hours of work were long, every kind of work, both in and out, being stented, or measured into tasks.

We all had to move along alert and active. I was then in my seventeenth year, and in my engagement I had stipulated to get to church, but the nature of my duties prevented me from giving attendance often during the winter, and I had bound myself to attend the Auld Kirk at Kinnettles, as distinguished from the New or so-called Free Kirk.

Kinnettles Church and its surroundings make up a scene of inland lovely landscape unsurpassed by anything of the same kind to be met with in this or the sister country.

The parish minister, Mr Lownie, was regarded as a very learned man, but weak as a preacher, and being, as "the Nons" said, "only a hireling," whose sixpence was assured with his day's work.

So what with the long hours of labour during the week, when I got to church I was not much interested or edified by what the rev. gentleman referred to or delivered. My master, with his two, and sometimes, all three sisters, sat immediately behind us, and saw me now and then fall asleep during the sermon. On our return from church they used to rally me on my slumbers during service, and I answered that if they would get Mr Lownie to " pit mair vim intae his discoorse, I widna dover " (sleep). Then some of them would declare they " war shuir he gied me mair than I cud mind, if I wid keep wauken;" and I offered to bet " I wid bring it a' hame, an' say it owre to them if they wid make the bet big aneuch," but they would not risk the odds. Before the winter expired they found reason to believe that I could repeat a sermon such as Mr Lownie's after once hearing it.

It was after a ministerial visit we had from Mr Lownie on a winter afternoon. In those days a visit from the minister was a stirring and important event in the life of a farm servant, and in some case due warning was given to prepare for it, and sometimes honest and earnest preparation was made to be able to answer the questions likely to be asked. Not much previous warning was given in the case of the visit I am now to record. We were told at mid-day to cease work and tidy up ourselves for " the catecheesin'," as the minister was coming, and about two p.m. we were all (the half-dozen) ushered into the parlour with due solemnity, where the parson and our employer, with his household, were seated. We, the servants, men and boys, and the maid-servant, stood around like a school class, and the dread trial began.

It would be difficult to describe the feelings of each member of that class, as depicted on their faces. But it would be safe to say that none of us knew what was coming; but Mr Lownie, as was customary, then fired his first shot from the " Single Carritches " (or Shorter Catechism), and between what he helped out himself, and what the catechised floundered through, the answers were repeated.

I do not remember the relation in which the questions were put to us, but the meaning of one asked after repetition brought a deadlock, and went the round of the class until it reached this waiting youth, who gave the meaning, and rather enlarged on it!

The old minister lifted his eyes and looked at me, and said, "Ah! my boy, your answer would not disgrace many a man of sixty years." Here was another spark added to the flame of my intellectual pride, but understand, dear reader, I was only a boy, with very little else then to be proud of, and if I did get a little uplifted by the praise bestowed then, I trust I shall be pardoned for mentioning it now!

The ladies of Samsonbank, who previous to this had doubted my ability to remember the minister's whole sermon, if I could keep awake during its delivery, changed their minds after this catechising incident.

Speaking of minding minister's sermons, and remarking on them at home, or on our way thither, recalls to me a rare summing up of a sermon I heard preached in Rescobie Kirk. The criticism on that discourse made by a young friend and comrade, now long gone home, was so terse and expressive that I think it worth repeating here.

The critic was Sandy, the son of auld Jamie, the smith at Gate-end of Pitandrew, and the preacher was the successor to Mr Lownie, who had that day come from Kinnettles. He had chosen his text from the narrative of our Saviour's temptation in the wilderness, and I thought he had handled it well. He came out very strong when describing and denouncing the Satanic devices.

As Sandy and I were walking home by the Loch-side I was commenting on the discourse we had just heard, and I finished my remarks with—

"Man, wisna yon fine when he 'summed up' the hale thing and gied yon partin' shot tae the deevil?"

Sandy was lame, and walked with a big limp by the help of a short staff. He stumped on for a little before he replied, and then he said—

"Ou, aye, he gied Clootie an awfu' tearin'—an' awfu' tearin'," repeated with emphasis.

It was the most graphic but shortest and truest description I ever heard of any sermon. My friend Sandy had a knack of replying to speculative questions peculiarly his own. One instance will suffice to illustrate Sandy's style of unconscious agnosticism. One day as I entered the smiddy (or shop) where he and his father worked, each at a forge, in either end of the place, there was lying on the middle of the floor an old iron hoe for pulling broom, which once belonged to a man sometime deceased, who had to end his days ekeing out a living at pulling broom for his neighbours, after he lost his means as a farmer and cattle-dealer.

The old smith was doing some little job at the anvil as I went in, while Sandy, with his hand on the bellows-handle, was standing blowing the iron hot, with his face to the door, and his back to the forge. Giving the old instrument a kick, I said—

"There's auld John Barbour's broom hyow."

"Ou' aye," quo' the old man, "John disna need his 'hyow' ony mair."

"I suppose not," says I, but immediately Sandy strikes in with

"Deed, fa'ther, ye dinna ken. There's maybe as muckle brume faur John is noo as there is here," and as he turned round to his fire he adds quite gravely, "Deed, aye, and maybe bigger fires tae!"

There was never the ghost of a smile on Sandy's broad pock-marked face when he uttered a saying like that, and his keen dark eyes looking out from below his dark bushy eyebrows, with his head of short black curly hair over-toping all, made his droll sayings very remarkable.

I did not think much about it at the time, as it was Sandy's way of looking at such questions. He was held to be a great reprobate, though then, and yet, I think, he had much good in him, and more real honest reverence for and belief in things unseen than many who considered themselves "unco guid" compared with poor Sandy.

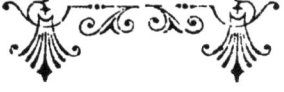

Chapter XXI.

> .... "*There is a history*
> *Figuring the nature of the times deceased;*
> *The which observed one may prophesy*
> *With a near aim of the main chance of things*
> *As yet not come to life, which, in their seeds,*
> *And weak beginnings, lie entreasured."*
>
> —SHAKESPERE.

1846. — An Early Spring. — Two Narrow Escapes from Serious Injury or Death. — A Hot Summer. — Description of the weather. — Strange Atmospheric Developments at first of Autumn. — Total Potato Blight. — Dismay of the Public and Farmers. — The old Brown-cloaked Lady's midnight Prophecy on the Dundee Road two years previous, now fulfilled in the Potato Blight. — The circulation of the news of Strange Events then, contrasted with the present time.

The spring of 1846 opened early, and vegetation came so rapidly forward that even before the middle of April the fields and woods wore such wealth of flowers and foliage as is only seen in this country about a score of times in the life of the longest liver. The previous winter being so open, mild, and free of frost, the ground by the second week of May was so dry that on open, easily-cultivated land, where soil was being prepared for the last of the green crop, it became like hot ashes.

About the end of the barley seed time at Samsonbank, I met with some thrilling experiences, and escaped on two occasions from what might have in either case caused me very serious injury, or even killed me outright. I had been sent one afternoon to assist in the harrowing down seed at the finishing of a newly-sown field, with a couple of fine young mares—rare beauties they were, too—and each had a foal from whom on this afternoon they were separated for the first time since the birth of the young ones. I was guiding them with only one rein attached to the near or left hand animal's head, and I should have walked near their heads, but there being another pair of horses with a brake of harrows leading, where the driver with double reins drove from the rear, I with my single rein drove from the same position, and did not observe until it was too late, that the patience of the handsome equine mothers was quite exhausted, and their only wish was for another meeting with their week-old progeny, so all of a sudden the couple tried to bolt for home.

I, of course, tried to prevent them, but with only the single hempen control, just brought the now fairly-roused animals round and round in a circle several times, while the iron-teethed implements were sometimes turning on their edges or being lifted bodily from the ground. The soil we were working being so dry and powdery, raised such clouds of dust as nearly blinded me. I called to the man in charge of the other pair of quiet old stagers to come and help me, but he stood petrified, apparently frightened to approach. However, I got the rein shortened hand over hand, and reached their heads and managed to restrain and soothe them, although they were both terribly roused, and fairly mad to get home, and, had the harrows' teeth touched them, they would most certainly have gone beyond my control, and a frightful accident might have been the result. Other two men were ploughing at the distant side of the field, but too far off for them to render help, even if they could have safely left their charges to come to my aid.

When we got home, in the evening, I was much praised by the spectators who witnessed the exciting struggle from a distance for my "heroic feat," as it was called, in preventing the excited animals from getting off altogether, while the "ither cuif," as they called the man, stood and looked on, and did not assist me. This was so far, so good, but next morning in the same field, and close by the same spot, while finishing the harrowing-in of the seed on the end and side-ridges, with the same team, a piece of old tin got among the harrow teeth, and off both animals bolted again.

Fortunately I did not have the reins placed in a loop round my neck, or waist, as we sometimes were wont to place them, and I held on till forced to let go my hold, through one rein breaking, and I was dragged down on my face. Then those couple of fleet gallopers went round that field in a style like racers training for the turf.

There were a pair or two of horses and ploughs finishing the tillage close-up to the stone fences, and two or three hands were digging-out the square corners of the field, but one and all cleared out of the way of the flying pair. Happily, the gearing gave way, and the fugitives, thus unencumbered, held on their mad career, with tails in the air, screaming as they went, and reached the farm-yard in about the same time it has taken me to describe their flight. The run was about half-a-mile distant. They were left to nurse their precious youngsters for the rest of that day.

My master met me after this exciting scene, with his face pale with rage, declaring I should never lay a hand on a horse of his again, but after he was told that I had held on till I was dragged down on my face, and that one rein broke; also how I had fought them with one rein and prevented them running off the previous afternoon, he quieted down nicely, and in less than a week he left me with the same pair yoked to a plough, and with only one guiding rein as before, and told me if they attempted to run off again, to let the plough into the soil down to the beam. This would hold them so long as the chains and harness kept whole; but they became quite manageable afterwards.

This young farmer used snuff very freely, and had reduced the art of taking it while at work to a science. He took a pride in showing how to bring round a pair of horses yoked in a plough at the end of a field, and take a pinch of snuff at the same time, without halting or losing a moment's time, or a foot of a new furrow, and he used to say, when showing me this rather clever act, that he was learning me to use snuff, and if I lived to be old I would blame him. Although I learned to use such a powder I had no trouble in giving up the habit many years ago.

He did not live to be old himself, for about three summers after this he returned home on a hot evening, perspiring very freely, and calling for a drink of butter milk, partook of such a draught as caused inflammation almost instantly, and although a strong man in his prime, in spite of the best medical assistance available there, he died on the third day after the seizure. During this summer (1846) the great heat, and dry weather, prevailed till the end of June, so that for about ten weeks we had never a drop of rain; but about the first week of July, and onward till well into August, there were at intervals the heaviest rain-showers, accompanied by short sharp thunderstorms, the downpours being remarkable for the weight of their volume. Many old people said they had never seen such a deluge of rain. The harvest turned out heavy, and early, but about the first of September strange close stifling fogs came up from the south and east seawards, and strong-smelling hot moisture filled the atmosphere.

About this time, when the bulk of the potato crop was ripening, that was when the fruit of that plant was appearing, and forming apples, after the bloom had fallen off; then all of a sudden whole fields, whose appearances were quite healthy in the morning or evening, in the course of the next day or night were seen with every stem laid prostrate, and blackened as if they had been blasted by lightning. On examining the roots it was found that some frightful distemper had struck both stem and root, the tubers, in about nine out of ten, were black in patches throughout, and useless.

Before this visitation the husbandman, the man of science, and every other man, stood mute and helpless, and so no one was found able to fathom or find out the cause of this dread pestilence.

Many theories were propounded as to its origin, but to this hour, and after the lapse of half-a-century, its true origin, and especially the propelling force of the speed at which it traversed every district, and the completeness of the havoc it wrought, has never been ascertained.

In the year 1845 a rumour came from the West of Scotland (and it is said that rumour originated in Ireland) that some unknown disease had made its appearance in the potato fields.

This report, when first passing around was looked upon as an idle tale.

I heard a weird story told one autumn evening in 1845, at Kirkton o' Lemlydale, which came back to my mind like a prophecy fulfilled. When in 1846 the complete potato blight became so widespread, the memory of that tale proved a sad presentiment in the case of thousands in the West of Ireland. The place where the prophecy was said to have been uttered, was somewhere on the turnpike road between Dundee and Forfar. Up to the date referred to, and until the two railway termini in Arbroath were connected, the old carriers plied their trade by the road, and their homeward journeys were generally made during the night. Those heavy-traffic "knights of the road," although not authorised to carry passengers, could sometimes be induced to grant a belated and tired way-farer a lift along, on the top of the high-loaded carts.

It was said that on one very dark night, and at a lonely part of the road, a Forfar carrier was accosted by what seemed an old woman enveloped in a long brown cloak or mantle, who asked for "a lift" along on the foremost cart, whereon sat the driver of the caravan, consisting of two or three loaded carts. The man (it is said) halted his horses, and assisted the sombre-looking figure to mount to the seat she had requested, and the teams were again started, and came jogging along at the usual three-miles-per-hour pace of the fine big and powerful horses.

In the course of the conversation with his newly-found passenger, the carrier inquired if she had heard of a hitherto unknown disease doing damage to the growing crops of potatoes in some parts of the country. The brown-robed stranger replied—

"Yes, she had heard of it, and," she added in an awe-inspiring oracular, half-sepulchral tone, that "next year there would be fewer potatoes left after the same disease than had ever been seen since the introduction of the root to this country, and by the second year (viz.—1847), thousands on thousands fewer people to eat them!" The carrier, rather struck by the manner and matter of this uncanny-looking interlocutor, ventured to inquire how she knew such things would happen?

She did not reveal how she knew, but said that they would come to pass as surely as she knew that there was a dead man on the top of his (the carrier's) rear-following cart!

Completely astonished now, and remembering that a few miles back, before he met what he now believed to be an oracle, he had allowed a tired male pedestrian to take a ride on the rear cart, the carrier dismounted and ran to the last cart, and on getting on the top thereof, lo! the man (who about two hours before had taken his seat there, and apparently in full health) was now lying dead, and stranger still, on rejoining his leading cart to take his seat as before, the old woman was gone! and the carrier saw her no more!

I have already mentioned that newspapers were much scarcer in 1846 than they are now, and they were only published in the larger and more enterprising towns, and except hearing the foregoing story orally repeated once, and much surprise expressed by them who listened to its narration, I do not call to remembrance that I ever heard the midnight prophecy on the Dundee Road mentioned again, until I have told it now, as I then heard it. The tale was not even referred to, so far as I know, when the total blight of the potato crop in 1846 became an accomplished fact, but whether the story is true or not, the loss of that year's crop was most complete and far-reaching in its consequences.

Chapter XXII.

"Hurrah! for the men that work;

. . . .

*Who earn their daily bread
By the sweat of an honest brow;
Hurrah! for the men who dig and delve,
And they who reap and plough."*

—RICHARDSON.

Repeal of Corn Taxes.—A Jubilee Day held in the County of Forfar in honour of Free Trade.—1846-47.— leave Sampson Bank and am engaged to Mr Daniel Pinetree, Sawmiller and Farmer, Rosinburn.—First Experience of Bothy Life.—Severe in its simplicity, and rude in its resources.—Old Joe—a Gigantic Quadruped.—Find I cannot stand that old horse, and also find that I have undersold myself.—I take leg-bail, and leave the place.

It is worthy of mention that on a day in August, 1846, the Act was sanctioned which repealed the legal authority which levied a tax on foreign grain imports, and to mark their appreciation and express their joy at the fulfilment of this long-promised relief, most of the towns in the county of Forfar proclaimed a day of jubilee.

Dundee, then only a royal ancient burgh, though now rejoicing in the title of a city, was a notable exception in the jubilee celebration. It was said the authorities there did not consider it would be safe for the preservation of the public peace to make any joy demonstration, or permit any trade, or political or public procession, owing to the unruly and factious population they had to govern, because at that time toleration of each other's views and beliefs, either political or religious, was not so well understood, even in Scotland, as it is now, and toleration was never practised then between the different sects of the professing but shamefully divided Christian Churches, as it is now. Protestants and Roman Catholics were ever ready to fly at each other's throats on every opportunity—so the day of public rejoicing observed in the other towns had to be repressed in the turbulent town referred to.

So was the popular report at least in Forfarshire, and I am in this case only repeating that report as I heard it.

Martinmas came round once more, and again I had to appear in the hated feein' market at Letham, as I refused to stay longer at Samsonbank, as odd horseman and cattleman, for I held that I had proved that I could work a pair of horses now, so in search of a pair I went forth.

The master I was leaving came to me in the fair, and kindly offered to assist me to a place, and when the hour and the new master came, my old employer came forward and gave me a first-class character in every respect, especially praising me as a great worker, and telling Mr Daniel Pinetree, who was trying to hire me, how well I had served him, remarking that although quite a boy I deserved to get and could really earn a man's wages. My late master, however, did not indicate what those wages should be, so when I was offered £9 sterling, for the next year, with the usual allowances of oatmeal and milk and bothy lodging, seeing I had only £5 for the year's service I had just ended, I thought I was getting a good advance, but I found afterwards I had made a great mistake, as farm-servants' wages had risen with a bound, owing to the scarcity of hands, who had been enticed from farm service to work at railway construction, now in full swing all around, and at which employment weekly wages had been advanced fully a shilling per day; so I found I had undersold myself for a year to the tune of about £3. I only found this out after it was too late to get it rectified, but its rectification came about during the year nevertheless.

My new employer, Mr Pinetree, was not only a farmer, but a wood merchant and sawmill owner as well. He had been a joiner to trade, and he and another journeyman mate were the first in the Arbroath district who started to work the steel circular saws, driven by water power, and make a trade of this operation. Previous to this the manual-wrought vertical saws, and saw-pits, were the only appliances used for the cutting-up of the giants of the forest, either home or foreign grown. The name of this sawmill and farm, where my lines had now fallen, was Rosinburn, and my work was driving one horse and cart, principally delivering newly-sawn wood into Montrose, which was about seven miles distant.

The horse I had in charge for this job was all that remained of what had been a most gigantic sample of the equine species. His name was Joe, and standing as he did, as he evidently had doubts about lying down, for if he had laid him down it would have been an engineer's job to set him up again. Between shoulder top and lower-foot he measured over twenty-two hands, and had his back been in a condition that I could have ridden thereon, I would then have rejoiced in occupying a place in the higher walks of life, and would have breathed a purer air at such an altitude.

I will describe hereafter how this unfortunate old horse affected the period of my service at Rosinburn, as the description of social and domestic life there will get the first place in this narrative.

This was my first essay of bothy life. Such a life at that time was so severe in its simplicity, and rude in its appointment, that now, recalling its history, I only marvel how we managed to turn out on Sundays and fair-days as respectable as we did, from places where the appliances for either moral or physical improvement were so scanty that one could not conceive by what mysterious process many bothy men dressed themselves as tastefully (if not more so) than their masters, who had all needful requisites for dress and adornment, whereas we, the down-trodden, often unjustly, despised bothy-dwellers in general, had nothing beyond a razor, a comb, and sometimes a sixpenny looking-glass, and in some instances a clothes brush, in addition to a set of shoe brushes, among half-a-dozen of us.

Then all the furniture provided by our masters for these dwellings consisted only of an iron pot and ladle, a saut bucket (i.e., a salt box) sometimes a wooden pail which had to do duty as a wash hand basin, besides having to contain or carry both cooking and drinking water, and sometimes the only drinking utensil to be found in such establishments was our wooden brose-caups, or a whisky dram-glass of the old pattern minus the foot. I have heard of an instance where a small crowd of the sons of the soil lived huddled into a place of the kind I am describing, when one night, on returning from a spree or entertainment of some kind, with one of their number overpowered either by drink or dancing, and supposed to be asleep, while another was ransacking the elegant mansion for some vessel wherewith to get a draught of water, were astonished when the supposed sleeper roused himself on his elbow, and to the surprise and boisterous delight of his fellows, cry out in half-sleepy drawl, "Tak' a drink wi' the aix" (axe).

At some places there was a meal bin for each man, separate with lock and key, if he cared to lock it, but I never saw one of them locked, and I never heard of an instance of one man tampering with the other's stores. To the afore-mentioned furniture was added a long four-legged form, or stool. This, placed across in front of the fire, and the meal bins, made up all the seats we were allowed. I never saw a table or chair in a bothy, and have known men who had inhabited such places from boyhood even on to grey-haired old age, who I verily believe could not have accustomed themselves to the use of either table or chair. Such were the furnishings and appointments of the first bothy I inhabited, and the inventory here given is a correct list of the full rig-out, only adding thereto beds, with in general plenty of bed clothes and sheets, which we were rigorous on insisting should be changed regularly, although we had at some places to make up and down our beds ourselves at all times, as in many ill-advised instances, the women servants were not allowed to set foot over the door of the bothy.

In such cases, when the day for changing the linen came, the bothy key was left at the milkhouse window, where our daily allowance of the lacteal fluid, fresh from the cow, was handed out, in general, twice a day. At some places on the day of changing the bed sheets, one of the maid servants went to the bothy when the men were absent, and changed the sheets, merely leaving the clean and taking away the soiled linen, not even being allowed to make up our beds.

I have termed such restrictive and prohibitory rules ill-advised, as tending, where young people of opposite sexes are thus prevented from meeting on the common ground of common employment, or in hours of leisure and recreation, while in the service of a common employer, instead of such measures tending to improve the relations between the sexes in its best sense, according to my observation, such unsocial and artificial means of regulating male and female intercourse, or trying to entirely prevent them meeting at all, has invariably defeated its object. In a majority of the farming population cases in several of the best agricultural districts of Scotland this restriction has brought about that deplorable state of matters such repressing measures are generally meant to prevent.

So much is this the case, both north and south, that our country has earned the name of a nation of hypocrites. And who is to blame? I think I hear some reader reply, and say, "Of course, the creatures themselves," but hold on, ye sapient moralists, and unjust censors of your fellow-men and women, and I will hereafter endeavour to show you that several true words can be said on both sides of the great question of who is responsible for the terribly lax and unsound thought there is abroad in our beloved land, on the great evils of the social life of the farm.

Let me furnish my record of experiences at Rosinburn in 1846-1847, and how old Joe, the big horse, and I got on. I found him the most willing uncomplaining creature I have ever met with, and he, poor beast, had something to complain of, which would have made many horses rebel and strike work altogether, for a sorely-wounded and supperating back under the saddle was his, and although there were numbers of more experienced hands for directing treatment and dressing for such a wound than I could then be, and although Pinetree himself was a Free Kirk elder, he caused this poor frame of a tortured animal to be driven, sometimes twice in a day, from the sawmill to Montrose, making the daily round 28 miles, and sometimes on both occasions drawing a load of one ton ten cwt. of newly-sawn timber, although the horse's condition was perfectly well known to his owner. There were two carts, and one was loaded while the other was on the way back.

Were such a cruelty practised now any owner would be heavily fined, and the driver punished also. In less than a fortnight, seeing I could get no opportunity of improving poor Joe's miserable state, I got so disgusted at the idea of being seen on the road with such an apparition, that I made up my mind to leave the place rather than drive him at all, so taking a Sunday evening to think it out, in the dark of next morning, and while my bothy mate was engaged in the stables with his pair of horses, I, after seeing poor Joe fed and dressed down, fastened and roped my small clothes-box, and without saying anything to anyone, except asking the assistance of one of the sawmillers to hoist my box on my back, and getting that assistant to pledge himself to silence regarding my departure, I took the road, and got soon under cover on a rough bye-way and reached Montreath Forest.

I walked on through the woods without laying down my burden, until I had put three miles between me and Rosinburn. I then came on a row of a few houses just within the edge of the woods, and near an open glade, which I learned had been let as a small farm, but which had to be trenched and drained, and the contractor for the job was on the ground engaging hands by the piece and by the day. I went to him and got work.

After engaging I went home to Merlin Brae and told my mother of my flight from Rosinburn, and the reason for that flight, and of the chance I had to bury myself in the depths of the forest till all search for me would be abandoned. My mother did not quite approve of the step I had taken, although she said I would have been quite right in refusing to work the horse in such a plight. She thought I should have made known my refusal first, and then left if the beast was not laid off until his wounded back healed.

Seeing my mother had some doubts of my earning a sufficient living at the work I had engaged for by the week, I tried to assure her that with three and sixpence worth of a steel-mouthed spade, neither I nor her had any need to fear the face of clay, animate or inanimate, and added that I had faith to believe neither of us would be disappointed for a pair of stockings or a breakfast through the step I had now taken. I walked back to Montreath Forest next morning and commenced work, and for two months was paid twelve shillings per week, getting very good lodgings at one shilling per week in the head-keeper's house, who had charge of the fowls of the air and the wild beasts of the forest and field which frequented the estate and that portion of the forest, which was once wholly a commonty, but is now claimed by the owner of the domain of Chalmersfield. The fine modern castle of the same name stands near that bridge which carries the road from Forfar across brae-borne Esk to the ancient city of Brechin, or St Ninians, whichever name you prefer.

I have heard it said that it was in the parish of Brechin the writer of these sketches was born, but never having seen the registry entry of that event, if such a thing did happen there, I, although credited with a rather retentive memory, cannot recall the event. If such a thing did really happen to me there, as the Paisley native declared, I could not help it.

However, after two months' labour in that part of the said parish, under the forest cover, at the end of that time I came out into the open once more, and took to navvying work at the construction of the railway to Aberdeen, which passes through part of the now cleared site of the ancient desmesne.

How Plaintree's sister saw me among the navvies, and reported to the man from whom I had deserted, and what measures he of timber and big hungry horses took to get me to fulfil my engagement with him, and how it all ended, will be told in the next chapter.

Chapter XXIII.

" Thou shall not kill !"—in times of dread
  The thrilling accents came,
Pealing from Sinai's hallowed head
  In thunder and in flame.
" Thou shall not kill !"—to Me alone
  Belongs the gift of life—
A gift I delegate to none
  In this dark world of strife. "

—RICHARD RUIGG.

After two months' absence, I am induced to return to Rosinburn on a new agreement. — I work that out and re-engage a third time. — John Singleton —A new master and a new place.—Miss Ovington, his housekeeper. — The Gulf between bothy men and their employers. — Moral Degradation of Bothy Life. — Carelessness and culpability of the Masters. — A Terrible Tragedy and a Hanging Judge. -- The feeble attempts and half-hearted methods for ameliorating the lot of Bothy-men.

I had not wrought a week at railway construction when Mr Daniel Pinetree made his appearance one fine clear winter afternoon, accompanied with the two special railway constables, who were employed by the authorities to preserve peace and order, where large numbers of workmen were employed at such works.

On our gaffer, or overlooker, sending a man to take my place, and asking me to go and speak to Mr Pinetree, I sent back word that as I had nothing to say to the gentleman referred to, I would not leave my place in the barrow run, so Mr Pinetree had perforce to come to me, which he did, and demanded " what I was doing there?" Like a thorough Scot I replied to his question by asking another, and inquired if he did not see what I was doing there? He gave it as his opinion that I had no business there, and that I was his servant. I replied that I became his servant through an error, and that now after two months, and under certain circumstances existing at the place, which caused me to leave his service, I did not think he had any claim upon me.

He threatened to call back the constables and have me arrested, and I said that if the officers could produce the County Sheriff's warrant for my apprehension I would surrender at once. He said they could soon get a warrant. I replied, "You can go then and get it, and by that time you will have to seek me elsewhere." There were no electric telegraphs or telephones in those days, and Mr Pinetree had to go as he came; but the gaffer on the job, and in whose house I lodged, told me in the evening that Pinetree was determined to give me trouble if I did not return to fulfil my agreement, or otherwise go next day and settle with him, so I resolved to take a walk to Merlin Brae, five or six miles distant, and consult the only counsellor I had to refer to (my mother).

When I stepped into her house about ten o'clock the same night, and surprised her by telling her that the master I had left two months before was after me, she was much excited, declaring I "was aye in a habble," and "windered," as she expressed it, "whaur a' my ups and downs wad land me." Her conclusion was I should return to the place unconditionally. I was as firmly resolved that I would do nothing of the kind, but I walked to the place the next day, and after a long negotiation it was arranged that I would resume duty and work out my agreement on condition that nothing was to be deducted from the first half-year's pay for the time I had been away, and specially that I was not to be asked to lay a hand on the old equine wreck, but would get a respectable-looking and proper horse to drive.

This compact was more than fulfilled, for the one horse and cart expanded into a pair of horses and carts, which I drove among the woods, and along some of the wildest and roughest roads in the district; but the experience gained at such work was of great value to me in the directing of the removal and loading and conveyance of all sorts of timber by road or rail in coming years.

However, the best part of this rather broken year's record is that notwithstanding our second agreement as to no deduction being made for the time I was absent through desertion, within a week of the Whitsunday term, 1847, I sought and obtained another advance of pay for next half-year, owing to having successfully managed the working of the two carts and horses in place of one. Martinmas came again, and having no intention of spending another winter at such rough and laborious work, although I had learned to be skilful at the handling of heavy timber, and although again offered more wages, I left, and took to farm service pure and simple, and saw bothy life in another district. Its phases were very similar to what has been described in the preceding chapter.

The years 1848-49 found me located twenty miles to the west of Montrose, a fine district, adjoining the beautiful parish of Kerbetbower. The name of my new parish was Eastern Kerbet, and the farm where I took service at the Martinmas term rejoiced in the name of Wintersheugh, owing I suppose to the sun never shining on it for the three winter months.

It was a fine large farm, occupying four pairs of horses. Our master, whose name was John Singleton, was a man past middle age, but unmarried. His niece, quite a modernised young farmer's daughter of the time, who had been brought straight from the boarding school, acted as mistress of her uncle's establishment. She was highly educated, I have no doubt in all the ornamental branches of learning, which then, as now were principally acquired for the purpose of developing, refining, and improving womankind, but this education left her with about as much practical knowledge of the common and useful duties of farm housekeeping and management as might be expected of the city school-girl who knows not grass from grain.

Miss Ovenston had the good sense not to show her ignorance, for we never saw her, except on very rare occasions, and I believe although we had all been laid up sick, or even dying, she would not have come to visit us. Yes, the gulf of class distinction was very wide between the hired servant and his master and mistress by this time, and the thing went on all unseen, and the gulf widened more and more while the moral and physical conditions were the same in Forfarshire till a terrible tragedy, the murder by a young man of a child of which he was the reputed father for which he suffered at the hands of the public executioner took place.

From the sadly pathetic and strongly extenuating circumstances of the crime, and the youth of the criminal, it was thought that a commutation of the capital sentence might be got, but Sir George Gray, who was Home Secretary at the time, refused to recommend

Her Majesty to interfere, and the culprit, a mere boy (he was only in his 21st year) paid the extreme penalty of the law in sight of a large and morbid-minded crowd of spectators, in front of the County Jail at Forfar. I remember the morning was one of the finest of that May, the season of the year, and fields and woods, moorlands, fells, and mountains were adorned in all the unspeakable grandeur which the great Decorator had spread over all His works! And yet this morning, bathed in light, the air laden with the odours from a thousand blossoms, and made vocal in the young summer chorus of a myriad of gossamer-winged and feathered minstrels, beheld that horrid though legal deed done in the land of Sabbaths and Christian gospel preaching.

It was said numbers of the spectators fainted when they saw the unfortunate youth thrown off. I think it served them right. No one except those who had the law's behests to obey had any call to be there, and whether public executions be right or wrong, their being veiled from the moribund gaze of the unwashed mob now, is one improvement we ought to be thankful for. It was said the unfortunate culprit was a very handsome youth, fair-haired and fine-featured, and stood six feet in height. I never saw him, but there is one thing I know, that if everyone had felt as much sorrow as I did that morning he died, there would have been no witnesses outside the county jail to look on what I believe to this hour was a judicial murder. His condemnation earned for the Lord of Justiciary who passed the sentence the name of the "hanging judge."

The Queen and Prince Albert were then occupying their retreat in the Highlands among the first years when they were there, and the history of this crime with its results sent such a thrill of horror through the hearts of Christian philanthropists, and laid bare such a state and manner of life in bothies, that social agricultural degeneration (as it was called) became a burning question, and a deputation, headed by the good and faithful minister of Oathlaw, who was chaplain of the County Prison at Forfar, went to Balmoral, I rather think at the request of Her Majesty and the Prince, and a great ado was made, and many schemes mooted for improving the dwelling-places of the farm-servants.

That alone seemed to be considered the only sore requiring to be healed. Better housing was urgently wanted, but except in some very special cases, even that improvement was not carried out. I thought it remarkable that no word was spoken among all that was proposed as to the need there was for some kindly personal interest being taken in our moral welfare by our masters, and especially that some hours more of relaxation should be granted to us, and that the same masters and mistresses should see that all reasonable facilities should be provided for their servants, both male and female, having open and decent daylight interviews. I used to inveigh loudly against the custom which relegated the meetings with sweethearts to only the midnight hour, as if courtship and marriage were things to be ashamed of, and I insisted that such duties, being inherent in our nature, were among the most sacred and honourable duties which both sexes are called on to fulfil. The ignoring of our rights in that respect, and our having to prowl about in hours of darkness, like thieves of the night, just made young men and maidens into robbers of purity of life, in place of representing to the world, as our beloved country was once famed for doing, a farm working class of both sexes, pure in morals, patriotic in spirit, God-loving, and God-loved.

We were fast becoming a morally polluted and loveless rabble, for in spite of certain educational advantages which were available to everyone, the behavious of both sexes, in very many instances, both north and south, was unworthy of responsible or rational beings.

It is nearly forty years since I left farm service, and I see much mechanical ingenious improvement in the modes of working, and hear a general outcry about farming not paying, or being a money-making trade. But the latter to my mind never was the primeval purpose or intention of farming, because a farm can produce all that man requires from the cradle to the grave, and where a man farms his own property, and the freehold in his own hands fulfil these conditions, there can only be found the true meaning of the finest words in our language, " Home, sweet home."

Chapter XXV.

*"Man's inhumanity to man
Makes countless thousands mourn."*
—BURNS.

I give up farm service and join the pavement quarriers in the Greyrigg Valley. — Details of the work.—Working Hours and Wages. —The seeming Contentment of the ordinary manual toiler then, contrasted with those of the present time.—Harvesting under new conditions in 1848.—The Harvest Contractor and his squad.—Soutar Mixitwell, the Village Publican in Winkleburn.—His raw-grain whisky, and its effects.--Our Lodgings and the scenes witnessed there.—Woman, what man makes her.

At Whitsunday, 1848, I severed my connection for a time from farm service, and after a few weeks at various kinds of work, I joined the pavement quarriers, near Greyrigg. That industry had revived for a few years since the time of the general failure in 1837, when the enforced retiral of my grandfather and other old hands took place. Quarry-work was then and always had been a very laborious and poor job for its employees. The work could only go on in dry weather, nor could the labour be carried on during hard frost. Some of the operations were rather dangerous, as very often the harder kinds of rock layers had to be broken up by blasting with gunpowder. The gelatine or dynamite cartridge was not then invented, nor the long safety fuse in use, as they are now.

The weekly wages ranged from twelve to fifteen shillings for a day of ten hours. And there were no Saturday half-holidays then, yet in some cases where an hour or two was made up by arrangement, we got off at 4 p.m. on Saturday. The steam-driven machinery, such as patent derrick cranes had not then made their appearance in quarries, and the handloom yet lingered in the land. So when winter came the frozen-out quarryman, the mason, and mason's labourer, and other fair-weather workmen, took refuge at the handloom during the dead time of the year, in order to provide themselves and their dependants with stockings and breakfast, and if possible procure at least " tatties an' saut " for the other two meals, till—

> " Spring wi' young and gladsome step,
> Wid cross the knowes again,
> And buds on trees o' every shape,
> Redeck the hill and plain."

These additions of indoor or storm-staid toilers swelled the number of the workers at the " four posts of misery," as the handloom industry was then named, while steam cranes, so needful to quarry working were not then in use.

Alongside of these inventions came the steam powerloom, which ousted the old handloom weaver, and filled his place with a young pale-faced, tea-drinking, half-starved race of operatives, who were forced into the hells and hovels of the insanitary overcrowded town or city dwellings of the old order, and while inventors, and those who profited by the inventions, became millionaires; the operative became only part of the millionaire's machinery. I have spoken of the gulf which had opened, and seemed ever widening, between master and servant long before I left the farm service. The chasm is no wider nor vaster than the division is now, which lies between other employers and employees. This chasm if not soon spanned over by the bridges of well-understood mutual interest, on the foundations of goodwill to men on both sides, can only otherwise widen until it engulphs the contending interests, and when the industrial war which has brought the catastrophe is ended our grand old country will have little left but her glorious history, which starving men with wives and children can neither eat nor wear.

It is a deplorable, because it is a true reflection on the progress of science and art, that after such an abridgement of time and space, which enables man to live more and accomplish more in a month than could be done in years previous, that the volume of human happiness seems less, and unrest and discontent among all classes much increased.

It appears to me, and to many more, better able to judge than me, that this terrible contagion of pride, selfishness, and ambition is more prevalent than ever.

Before the harvest of 1848 arrived another crisis and collapse took place in the pavement quarrying trade, and I had to seek other employment, and got engaged as a scythe-man to a reaping contractor, a new kind of employer in our district, who had contracted for the cutting-down of all kinds of grain on several farms, at so much per acre.

The experience of the wet harvest of 1841 had in the interval dispensed with the ordinary sickle, or reaping-hook, which for so many generations had been the handloom weavers' hope and stay in guaranteeing the year's moderate rent for the

"Wee kailyard and the hoose abune his heid."

The contractor with whom I engaged had a partner who was lessee of the public-house in the village of Winkleburn. His name was Souter Mixitwell, which was sometimes pronounced Makesweel, but then it was a gross libel on the idea of wellbeing, or making well. For it is no exaggeration when I say that the stuff he sold under the name of whisky was the vilest compound ever dealt out to a man or woman under Her Majesty's license. Yet several of my fellow-workmen, aye, and women too, had actually undertaken by contract to spend a part of their hard-won earnings in this wretched public-house. They could scarcely have yielded a more loyal fulfilment of such a nefarious bargain. We all lodged in an old castle on the principal farm where we harvested. We cooked and ate our meals in the great gloomy dungeon-looking hall, where darkness was made visible only through the ancient loopholes in the thick walls, or by the glow from the great arched fireplace, when the fire burned on the hearth.

Our bedrooms were in separate apartments of this old stronghold, the men's in the upper, and the women's in the lower regions. Had the late medieval owners or occupiers of this historic mansion been permitted to step out of their graves hard by, and under the light of the lovely harvest moon, have witnessed the scenes enacted in the hall of their fathers by this band of harvesters, when they returned from Mixitwell's poison drug-shop, I believe these ghosts would have fled back to their graves at a pace double-quick, even for ghosts!

I may close the account of my disagreeable experience here by recording that in less than a week's association with this company I changed my lodgings, and for the remainder of the harvest-time I walked to and from my home at Merlin Brae, a distance of over two miles, every morning and evening. I found it no very easy matter to bear the persecution and obloquy which my avoidance of this company in the hours of leisure gave rise to, and holding aloof from their revels, etc., sometimes exposed me to such a storm of derision as took all, and more than all the philosophy of the religion I had yet learned, to enable me to resist and keep clear of their company.

Yes, as a young man I saw much rough behaviour and heard language objectionable and wicked at most country places in every district, and I never failed to denounce the bad habits, and warn the males, young and old, when I got them in quiet times individually. It seemed to me rather remarkable that in most cases when I thus reasoned with those of my fellow-workmen on sobriety, probity, and purity of speech and behaviour, they generally agreed with me, but at the same time very often had some plausible excuse whereby they exonerated their conduct, a proof that Burns was right in saying—

"When rantin' roond in pleasure's ring,
    Religion may be blinded,
Or if she gi'e a random sting,
    It may be little minded."

I have mentioned only warning my fellow workmen. I never checked or warned any of the other sex, as I have a theory, whether it be right or wrong I have held it since I began to think on the relation of the sexes, that woman, especially the truly domestic woman, is exactly what man makes her.

Notwithstanding all we see, hear, and read about "the new woman," she is still, and will ever remain, what man makes her; aye, even in all sorts and conditions of life this has held, and will ever hold good. But the manlier woman becomes, in the best sense, through her imitation of all that is truly noble and manly, but only so far as her mental and physical endowments permit, then so much the better fitted will she be, to be man's companion —not his equal—in these attributes of mind and body which are essential to man's highest attainments. She is his superior in the qualities which charm, adorn, and cheer our earthly habitations. Amid all the vicissitudes of man's and woman's earthly lot, I look on the rubbish which is often spoken about "woman's rights," and "woman's equality," and of woman's and man's interests being separated, as a wicked modern heresy.

However, the opinion of an obscure and unknown quantity like me will be of very little account in this age, when every man and nearly every other woman, old or young, think themselves possessed of more than the wisdom of Solomon, or all the sages of ancient days!

Chapter XXV.

"Death! grim Death!
Will fold me in his leaden arms and press
Me close to his cold clayey breast."
—CONGRIEVE.

" Of all who flock'd to swell or see the show
Who car'd about the corpse! The funeral
Made the attraction and the black the woe,
There throbbed not there one heart that pierc'd the pall."
—BYRON.

1850.— I join the navvies at the Construction of the Railway to Aberdeen. -- Sudden Accidental Death of my first work-mate from Bristol. — Description of his funeral, the most novel procession I ever took part in.

I continued at various kinds of out-door piece-work during the greater part of 1848-49-50, and wrought as an ordinary navvy at the completing of a part of the railway to Aberdeen from Montrose, on to three miles beyond Stonehaven. The latter is the capital of the county of the Mearns. The finish of this left but thirteen miles of that line to complete to the terminus, but those remaining miles were not opened through to the north bank of the River Dee till some time in 1851.

There are only two incidents that I remember worth mentioning which took place during my navvy experience. The first was the accidental death of a work-mate, a fine young man from Bristol; his name was William Hollinbay.

He was a manly specimen of an Englishman, stood rather over six feet in his stockings, a handsome fellow, and was only in his twenty-second year. He was not like the average of railway navvies, but was more intelligent, of nice manners, and an energetic worker, and I heard after his lamented death that he had no need to have taken to that kind of work. The accident came about as follows:—We were working at the banking-up of the abutments of a new bridge which spans a mountain stream that rises in a Grampian glen, and traversing one parish passes below the railway we were finishing. The material for the abutments was being taken from a field alongside the line, this was being filled into wagons, of which there were two trains of eight each in use. There were two bank-faces cut in the mound of earth we were removing, so that one train was filled while the drivers brought forward the other train of empties.

Hollinbay and I and another were in our turn of the farthest inward, or gullet wagon, as this was called, and when going and returning between the two trains of trucks we walked along the top of the bank from which the material was taken, and on our return to about the third train to be filled on the first Monday morning after only one week's comradeship, when we had descended at the end of the row of trucks, and were stepping in between the face of our truck, the cry "ware out!" came from above. I backed at once about three paces and on looking up I saw the whole face, about twenty-three feet high, bulging out.

Poor Hollinbay was before me, and the third man was outside the train of wagons, and safe. I saw Hollinbay look up and note the danger, but instead of running forward, which would have cleared him, he made to mount over the second wagon, but while he had his foot on one wheel and his hand grasping the side, in less than a second, before he could make the spring which would have landed him in safety, the mass came down with a great crash and pinned him against the wagon with such a force that the rails started the spikes which held them to the sleepers through the blow given to the wagon wheels.

The thing was all so sudden I did not realise for a second or two what had happened, until I saw my mate's hands relax their grasp and quiver for about another second, and all was over! But the full meaning of the accident did not strike me till a shout of horror was heard from the row of men standing outside, in which a shrill but musical and mournful wail arose from our brothers of the Emerald Isle, whose voices in sorrow or joy are always expressive and eloquent. "Oh! the man is killed!" was what they called out to each other.

Then many willing and strong hands seized the wagon and turned it right over, and the lifeless body of my comrade fell forward, but not flat to the ground, as it was held fast by the knees in the earth and stones which surrounded it. I yet see! for the scene is all before me now! how carefully these rough men removed the debris from around the lifeless clay, while others held the body erect; then with what sad-eyed reverence they laid it softly on the improvised bier of rough boards and summer broom! then laid the whole aside, while we all stood silent and dismayed in that terrible presence which had descended so swiftly among us on this lovely summer morning!

A doctor came soon, but his services were of no avail, only he told us that the victim had died a painless death. Not a bone was broken, and the only mark of violence was a red line across the breast, in the region of the heart. The medical man said the blow on the back which pinned him to the truck had caused rupture of the heart. They bore the body to the cottage where he had been lodging, about a mile to the west.

We wrought no more that day, for we were all upset and saddened by the suddenness of the accident. There had been some time lost the previous week, and as I left my lodging at the breakfast hour that morning, it did not look like being a fair day. I said to my landlady that it looked like another bad day, and added that it would be another case of lost time. When I went back, stopped for the day, she said, "Now you have got a case, and a sad case, with something more in it than lost time." This was the first time I had been so near the King of Terrors, or seen a death by accident. I have witnessed several fatalities since then, but none of them have impressed me so much as this one did.

During the filling of the raik before he fell, my young friend remarked that he had lost the Friday previous through taking some "Scotch" whisky on the Thursday night, and then he lost the Saturday through wet weather, and he vowed he would never taste whisky again while in Scotland. I believe he would have kept his word, if he had lived, but he was taken away from the evil to come, and never again had the chance to break his vow.

We buried him on the third day after, and the whole squad attended the funeral in our working clothes, as requested. The conveyance was a long-cart which had been conveying lime and building materials about the works, and the beast of burden drawing this temporary hearse was a great swift-stepping black mare. It appeared to me the most unique and novel-looking funeral procession I ever before or since joined in. The day was hot, and the mare went on at a great speed, and until the driver slowed down a little we were all kept half-running, with the sweat pouring down our faces. There was one tall, lounging, lazy fellow in the procession, who gave up, but instead of falling by the way he mounted the cart and seated himself on the coffin, which lay there covered with a black mortcloth or pall. He was said to be a native of Auchterarder, and was known in the squad by the name of that celebrated lang toon.

Before joining this squad Auchterarder had been working among red quarry stones, or red ore or clay, and with his long sun-burnt face and red-stained clothing, his great gaunt figure, sitting bolt upright on the dead man's black pall, in the midst of the white lime-stained cart, with about sixty men in hob-nailed boots, and apparelled in fustian and corduroy, running behind made up such a picture as I cannot describe, but which I can never forget.

When some of the procession saw this figure in terra-cotta sitting on the dead man's coffin, they raised a howl of execration, and shouted to him to get out of that! Some took up stones and tried to hit him, but there he sat, like a great heathen idol in red, not moving a muscle of his long solemn face, but ducking and dodging his head to avoid the missiles which were flying about him. The man in charge of the funeral stopped the stone-throwing, and that red painted figure kept his seat until we reached the quiet kirk-yard.

It was a sweet sequestered spot at the bottom of a green glade, surrounding a grey auld parish kirk of Scotland. There in a corner of the ground reserved for strangers, beneath the cool shade of some grand old trees, we laid our early fated brother's remains at rest, while the feathered choristers in their leaf-screened bowers overhead sang his requiem! The remembrance of that requiem, often since that sad day, amid many of my life's vicissitudes, has reminded me that there are worse things to be met with in life than an early death, and has taught me to think with the poet, who says—

"Weep not for those who in life's early morning
The veil of the tomb hath hid from your eyes."

Chapter XXVI.

"*Now one's the better—than the other best,
Both tugging to be victor, breast to breast.*"
— SHAKESPERE.

"*How like a fiend may man be made,
Plyiny the foul and monstrous trade,
Quenching with reckless hands in blood
Sparks kindled by the breath of God.*"
— WHITTIER.

The Village of Drumlithie and its new Steeple.—Opening of the Railway to within twelve miles of Aberdeen in September, 1850. — A pitched ring fight in which I act second to a Forfar man.—Victory of my man. — An International Navvy Battle, wherein our Brothers over the water were worsted, and driven from the village.—Treachery of the villagers.

The other notable occurrence which took place during my railway-constructing time was on the opening of the afore-mentioned length of line in the autumn of 1850, when a kind of international riot took place, and a navvies' battle was fought between the Irish workmen on the one side and a combined force of English, Highlanders, and native Scotch on the other, near the village of Drumlithie, where all four nationalities lodged.

This village, I may mention, is noted as the place where it is said the public steeple, for some time after its erection, was removed indoors during the night! Whether this was meant to preserve its health, or prevent its being stolen, history saith not.

The breaking out of hostilities came about in a very simple way. The contractor for whom I and a large number belonging to the different races worked treated his hands to two hogsheads of English stout, to celebrate the opening of the extension. The contents of the first cask were run off from a cart unyoked on a small bog-meadow near the village, and the distribution took place in the evening immediately after the first train passed conveying the different contractors and directors of the Railway Company.

By some oversight on the part of those in charge of the liquor, it was discovered, when too late, that a whole Irish contingent from another section had pushed forward, and had drunk all the beverage meant only for our squad. Next day was held as a holiday, and all work was suspended. The second cask of stout having been reserved for this holiday, a better plan was adopted in its distribution. We being all first identified by calling the roll, were ordered to sit in rows, and the liquor was then fairly dealt out to those for whom it was intended.

That part of the business was soon over. Then it was found that the clever Pats and Barneys who ousted our squad the evening previous were now present, and had been watching while we were being regaled. They were fully arrayed in gala attire, but in addition to their holiday ornaments, it was revealed afterwards that each man of them had provided himself with the Irishman's weapon of persuasion and offence, viz., the time-honoured shillelagh! It was said each had this artfully concealed in a limb of his pants. Their treacherous designs were only found out when the melee began.

The signal for its commencement, evidently preconcerted, was an assault on our employer's brother, a big Lancashire man. I did not see the beginning of the battle in the meadow, as I had my attention drawn at the time to the preliminaries of another difficulty which had occurred, where the articles were being signed for a pitched battle between two single belligerents. One of the principles was from my native county town of Forfar, his opponent being the landlord of the house where my friend lodged, both members of our squad. Yet the trouble was considered by each of such a grievous nature, it was thought honour could only be vindicated by fighting it out. My district countrymen were known along the works upon this line as "the Forfar light infantry," also as the bravest and fairest in a stand-up fight, always using their fists, and never taking any undue advantage of an opponent, or hitting him when down.

On this occasion I saw that the Forfar man was all alone, with no one to see fair play to him, or to take his part, and the landlord being a native of the village the crowd around the ring seemed all for him. On seeing this my sympathy took fire, and would not allow me to remain neutral, so I leapt into the ring, and called on the Forfarian to follow suit, and I would be his second.

The reader must understand I was just fresh from having my share of the London stout, and was thereby stoutly inclined for deeds of daring, especially where the honour of my native district was at stake! So the memorable fight began, under honour's regular rules, and my distinguished patronage! The contest was soon decided. Forfar, true to her time-honoured record, in the person of her brave and skilful son, was very soon the victor! He doubled up this landlord in three rounds by knocking him down fair and square each time, and I led my man in triumph from that blood-stained field!

But while I had been engaged seeing fairplay to my countryman, the riot had been going on between the Irishmen and the whole of the other nationalities, in another part of the field, and while I and the victor from the ring fight were making our way to the village to seek fresh quarters for my newly-found friend, we heard a noise of contending men behind us, and on looking round, lo! we saw the whole Irish host in full flight from where they had taken their stand!

The rout soon overtook and passed us at a pace which only men fleeing for their lives can do, their holiday clothes in numerous instances in rags, flying in the wind, while many had their faces streaming with blood; they were closely pursued by the victorious enemy!

Those pursuers seemed not to have won the battle scathless, for many had hands and faces wounded and bleeding. Nearly all were armed with some sort of weapon; the vanquished had thrown away their "shillelaghs," but many of the pursuers carried pick shafts or formidable-looking sticks. I observed one man in pursuit with only his boots, pants, and shirt on, and he carried a big open knife in one hand and a pick-shaft in the other. I knew this man at the works as one of the quietest and most steady of men. I saw another with his underclothing torn from his back, leaving his body exposed from the waist upwards, and hearing the cry, "Clear the place of the Irish!" Poor fellows, they had for some weeks past been blamed for all midnight garden robberies, etc., but who, I do not believe, were more frequently the robbers than others of the different races there. A few foolish characters had begun this breach of the peace. Their conduct of the previous evening had aggravated their offence, and made the victims determined to expel the whole race, good and bad.

Seeing that nothing but a clean sweep-out would quell the disturbance, I ran to the lodgings of a nice Irish work-mate, whom I wished to warn to keep out of the way till the storm would blow over. When I reached the place I found my favourite gone, and we never met again!

Finding the majority bent on following up their threat of clearing the town of the now rightly or wrongly obnoxious race, and being in fine fighting trim, I actually went to my lodgings, and divested myself of my coat and vest, put on my working belt, sallied forth again, was pressed into the service of the victorious party, and took the field at the head of one of the house-searching brigades who stormed the dwellings, and turned out the fugitives.

The victors went about the work of expulsion after this on a thoroughly systematic plan, and with an energy and method, so that by three p.m. not a man was left in Drumlithie who did not pronounce the words "king," or "guinea," with the same accent as in the word read.

That was a shibboleth or linguistic test applied to the Emerald Isle nationality, and it proved most effective. It was the first and last riot or fight I ever had a hand in, and the part I took in both affairs astonished me, and does so yet, when I remember that as a boy I would never mix in any fight. However, I was not more surprised at my own conduct in this than at that of some of the quietest and steadiest men I had seen in our squad engaged in the rather serious melee, and my experience then convinces me that most men, and especially Scotchmen, will fight when aroused to it in the face of a common danger.

There was not much damage done in this riot, but it was far-reaching in its results, and were the same occurring anywhere now, it would be magnified, and the whole proceedings given in the daily press, with embellishment of language and a minutiæ of detail which the lover of newspaper gossip really lives on.

I think I hear the reader denounce the fighting and rioting as very wicked and lawless. In this I quite agree, although I did not lay a violent hand on any of the unfortunate fugitives, and there were no bones broken. I, with a number, who took a prominent part as leaders of the chuckers-out, thought we were only doing a public and meritorious work, for the householders had been clamouring for months previous against the Irish, and saying they should be cleared out of the place. When this was brought about by the ill-advised race themselves, those weak-willed and vacillating inhabitants got into a great panic. While the expulsion was going on they despatched a mounted messenger to the county town for police or military to quell the disturbance, and about twenty constables arrived in two brakes about three o'clock, but by this time the place was as quiet as a church, because we had cast out the authors of the riot.

Then the treacherous inhabitants turned on us, and gave information to the authorities regarding this one and that one, who had been conspicuous in their efforts to restore peace to their miserable hamlet, in the very way those deceitful householders had expressed a wish for. I own the method was rough and ready, and I never had a hand in anything I was more heartily ashamed of. But the conduct of those cowardly informers so disgusted me, and fearing I might be marked out for capture and punishment for the very small share I had in the fracas, I left the village, and the work of a navvy, and found my way towards my own district, and then at the Martinmas of 1850 took my way north beyond Aberdeen, even to Gordon's land, the land of kail and castocks! My adventures there for the next two years will be duly recorded in the following chapters.

Chapter XXVII.

"*Heely, heely, Tam, ye glaiket stirk—ye hinna on the hin' shelvin' o' the cairt. Fat hae ye been haiverin' at, min? That cauff saick 'll be tint ower the back-door afore we win a mile fae hame. See't yer belly-ban' be ticht eneuch, noo. Woe, lassie! Man, ye've been makin' a hantle mair adee about blaikin' that graith o' yours, and kaimin' the mear's tail, nor balancin' yer cairt, an' gettin' the things pack't in till't.*"

"*Ou, fat's the eese o' that lang stoups ahin, aw wad like to ken! Lay that bauk across; an' tak' the aul' pleuch-ryn there an' wup it ticht atween the stays; we canna hae the beasts' maet trachel't amo' their feet.*"

"*An orpeit peekin' little sinner,*"
"*A preen-heidit ablach,*"
"*A peer win'y smatchet.*"

Specimens of Aberdeenshire Dialect, from

ALEXANDER'S "JOHNNY GIBB OF GUSHETNEUK."

Arrived in Foremartin District, sixteen miles N. E. of Aberdeen, in 1850; in Logie Buchan. — Among a People speaking a quaint but not uncouth, though a kind of strange dialect.—Folks with very little idea of distance, or of points of the compass, yet not ignorant.

The Martinmas term of 1850 found me sixteen miles northeast of Aberdeen in the land of the Gordons, not the parish, but not far from that parish where once lived the

"Logie o' Buchan, even Logie, the laird,
 Wha wiled awa Jamie that delved i' the yaird,
 Wha played on his pipe and viol sae sma."

and by these accomplishments and his handsome person, was declared by his admirers as the "floo'er o' them a'!"

This was an entirely new district to me, where the manner of conducting farm-work, and the working hours as well as social manners, were entirely different from all those of my own native county. I also found myself among a people speaking a quaint-sounding and strange Scotch dialect, not exactly uncouth, rather musical, but much of it really silly in its idioms, and very redundant in its colloquialisms, where the Scotch adjective diminutive was used to almost everything, and everybody, large or small, and where in the case of a stranger asking his way on the country roads, and the distance to the place he wished to arrive at, he was told it might be a mile, or any number of miles, " an' a bittie," this gait, or that gait, while the distance undefined, but said to be " a bittie," in the informant's reply, was generally longer than the number of miles. This gait, or that gait, might denote any of the points of the compass, and the bewildered pedestrian could never know, except he carried a pocket compass, in what direction on the King's highway he was proceeding.

But even with all these odd-looking, and to me strange traits, I found them a kind and generous-minded folk. Even with their indirect answers, and their apparent want of geographical terms, they were in general very fairly informed, although for many years previous, and for seventeen years following the year 1850, both that county and the burghs therein were represented in our Legislative Councils by a high-and-dry Tory, of the old blue-blooded order. Yet even with this depressing and progress-staying school of politics dominating their minds, my fellow-servants there were not more ignorant of public affairs than districts south of

Aberdeen, where the democratic and Liberal element was more in the ascendant. In fact, so far as news from a distance were concerned, I think they kept themselves better informed, for at most farms the men-servants clubbed their pence and had the "Aberdeen Journal" posted to them weekly from that ancient University City. That paper, including the stamp, cost 4½d, plus postage, which was not less than 1d per copy. The same publication has now a morning and an evening issue, selling at one penny and a halfpenny respectively.

I may mention as a delightful reminiscence that during my two years' sojourn in that district of rolling but almost closely-cultivated heights and hollows, peat moss, and treeless fields, I heard more old pithy Scotch proverbs and maxims in daily use, in their queer old tongue, than I ever heard before or since, and at the farm kitchen firesides of Logie Buchan, I listened to a greater number of Scotland's fine old songs than I had ever heard before. I was delighted with all those homely and heart-warming influences, with living in the farm kitchens, and having a most ample though almost entirely vegetarian diet always prepared for us by the deft hands of women, generally young and handsome, who oft in our well-won leisure hours with their sweet voices waked the kitchen echoes

"By vocal music's magic art,
　Which aye with Scotland's ancient lays,
　Thrills every Scottish heart,"

Yet, with all this, I saw much to perplex and sadden, and much which detracted from the character of a life and occupation which I have long thought should, even in this imperfect state of existence, be the purest and the best, because being without the artifices, and free from the thousand and one inventions for evil which so abound where large numbers of our undeveloped race are crowded together. I think that the farm servant, or husbandman, and the shepherd on the hillsides, and on the open fields stand much nearer to God, as they have the never-ceasing but ever-changing charm of Nature's sights and sounds in their ears, and before their eyes! These toilers in the open have the best opportunity for that mind occupation in which the shepherds of old, and the tender of flocks in all ages, as also the tiller of the fields from the earliest time down to the days of our own ploughman poet, who sang—

> "I ha'e been blithe wi' comrades dear,
> I hae been merry drinkin'
> I hae been busy gatherin' gear,
> An' I've been happy thinkin'."

Yes! I think the country man or woman has the best opportunity for happy thinkin', and that happy thinkin' can only be in the heart, which, through the eye of the soul, sees, as the untutored Indian sees—"God in everything, and hears Him in the wind."

Chapter XXVIII.

*"The halesome parritch, chief of Scotia's food;
The soupe their only hawkie does afford,
That 'yont the hallan snugly chows her cood."*

—BURNS.

Peculiar Names of Farms—Auchmasquabble, and Sandy Sharpset, my new Master — A startler the first morning—I object to turnip brose for dinner — A New way to kill Rats.

The district in which I was now engaged to serve is peculiar, in that the names of many of the farms begin with "Auch." This, I was informed, denotes a Gaelic origin for such names, and is common all over the land of the Gordons and other districts in the adjoining counties.

My new home, I may mention, was named Auchmasquabble. This is a fancy name, but not inappropriate, as my new master when about the farm was continually squabbling with some one. His name was Alexander, but commonly styled Sawney Sharpset. Fortunately for peace at the farm, he carried on a corn merchant's business at Aberdeen, and was only the first half of the week in the country.

I had been hired by him the morning after the hiring fair at that city, a week before the flitting-day, and as my new service did not begin till the flitting-day, I returned south to Merlin Brae to bid farewell to my friends at home, as going to a distance of ninety miles from the native heath, was at that time quite a long journey. My wages were fixed at £6 for the following half-year, or £1 per month, with the usual board and lodging added. The wages here noted were about half what they are now. Of course foremen, or those having charge, had from £7 10s to £9, with board and lodging for the half-year. The higher figures were paid to hands experienced and skilful in all kinds of farm work, either in byre, barn, or field, or for head-cattlemen, feeding and rearing live stock, the chief farming industry all over the country, and very much the chief pursuit in the less productive of grain-growing counties adjoining.

Gordon's land carried the bell at this time for fine-fed meat, and that meat commanded for a number of years the very highest prices in the markets of the populous towns and cities of the south, especially in the British metropolis. On my way north, at the time appointed for me to enter on this new district's experiences, I went by rail and coach from Forfar, booked through as a passenger to Aberdeen. Passengers had to change from the railway train to a four-horse stage-coach at the temporary terminus. The opening for traffic to which terminus, and the lively festivities which took place on the occasion at Drumlithie, are before described at length in chapter xxvi. The day I went north the coach was crowded. I had an inside seat, and when a start was made we were rather hard pressed for room.

There was a stout English commercial on my left, and he seemed to be very uncomfortable; indeed, I thought from his behaviour, and the trouble he made for room, that he felt his dignity compromised because a farm servant was seated beside him, but I considered myself as good as he, and I saw his cup of misery was filled more to overflowing when the conductor took up a young country woman on the road, and made a still greater contraction of the discontented man's room.

When the lady was being seated he seized hold of me by the clothes and tried to telescope me into the passenger next me on the right. I bore that sort of assault quite calmly, and did not utter a word, but I expected to get a word with him before we parted.

While the coach rattled along, swinging from side to side, over rough and smooth, I rather enjoyed the shaking up which I saw the great Englishman's corporation was getting, and the heat kept him in a very unenviable temperature. I whistled a tune to myself in a minor key! At this the big man cocked his ears, and in mock surprise exclaimed,

"Ah, art thee wheesling? Can'st thee sing any?"

In my best deliberate Scotch drawl, I replied, "Na, I canna get room for big grumblin' Englishmen, aither to wheesle or sing, as ye speir!"

The explosion of laughter which followed this answer from the other commercials on the opposite seat covered my tormentor with confusion, and he looked unutterable things, but did not trouble me with further attention during the journey.

At length the coach rattled along Union Street, and we landed at the Royal Mail and General Coach Office in Aberdeen. This is the place described by the late Shirley Brookes, editor of "Punch," in his notes of a holiday in the north, as "a fine city, with plenty of strawberries and cream, built of granite," it being left by the printer of that note to the reader's imagination to guess whether the city or the strawberries and cream are granite built.

From the coach office, with the assistance of a porter carrying my clothes chest, I found my way to my new master's residence in the suburbs, where under the shadow of an ancient and famous University, Mrs Sharpset, with her numerous family of boys and girls lived. About three p.m. I started for the farm, sixteen miles inland. The sun went down in about an hour after we left the city, but the weather was clear, and on the fourteen miles of main road we traversed before turning off to the left on to a cross road, I counted eight whisky shops, or public-houses. My escort and conveyance were two men with two pairs of horses and four carts who had left the farm at three o'clock that morning with grain for the city. We arrived at the farm at about half-past seven, and when the horses were put up, groomed, and fed for the night, we went for our own supper, and I found the farm-house a great tall castle-looking erection, quite unlike the ordinary run of two-storey one-room wide farm-houses, but more like a laird's or proprietor's mansion. And it turned out that it had been so when erected.

There was a great fire of peats burning on the open hearth within the wide-arched fireplace in the kitchen, where also stood a long white deal table, with a form for sitters at each side, and a chair or two at the head and foot. The foreman took his place on a chair at the head of the board, but he did not say a grace or ask a blessing on the food. I had forgot up till now that I was now in the home of seven kinds of brose, and the first dish put before us now was the celebrated "curly kail brose," which, when well made is a dish fit for a king! This was followed by the greens mashed by themselves after being drained of the liquid, which, with the oatmeal and salt had formed the first dish. Those mashed greens, properly boiled and mixed with cream, form a food compound or salad (as the fashionable gastronomic would call it) which by itself is really delicious, and tastes the nearest like prime boiled ox beef of anything I can compare it with. Although much prime beef was raised in the district, very little, in some cases none, ever found its way to the farm servants' table, and we might have sung the old Forfar song which says:—

"For beef wis ne'er in ower oor door,
But just a pund at Yule, sir."

However, I have long thought that much flesh meat of any kind is not a help but a hindrance to both health and strength in many occupations, and I never had better health than during the two years I lived in Gordon's Land as a farm servant.

Continuing the story of working my term of service at Auchmasquabble. After we had supped we left the kitchen about half-past nine o'clock this first night, but nine o'clock was the regulation hour, and in most cases it is rigidly adhered to. When the foreman had lighted the "baut," or stable lantern, he led the way to an apartment styled "the chaumer," a small square room on the ground floor of the steading, and alongside the stable, but separated by a stone wall. It had no fireplace, and only one window facing the door. There were two close box-beds on one side, and one on the other, with five sleepers, and there under the clear quiet stars of this calm winter night I slept the dreamless and health-giving sleep I was so much in want of, after the longest journey in one day I had up to this time made.

We were all aroused at a quarter to five o'clock in the morning. The watering of the horses was the first thing we did, while the foreman dealt out their breakfast of bruised oats. Then, leaving one man to clean out the stables and groom the regular working stud, the rest of us followed the foreman to the corn-room where by the light of a barn lamp we winnowed and dressed with hand fanners the oats which had been threshed the previous afternoon. At half-past seven we assembled at breakfast in the kitchen. This meal consisted of oatmeal and water brose, which each compounded for himself, and to each man and boy was handed a tin basin, as clear as a sixpence, filled with milk set aside the night before, and now carrying a coping of rich cream as thick as an old copper penny. This cream we run off the top, and on to the oatmeal salad, or scalded oatmeal, and all along to this day I maintain there is not a more digestible or healthier morning diet. This was followed by girdle cakes of oatmeal, as many as we chose, which, along with the balance of the milk, completed our breakfast, summer or winter. To some constitutions this morning diet is not kindly, but it is oftener because they are not aware of the true way to compound the dish to suit their stomachs, or if the oatmeal is not pure, and well made, or if they take too big a feed at a time. I never knew a case of any one being ill through using oatmeal if the dish was properly made, and modified by the various changes or kinds of liquor those dishes were made with.

Continuing my record of experiences here, the first morning was a Saturday, and a strong white frost rime lay on the ground. At eight o'clock we all turned out to stubble ploughing, three pairs of horses, and one pair of oxen, or " owsen," as they were named. All farming or field implements were of iron by this time all over the district. I felt the sharp cold on my hands very keen, and having a pair of black kid gloves in my pocket I put them on. Fancy a stripling at the plough in kid gloves! They would appear to one now nearly as much out of place as where some very absurdly ignorant artist shows a Scotsman at the plough in tartan kilts. I had only gone a few land lengths each way when, oh, horror! I saw my new master, even Mr Sharpset, coming along the public road which ran alonng the top of the field. Did not my kids get off my hands and into my pocket in the twinkling of an eye. Mr Sharpset came up and waited till I was turning in the horses again, and looking at me half amused, and half something else, he, in a kind of nasal accent, exclaimed—

"Gweedsake, man! Saw ye ever a pleugh in yer life afore?"

This was a startler to begin with.

"O, yes," I replied, "I have seen lots o' pleughs."

"It strikes me," quoth he, "it maun hae been at 'e same distance as Moses saw the promised land! Dae ye nae see the pleugh-yok's crookit?"

I said I saw that, but "I thocht it was meant i' the mak' o' the thing."

Then he inquired if "I thocht it was i' the mak' o' things tae yoke the land beest wi' ane o' the chain traces about a fit langer nor the ither? Or is't the fashion faur ye come frae 'at the land beest gings sidie-weys i' the pleugh?"

"No," I replied, "that's no' a sooth fashion."

At this he laughed in spite of himself, then he took off the yoke, laid one end on a stone, and with another stone he hit the bend several smart blows which straightened it out. He then snapped it on the swing bars, took off the unequal traces from the land horse, compared them and put a knot on the longest and fitted them on, then said, pointing to the foreman's pair some ridges across,

"Dae ye see thae twa black horse across there?"

I answered "Yes."

"Weel," says he, "yer tae ging roond for roond wi' them."

"Oh," I replied, I'm twa roonds afore them already."

Then he snaps out—"It's damned easy for ye tae be that! Ye've been haudin' a furr no' abeen fower inch deep! Mind," he says, "my stibbles maun be pleughed aucht inch deep; that's aboot as deep as the moold breerd o' the pleugh," and with this he left me, and never interfered with me again, till one spring morning when some carts were getting loaded with oats in bags to be taken to a field for sowing. The foreman was in the city at the time with his horses and implements, ploughing, sowing, and doing all the spring needfuls to a small field there rented along with the city dwelling. Sharpset remained with us at the farm this week, and on the morning here noted he came to the mill-loft and commenced in a great hurry to shove the sacks down a wooden stair faster than two or three of us could get them lifted to the carts. This went on for a little until he shot down a bag which hit the one I had just hoisted to my back. I then called to him to "ca' canny," and not do so again, "or there wad be broken necks amon's!"

The man looked thunderstruck at my temerity, but immediately ordered the other hands to stand aside, and made me carry the whole remaining lot of bags, and when the carts were loaded up I turned to him and said,

"Now, I'll carry them all up again, or tak' bag aboot wi' ye up that wooden trap."

His only reply was, "Man, fan ye cam' here ye cudna deen that, and didna ken hardly hoo tae yoke a horse."

My reply was, "Tell me not what I wis. You an' me hae only tae dae wi' what I am noo."

That answer sent him aff "wi' a flea in his lug." I was a little curious to learn what had nettled him, and caused him to cut up as he had done, and I found out the cause of his chagrin when that day's work was over. On the day previous the dinner provided for us was one of the seven varieties, even turnip brose, but being now well into April month, such roots had lost much of their proper quality for making such a dish, so I refused to partake of them, or of the mashed and cream-dressed turnips either, and as I shoved them aside I, being foreman, or dinner president, said to the other diners, "Do not take any example from me, but eat what is before you, if you like it, but I will not dine on mashed neeps, and neep brose, twa days rinnin' after this time o' year." So I dined on bread and milk, not a bad dinner for a warm day either.

My example was followed by all the rest at table, and the master, in passing through the kitchen, happened to see the left viands, and demanded to hear the reason. When the housekeeper told him I refused the food, and all the others did the same, she said he flew in a passion, and ordered her to let him know if I ever refused an article of food set before me again, and he swore "by God! he would send me to a J.P. with the rejected stuff in a basket."

He never referred to my refusal of the food by a single word to myself. However, I connected the outbreak of this morning with his chagrin at me for refusing the precious dish of food which I considered too frequently offered us at that season. Sharpset of Auchmasquabble was counted the greatest Tartar as a master in that district, yet I served out my time, and satisfied him, and he gave me a good character when I left at Whitsunday 1851.

Then, when I had been out of his service a year, I re-engaged with him at the Whitsunday of 1852, and spent my last half-year of farm service in that region with Sharpset. He had a brother who rented and occupied a farm about fifteen miles to the west. That was in what the natives called the "doon throu" district. A good story is told of an amusing swindle successfully practised on the two brothers, and this with all their sharpness. The one's farm furthest off being rat-infested, and the place very much overrun, an advertisement came under the notice of our master in his perusal of some English newspapers which said that for a remittance of £1 the subscriber would send an infallible recipe and instructions which would exterminate the pests at once. So the brothers sent the money, and in due time they had the recipe returned, which merely read as follows:—"To destroy Rats.—Catch 'em and put salt on their tails!"

A friend of mine who served as a boy at the rat-infested farm saw the first meeting between the two adventurers after the arrival of this unique recipe, and he says their remarks to each other were much more expressive than elegant or edifying.

Chapter XXIX.

"*Blest are the pure, whose hearts are clean,
From the defiling power of sin,
With endless pleasure they shall see
A God of spotless purity.*"

—WATTS.

"*And oh! be sure to fear the Lord alway;
And mind your duty, duly, morn and night;
Lest in temptation's path ye gang astray,
Implore His counsel and assisting might;
They never sought in vain that sought the Lord aright.*"

—BURNS.

Whitsunday, 1851.—The first International Exhibition.—The Interest taken in it even among Farm Servants in Gordon's Land.—I take Service at a new place.—A general description of the surroundings.—My new Master—a Big Silent Man. The Chaumer, and Chaumers in general.—The Beeves of Buchan and Foremartin and the severe Economics as applied to Swine and Servants there.—The want of facilities for proper and decent hours for interviews between young servants of both sexes.—The Hindrances to Purity of Morals, Conduct, and Conversation and Happy Home Life.—Mention made of some notable Exceptions to the General Neglect of the Masters

At Whitsunday, 1851, when the first Exhibition of the Arts and Industries, gathered from all regions of the civilised or uncivilised world, had been about three weeks opened to the public in that wonderful building of rare design in glass and iron, which the ingenuity of man had up to this time conceived, the accounts of these marvels were the theme of all newspaper writers and readers in and out of London. This great Exhibition was also the all-engrossing topic among us, the sons of the soil, who tilled the broad fields of Gordon's Land.

At this term I had found service at a new place, separated from my old quarters only by a peat moss, and about one-eighth of a mile distant. The farm steading rested on a height dignified by the name of a hill, but scarcely worthy of that dignity, as it stood not more than between 300 or 400 feet above the level of the North Sea, over whose broad bosom in clear weather we saw a great distance. We could also see far inland on that treeless and mountainless landscape, and the scene, though neither exactly pastoral, and certainly not sylvan, with its closely-cultivated fields of all shapes and sizes, showed to full advantage their different products in early summer, when all the earth was green!

The pastures filled with herds of cattle of many breeds, all skilfully selected, together with the white-washed farms and crofters' habitations, set like sapphires amid the emerald meadows, not surrounded with snow-white bud-laden hawthorn, but instead thereof by the beloved national whin hedges, abaze at such seasons in golden blossom!

In the early morning, as we went forth in the presence of all this terrestrial beauty on the one side, turning our eyes ocean-ward to cloudless eastern sky, we could see the king of day rising from the great deep, spreading that light which gives life and vigour to all mundane things.

It is a very dull and saddened heart which does not, as George Macdonald says, like the lark at such seasons, and amid such scenes—

> "Spring aloft on its ain sang borne,
> And in loud shout and jubilee hail such a morn.
> For the hert should be fu' o' the hert o' the licht,
> Then come winter or darkness a' maun be richt."

To resume my reminiscences of life at Cairn Craig, for that was the name of my new "place."

My new master was a big silent man, reputed rich, who never condescended to quote the Queen's language, nor the northern doric of even " Gweed bless ye," with any servant about his place below the rank of his " grieve," as the foreman was styled in this district of proud but shrewd and successful farmers, proud of their success as breeders and feeders of " nowt," as the prime beeves spread over the green pastures were called. Those farmers, in the days I speak of, were tacitly if not openly registered in a union which made every member of the fraternity likewise proud of every pound or shilling they could wring out of those who tilled their fields and fed their " nowt."

While the severe economies applied to the vegetarian diet of seven kinds of brose made an extra thrifty farm dame of the district exclaim, in Dichty-water English, " that it was truly yawfu' the quantities o' neeps swine and servants ga'ed throu!" The swine came first! At the same time we were lodged in holes of lofts and outhouses, in many instances inferior to the stalls wherein they lodged their horses and oxen.

For instance, at Cairn Craig, the " chaumer " was lighted only by the door, and paved with big water-worn stones, the surface so irregular as made even a native of Shetland (one of our number) swear and pray such prayers in Norse language for our master as ought to have swamped that haughty-looking silent individual, who in common with all the more extensive farmers in this district, neither seemed to know or care for either the comfort of the bodies or the interest of the souls of their servants.

In fact, in the majority of instances, the big farmers hereabout looked askance and suspicious when a servant, either male or female, gave promise of possessing any superiority in intellect or culture beyond what they considered the scope of the clodhopper.

But in spite of the callousness and indifference of the would-be fashionable farmers, there yet lingered many kindly old customs and homely ways, and there were likewise masters who took a kindly interest in both the bodily and spiritual welfare of those who wrought for them, and who by law were, and are even now, at the call of their master by night and day during the period of hire or agreement. This would seem in some instances not understood by the hired servant of to-day, but the law has never been abrogated or repealed, and the relations of hired servant and hiring master, are second only to the relation of parent and child. In some notable examples in the district I am describing there were heads of farm households who gathered their servants and family around them nightly, and in some cases even at morning too, and as sincere and humble Christian fathers, directed their own and their household's prayers to the Hearer and Answerer of true prayer, acknowledging God in all their ways, and in every such case blessing and being blest with the things that enrich and which add no sorrow!

But for one master or mistress who set this example, and whose walk and conversation, and dealings with their farm servants were consistent with their high responsibility, and a virtuous life, there were ten who totally, and in the most culpable manner, simply ignored all rights, or needs, their servants had, either for average bodily comfort, or the improvement of their minds, and the cultivation of pure and virtuous lives!—ideals which have ever been, and ever will be accounted the true watermark of manly worth and woman's holy sphere!

The greatest disadvantage under which the unmarried servants laboured in this district, and in many other districts, was that with the suppression of "crofts," or small farms, for the sake of higher rents, croft was added to croft, and large farms were formed, but the cottar or hired man's dwelling, in many cases, was entirely forgotten. In very rare instances was a cottar or hired man's house provided, unless for a foreman or "grieve," and sometimes also a head cattleman's house. This was a sparsely-populated district, even void of villages, except at long distances from each other, and sufficient hands could not be raised, either male or female, to do the necessary odd work of the farm.

This caused a great number of the young men and women to be hired, and living together as they did in kitchen and "chaumers," masters and mistresses took no heed of their servants' interests, beyond what work they could get out of them, at the least possible expense. The wholly absurd, and more than stupid restrictions as to the time the men servants, especially in winter, were allowed to remain in the kitchen with those of the opposite sex were thus much curtailed.

Through such restrictions, if a love affair arose, every facility for open courtship, and interviews in decent hours were denied them. If marriage was anticipated and promised, as in the majority of unfortunate results I believe they were, the idea of getting married, and securing a house to settle down in on the farm where their betrothal had taken place, was in most cases a sheer impossibility.

Under such conditions the stolen midnight meetings between some unfortunate youths and maidens could have no other result than the one we saw and still see—the terrible scourge of illegitimacy in the country districts, with the attendant ills of poverty and pauperism, and the breaking down of the beneficent and holy influence of wedded home life.

To all these drawbacks and hindrances to social purity in the farm servants' life in Gordon's Land, when I sojourned there, was added the very low-toned and coarse standard by which modesty and chastity, in speech and behaviour, was measured.

I have lived on a farm there, where one never heard an oath or wicked imprecation used, but where the common conversation of men, and women too, would have been unworthy of the beasts of the stall, had the dumb brutes been endowed with speech.

Farming for some farmers is not a money-making vocation now, and may never be so again, yet there can be nothing surely to hinder better dwellings for hired hands, and a better sense of each others' mutual wellbeing, understood by master and servant alike. It must be obvious to the dullest capacity, that with the increased educational advantages which the youth of our time now enjoy, giving a fuller knowledge of sanitary and bodily comfort, there should be more equality between master and servant.

Such equality, though not yet fully recognised, has increased to a certain degree of late; but so long as the mere interest of £. s. d. remains the only link which binds the two, so long will the one idea remain with the master of having as much out of the servant as he can by force or fraud compel, while the servant on his part, rightly or wrongly, determines to render no more than he or she thinks due. Such a state in the relation of both parties to a bargain of service like farm service can never form the true give-and-take in life's fulfilment, for without an honest give-and-take on both sides, the doctrine of doing as we would be done by is lost sight of entirely.

Chapter XXX.

*"Her feet beneath her petticoat,
Like little mice, stole in and out,
As if they feared the light.
And oh! she dances such a way,
No sun upon an Easter Day
Is half so fine a sight."*
—SUCKLING.

*"A thousand hearts beat happily; and when
Music arose with its voluptuous swell,
Soft eyes look'd love to eyes which spake again,
And all went merry as a marriage-bell!*

. . . . .

*On with the dance! Let joy be unconfined,
No sleep till morn, when youth and pleasure meet
To chase the glowing hours with flying feet."*
—BYRON.

A Harvest Home at Pearlbank House, and full description of that grand festivity.

At the end of the harvest of 1851, along with a large number of male and female servants on the estate where our farm was located, I got the opportunity, through the kindness of "the laird," of taking part in and enjoying a "harvest home," at the mansion-house of Pearl Bank. This Pearl Bank estate marches with the historic parish I have mentioned in my record of life in Gordon's Land, and my first dwelling-place there. The river Ythan flows on from the north-west to south-east till it joins its waters with the North Sea, at a small seaport, which from the south-east bank of the river aforesaid overlooks the site of a whole seaboard parish, Forgue by name, which, tradition says, was completely overwhelmed by a sand-storm and great tidal wave, in one night, some hundreds of years ago.

Returning to my recollection of the harvest home at Pearl Bank House. This was a very fine entertainment, in the form of a soiree, concert, and ball, and was the last of the only two dancing balls I ever attended. In previous years, I was told, the evening's entertainment was preceded by a dinner to the tenantry, held in the mansion-house, but on the occasion I am recording that dinner was not given, but a fine lithographed card, bearing the Pearl Bank house crest and coat-of-arms, was delivered at each farm by a mounted messenger, clothed with the Gordon livery. That card, signed by the laird, requested that the master and mistress at each place would allow so many couples of their servants, male and female, numbers equal, to attend a harvest home at the mansion-house.

It was said the tenantry were much chagrined at the masters and mistresses not being entertained first, but "they durstna anger the laird" by refusing us permission to attend. Three couples went from Cairn Craig, and the recollections of the joys of that one night of unalloyed and innocent pleasure! has remained a memorial with me as one of the nearest approaches I have ever made to a joy which I thought the nearest to those of Paradise! or that I had experienced since the days of happy childhood.

There were many circumstances combined which made that night supremely enjoyable. The summer had been fine, and the harvest was now all gathered in. Yet much of the summer's beauty lingered all around! Along the main avenue to the mansion-house about one hundred couples of both sexes marched down arm-in-arm under the grand old trees, in the full moonbeams of that lovely September night!

This made a scene of such charming beauty, as kept the processionists actually spell-bound, for I do not remember of hearing a word above a whisper spoken, until the ladies of the house, with the butler at their head, called out, "this way, ladies!" and forthwith took our partners to the house itself, where their superfluous cloaks, shawls, and such like, were laid aside, and the ball-room requisites then in fashion touched up and re-adjusted.

The men were directed to a hall at the coach-houses, there to await the opening proceedings. After a little we found our way up a broad stair, on reaching the head of which such a flood of light was shed from over a hundred richly-decorated wax candles. These lights, with the floral adornments of that charming place, fairly dazzled the eye, and whatever the others thought of it, I remember I thought it like a scene from the Arabian Nights Entertainments, those grand tales of Oriental splendour!

After waiting a short time we were joined by our partners, in all their array of rural attractiveness and blushing beauty, and although among this crowd of the daughters of the soil there was not seen many costly jewels, or gold or silver ornaments, yet then and there I could have challenged broad Scotland to show an equal number of finer-looking, healthy, and apparently happy young women!

When all were seated, the men on one side, and our partners opposite, the M.C., who was one of the partners of a grocery firm at Aberdeen, and who were purveyors to the Queen, called on the company to stand up! Then the splendid string band of four instrumentalists played the " National Anthem," in fine style, and several male voices joined in the majestic strains. There could be no mistaking the notes of loyalty which awoke the echoes of that lovely scene and rang through the surrounding woods!

After we had all partaken of substantial but non-intoxicant refreshments, not composed of whitey-brown tea, with pastry of doubtful origin, which so often grace the board at gratis entertainments or so-called " festive occasions," the ball was opened by our host's housekeeper and his chief boatman from the ferry on the river. Both those retainers were each over seventy years of age, yet when they stood up, and the gentleman bowed and the lady dropped her curtsey, the simple, natural, and unforced charm of their salutation showed all the grace of a day which was then fast dying out among common working people. As the music struck up it was most delightful to see how stately and in how correct measure this aged yet comely couple kept time to the cadence of the well-handled violins, whose magic art can warm the dullest fibre! of even an ice-cold heart! After the opening the dances went on in close and regular order, and it appeared as if the whole assembly had been trained to the exhilerating terpsichorean art.

In the intervals we had promenading, and were served with substantial refreshments, and enlivened with hearty song, not the unmeaning oddly-worded, and as they seem to me, idiotic ditties of the modern music hall order. They were the pithy, the pathetic, and never-to-die songs of " the land of the mountain and the flood," of whom the gifted Kennedy, one of their best exponents, says:—

> " Where have love's impassioned throes
>   E'er found so sweet a tongue?
> No mimic frenzy mocks the heart,
>   When Scotland's songs are sung.

> Their artless words, their liquid notes,
>   In perfect tones express,
> The matchless might of manly grace
>   And woman's tenderness."

The M.C. sang an old Scotch comic song in character, and when in after days I had attained a different position, I got very well acquainted with the gentleman, and used to visit his house by invitation at New-Year festive times in Aberdeen. Although he knew that I had come from following the plough, and would ask me about country-life phases I had seen, I never reminded him of the night at Pearl Bank in the years long gone, when he dressed as an old lady, and mimicking a young one, sang that delicious old song, "There cam' a young man to my daddy's door!"

Continuing my reminiscences of the Pearl Bank harvest home, the best and most picturesque part came about midnight. An interval was called, and four stewards were seen conveying a large white wicker-basket to the upper-end of the ball-room. They placed it on a raised platform, overcanopied by an arch of beautiful flowers and green foliage. One of the stewards next went around with a silver salver, filled with a number of sealed envelopes, and all the ladies, married and unmarried, were invited to select one each. When the drawing was completed the laird made his appearance, radiant in a ball costume which had been in fashion many generations previous. He was a most dazzling and picturesque figure; he wore a white-powdered, full-bottomed wig, stiff high collar, and gorgeous neck-tie, white ruffled shirt, the breast glittering with jewels, deep-flapped white silk vest, blue cloth dress-coat, with gold lace facings and buttons of the same material, white knee-breeches, silk stockings, and gold-buckled shoes!

Having taken his seat on the platform alongside the big basket, each lady, beginning at the far end of the row, was led up to the front of the platform where her sealed envelope was opened, a slip of paper therefrom telling the name of an article drawn, and this the laird, with a kindly word or two, presented as a prize to the lady. There were no blanks, and every lady got something, and all articles were good and useful, some getting dress-pieces, others got shawls, etc. It was the prettiest and most unostentatiously generous distribution of presents, totally unexpected, that I have ever heard of; for not one of the recipients had the remotest idea of what was in store for them, when the envelopes were handed round. When the gifts had been distributed, the M.C., without any long laudatory speech, called for three cheers for Sir Charles (the laird). These were given with great spirit, and again and again renewed with such energy as awoke the feathered heralds of day, and chanticleer gave forth his morning notes two hours before his usual time! The singing of "Gude nicht and joy be wi' ye a'," brought this unique and happy harvest festivity to an end!

I have mentioned at the beginning of the harvest home reminiscence that this was the second and last dancing ball I ever attended; but I do not decry dancing, or other innocent, healthy, and happy amusement of any kind. This function, nor the first "ball" I attended, were not "promiscuous dances." Such were not common in that quarter, and the dancings which go on at hiring fairs in the south and west of Scotland were not a practice in Aberdeenshire.

Any stranger attending a dance in Gordon's Land had very little chance of getting a step therein, unless he took a partner with him, and as only the female outdoor workers attended hiring fairs in that locality there was little likelihood of "promiscuous dancing" becoming common.

Chapter XXXI.

" But what avail her unexhausted stores,
Her blooming mountains and her sunny shores,
With all the gifts that heaven and earth impart,
The smiles of nature and the charms of art,
While proud oppression in her valley reigns,
And tyranny usurps her happy plains."
—ADDISON.

Mains of Ravenbank.—A bad investment.—Full account of the persecutions by a bad master.—My enlistment in 92nd Gordon Highlanders, and how I did not join.—Return to Ravenbank.—My tyrant master.—Bad usage reaches a climax.—I throw up my job.—Description of bed and dressing-room here.—I sue for my month's wages, but lose them and expenses.

On leaving Rock Cairn at Martinmas 1851, I got engaged for the following half-year to a farm almost alongside, named Mains of Raven Bank. This engagement turned out a failure, as the farmer there proved a despot. His overseer, the only master who by my engagement I was to obey, did not assert his position, and keep his chief from interfering, and anyone who resented the tyrannical conduct of that great tyrant was marked out for all the ill-usage, short of personal violence, which a mean and spiteful nature could invent. In short, I found life so intolerable at Raven Bank that I sought leave of absence for one day and walked to Aberdeen, a distance of sixteen miles, and tried to enlist in the 92nd, now the Gordon Highlanders, but the army being then on a peace footing, my military scheme did not succeed, as I was a quarter of an inch short of the standard height. As I would not risk staying that day and the following night in the city to get rested, when the officer said I would stand the height certain, and as I thought that if I did not pass then it would be said I had run off from the unhappy place, I walked back the way I came, and did the thirty-five miles there and back between 5.30 a.m. and 6 p.m. on threepence worth of wheaten bread and a mouthful of water two or three times by the way.

I stayed about an hour in the city, but went into no place there except the recruiting depot quarters, where I did not sit down, nor indeed, for the whole twelve and a half hours between my departure and return I was never off my feet. I have often thought since then that although I was rejected as being one quarter of an inch short of the standard height, my endurance on the march would have stood even a severer test than twelve and a half hours; but though recruiting officers in November, 1851, were thus particular, even to a quarter of an inch, the War Office authorities got a rude awakening from their peaceful dream, in less than three years afterwards, when in 1854 the dreadful sound of war was heard, and Europe's Eastern border saw garments rolled in blood!

But though baulked in my intention to join Her Majesty's service at this time, I got the hateful service at Raven Bank left, as one evening about a fortnight later, in presence of all my mates, in the stable, this ruffian farmer insulted me and swore at me, at the same time blaming me for an omission of duty which I had not had an opportunity either to perform or neglect. I then threw up the job, and told him I would not lift another hand in his service, and took my neighbours as witnesses of his conduct towards me all along, which I held justified me in terminating my engagement because he would not allow me to fulfil it in peace. At the same time I intimated that I would try to make him amenable to me, and on the evidence of those around me, cause him to pay my half-year's wages.

The tyrant looked stunned by my outburst at first, but feeling certain that the witnesses I had invoked were in his power, and could be prevented from giving unbiased evidence, he followed me up a wooden stair which led to the dark attic-loft where we slept, and where our clothes chests were. No burning lamp, or other artificial light was ever permitted to enter here, and the free rays of heaven's light were only admitted by two roof openings, which at this wintry season, scarcely made darkness visible. In this place a man of ordinary stature could only stand erect if he kept in the centre of it, and a tall man had either to stoop half-bent, or thrust himself up through a roof-light opening before he could get inside his pants.

Here we had to dress and undress in the dark evening and morning on week days, and Sundays, our basin-stand being the pump and horse watering-trough at the opposite side of the public road, from which after our morning and evening ablutions we had to mount to this nineteenth-century dressing-room, and at our small mirrors, hung from a rafter beam, in a gloom denser than twilight, try to make ourselves presentable for either kirk or market. I have been thus minute, and at the risk of being tedious in my description of this sleeping chamber and dressing-room, as the outward appearance of this notable farmer's steading and dwelling-house gave no sign of such a barbarous state of matters existing there in the housing of over half-a-dozen hard-worked sons of the soil; and no outside spectator, unless he could have got inside and seen it, would have believed its existence possible in that pretending and rather boastful region. There is nothing at all exaggerated in the description I have here given.

It was up that wooden stair, or trap, the persecutor against whose demoralising and brutal treatment I had struck now followed me, but he stopped short at the top of the stair, and calling on the first horseman to join him there he told that trembling serf that he would hold him responsible that I removed nothing from that attic, until he was satisfied. I said he could not keep me from my own property. Then he threatened that if I did not desist from opening my chest he and his assistant would throw me down the stair.

I replied that if "either of you attempt to lay a hand on me, I will defend myself with the first article I can lay hold on, but as you are two to one, I will leave my things alone for the present, but I will have access to my own property when I come up here again."

I was wrong here, as the Superintendent of Police, on whom I called that night for some advice, told me I should have gone on opening my chest, and let them assault me, and then the officer would have taken both of my assailants into custody.

However, there I was, adrift and homeless on that winter night, without a shilling in my pocket, as the small sum I had over the past half-year's wages, was in my lock-fast chest. But the police officer was very kind, and directed me to go to a certain hotel, which he named, and tell them that he had sent me, but first he advised me to call on a Sheriff Officer, whom he also named, and get him to accompany me to Raven Bank next morning, where I would require to offer to resume my service if I was to be allowed to fulfil my engagement on its original terms, and if this was refused then I should raise an action for the half-year's wages and board wages.

After calling on the Sheriff Officer, and arranging as advised, I went to the hotel the Police Superintendent recommended, and was very kindly received by the landlady, who knew the unprincipled man I had left, for she said she served a half-year at the same place in her youth, when this man's father was alive, and because she would not encourage this son's villainous advances, that libertine took such an ill-will at her that he made the remaining time of her sojourn at the place almost unbearable. When I told her I had no money to pay for my night's lodging, as I had been prevented access to my money and chest, she said, "Oh, he cannot keep your clothes nor anything else;" adding she would take her chance of payment, and she hoped I would beat the scoundrel. She then ordered her servants to give me food, but I could not eat. I was put up very comfortably, and after a good breakfast next morning I again called on the law officer, who, along with his son as a witness, went with me to Raven Bank.

We met the farmer close by the farm-house, and in the presence of the witnesses I had, I offered myself back on condition that I would be allowed to work my agreement as originally undertaken. The reply my persecutor made was that he had nothing to say to me; that, as I had broken my bargain with him I would have to abide by the consequences. I said, I would prove that he, and not I, had violated the bargain.

He then invited the Sheriff's Officer and his concurrent into the farm-house, while I waited about for a little till the officer and his son came out again. Then the old fox told a fine story of how he and the farmer's wife had tried to get her husband to let me resume work, and allow the grieve, who, I insisted, was the one I was engaged to obey, to deal with me; but this deceitful old man said the farmer was bent on punishing me for breach of bargain, though he had at last agreed to let me go if I would pay the expense of the summons and its service, which this "old beagle" now held in his hands. The officer meant me to believe the summons had been applied for the night before, but I yet believe had been written out a few minutes before in the farm-house parlour. I said to the old sinner he had deceived me, as I thought he should have served me with the summons when I met him in the morning.

Now, seeing I could not depend on any witnesses I might bring forward, as I remembered that the other servants were all at the tyrant's mercy, and recollecting also that I was among a people of whom it was said long ago, that not a man of them would stand to the word that would hurt them, I got access to my chest, and from the few shillings I had, paid this cunning old man four shillings odds, and left the place, after telling him and his son, that if I had been as near Forfar as we were to Aberdeen I would read them all another version of the law of master and servant as applied in cases such as mine!

Chapter XXXII.

*"Do not suffer nought in vain;
Let no trifle trifling be;
If the salt of life is pain,
Let e'en wrongs bring good to thee,"*
—EBENEZER ELLIOTT.

January, 1852.—Engaged at road-making near Old Meldrum, in Aberdeenshire,—Eight shillings per week, and eight hours per day.—Good board and lodging at four shillings per week, in the cleanest house in the kingdom.—Hired from Candlemas till Whitsunday at Cairnochill.—A master of the right sort.

Having now lost a month's wages, and actually paid something to be allowed to escape from what to me had proved worse than slavery, after finding a house wherein to bestow my belongings I set out to find work, and succeeded in getting a job the same afternoon at the making of a new service road. It was about four miles further inland, near the small town of Old Meldrum, and about two miles from the seat of the Chief of the Gordon Clan.

We only wrought from eight in the morning till sundown, making a day of about eight hours, or forty-eight hours a week. Our wages were eight shillings per week. This was at the New Year of 1852. I and another man lodged in a crofter's house on the Gordon's estate, and we paid four shillings per week for bed and board! I have often since then found no better lodging or food for twice that amount per day! Our "fair" was mostly vegetarian, except that we got eggs often, and had a tea diet twice on Sundays.

The place was most fitly named "Sunnyside," and the amount of sunny sweetness and light which was there was really delightful. I am justified in recording, that after a very wide experience of different lodging-houses, and different kinds of cookery, not even in the finest hotels have I found food better cooked, or seen cleanliness in rarer perfection, than in Mrs Watson's house at Sunnyside in Gordon's Land. She was one of those crisply clean ladies not often met with, who kept her tea-kettle, and "the crook" on which she hung that vessel over the fire, both as clear as a new sixpence.

Cheap as bread stuffs are at this time, I believe it would puzzle the strictest economist among all our young men of this day, to get put up and provisioned, as we were in 1852, for double the money, although I believe among non-union wages-men, in these days of labour wars, many a man has to exist on less than four shillings per week. But we not only existed, we lived! and fared sumptuously every day!

The first of March came, and with it came spring, and the new road was finished, and I had to betake myself to a spring hiring fair, near where the bonnie burn o' Ury joins the River Don, which runs from Benachie. At this fair I met the farmer through whose grounds we had made the road I have mentioned, and he hired me for the quarter of a year up to Whitsunday, 1852.

This was truly a worthy man, an upright and sincere Christian, who called us around him on the evening of the Day of Rest, read to us, and held true worship, speaking of both his own and our responsibilities as professing Christians, and of the lives we all ought to live as became those who were the inheritors of that blessed patrimony handed down through the ages from sire to son, since the advent of the Man of Galilee, who made himself of no repute, but took upon Him the form of a servant!

This was the best place I had yet found in that district, and I could have re-engaged with this master, but he had a curious custom, that when he could not re-engage his first horseman none of the unmarried men were asked to renew their engagement. He told me this on the term-day when paying my wages, by way of apology for not asking me to stay. I remember that when we were all returning from the half-yearly hiring fair at Ellon, he came up with us on the road, and pulled up his horse and gig and complimented us on the hour and the manner in which we were going home.

It was between six and seven, on a beautiful evening in May, when all nature was smiling in the young summer radiance! The fields were clothed in their matchless green mantle, and embellished with all the floral jewellery of a lovely season, while the mavis and the blackbird, and all the feathered choir, were in full song, pouring forth their loves and joys to the western sun! The glorious day-king's beams were falling to their evening altitude, and shedding level rays on Benachie's broad slopes, and the same golden beams were lighting the north-western heights of the Tap o' North, in the same splendour in which all succeeding summer evening suns had arrayed that scene, down through time's cycles, from the hour when first those lofty heights emerged from this great globe's internal conflict!

So on this fine evening, as our master passed us, he gave us a few words of praise and encouragement, and said he was "proud of us." On the flitting-day he asked me if I had got a place, and I told him I was engaged for the coming half-year to go back to Auchmasquabble, and at the end of that engagement I expected to return to my own district, as I had now learned that farm-servants' wages were better in the south.

Mr Manbred said that if I wished to get the best wages which were paid in his district I should take to the study of tending and the rearing of prize cattle, as he said I was not like the ordinary run of farm servants, and he thought I would make a very valuable head herdsman. I thanked him, but replied that I had no intention of becoming a head prize-stock-man, but said that I would try and get hired to some place near a town or village, where the means of improving and adding to my little stock of education could be found in my leisure time, as I intended to train and qualify myself for taking the place of a first-class farm overseer or bailiff. So I parted with this really worthy master.

Nearly thirty years after this, when I called at this beautiful farm (Cairnochill by name) as a commercial traveller, I found my worthy friend of 1852 had removed to Aberdeen, and retired from the anxiety and trouble of farm life. His place now (in 1880) was occupied by his eldest son, who was only three years old when I sojourned there. This gentleman, now thirty-three years of age, stared somewhat when I told him I once served his father there. I gave him dates, and the names of people who once lived on his farm, and in the neighbourhood, not forgetting my old landlord and landlady of Sunnyside. This proved my bona-fides. Yet this son of a very worthy father did not give me an order, although the article I was taking orders for had wont to be extensively used all over this district by the rearers of prize stock.

Chapter XXXIII.

> "*Love is a plant of holier birth,*
> *Than any that takes root on earth ;*
> *A flower from heaven, which 'tis a crime,*
> *To number with the things of time ;*
> *Love shall live, and live for ever,*
> *And chance and change shall reach it never.*"
> —HENRY NEELE.

> "*Half our daylight faith is a fable ;*
> *Sleep desports with shadows too,*
> *Seeming in their turn as stable*
> *As the world we wake to view.*"
> —CAMPBELL.

1852.—I return to Auchmasquabble and Mr Sharpset—A yoke of owsen (or oxen).—Summer and the working-day here.—The shrine of my first and life-long love.—Evening Songs of the Lays of the "Land of the Mountain and Flood."—Almost a total eclipse of the sun described.—Yoking a young ox, and learning him to plough.—Stirring and amusing incident described thereanent.

At this Whitsunday of 1852 I returned as agreed to the place where I had worked first in this district, even to serve Mr Sharpset, at Auchmasquabble, this time to work a pair of oxen. My team was mostly employed ploughing, and the principal operation on hand was, at this fine early season, ridging—raising drills for turnip seeds, and closing the same when manured for seeding. This, in the district vernacular, was called "neep seed-time," and from the extent of acreage employed all over Gordon's Land it was one of the most important of all the seed-times. When the weather was suitable, and the soil in good order, it was the hardest wrought and most urgent of all seasons.

At this farm we wrought twelve hours per day, commencing at half-past four in the morning, leaving off for breakfast at half-past eight, commencing again at half-past nine, leaving off at one o'clock, and beginning again at two, and going on till six in the evening. All the horses wrought twelve hours, but my team of oxen required longer to rest and feed, and they wrought eight hours, divided into the morning and afternoon shifts, or "yokin's," as the spells of work were named. Between the number of hours of field work and the preparation of getting our cattle in order, and going and returning to the farm buildings another hour and a half was spent, making our day of toil fourteen hours.

There was not much leisure for relaxation or home enjoyment, yet we often found time to gather on the green grassy terrace which surrounded the empty stack-yard, to hold an open-air evening concert, singing the songs of Burns, or Tannahill, or some other author; those never-dying, and heart-stirring melodies so dear to every Scottish heart! How the memories of those beautiful songs, and the voices which intoned them, yet lives with me! and in hours which would otherwise prove lonely their remembrance comes back to cheer my heart, and to console me with the heaven-born hope that although the voices who joined in those thrilling melodies I shall never hear again on earth! yet I have every reason to believe that many of those singers have joined that choir whereof the bards of every age have sung the Eternal Joy!

Long as our hours of work were, and hard as the toil often

was, I may be permitted to mention that I never was so tired but that I could, under the beautiful summer twilights, find my way to the shrine of that "divinity," who a year before had captivated my heart's affections, and who from that time onward till the present hour, has held sway there! Oh, yes, although I had to cross a treacherous moss, and risk meeting a great savage watch-dog which was often let loose at night, yet, to quote the lines of the song which says—

"Short is the way and light the heart,
    When bound in Love's soft spell,"

I may add, to complete the verse—

"I crossed the bog and braved the dog!
For her I lo'ed so well!"

There was one occurrence in the astronomy of this lovely summer which is well worthy of mention. This was an almost total eclipse of the sun, which took place about the end of July. I remember it was a splendid day, and in a cloudless sky the shadow began to pass between us and the sun between one and two o'clock in the afternoon. Soon the fields, the whin hedges, trees, houses, and all the land, as far as we could see, took on a marvellous light-brown colour, which deepened and darkened till the whole earth looked a dark copper colour, which increased every minute with the progress of the obscuration, and the moon's disc looked as if a great black cover was gradually moving across the face of the sun, till only what appeared to the naked eye as a small rim of gold-coloured light was visible, gleaming half-way round the sun's upper edge! It was the most wonderful and awe-inspiring sight I ever beheld. All Nature seemed to listen, and one could imagine that the great sphere stood still! The wild birds hushed their song, and the farm-yard poultry in some instances roosted up as if night had drawn its sable mantle over the land at a little past mid-day. The darkness more or less passed off in a little over an hour, and the unveiled splendour of summer shone over the land again!

Then the sultans of the feathered seraglios, from farm and croft around, sounded their trumpets of greeting or defiance with as much apparent boast and confidence as if they had cleared away the darkness!

It was curious to hear the comments which were made by some of my mates on this beautiful celestial phenomenon. We were pulling weeds from the growing corn, which was then in full ear. There were six of us thus employed, two in each of three fields, and when I inquired at the foreman in the evening what he thought of the eclipse—"Oh," says he, "Jamie and me thocht the hin'most day wis come, and we wis makin' up oor minds tae lie doon in ithers' arms, an' juist dee faur we wis, till ance we minded o' the 'clips, syne we were a' richt, and eh, man, it was bonnie, but it wis fearsome!"

The only other incident worth mentioning as occurring in my last half-year's service in the land of the Gordons was connected with my ox team. I here wish to mention, notwithstanding what any crack ploughman may say in favour of horse haulage in the plough, that no pair of horses I ever held a plough behind can equal a pair of ordinary-sized oxen in the sound steadiness of draught, or the unswerving straight line in which they walk, and if properly fed and tended, and not overdriven, they will turn over as much land in the same time as the same number of horses, while in soft or mossy ground they will pass where a horse would sink up to the girths. The pair of oxen I had at this place were both polled, and light-grey in colour, pretty heavy, but not kept fat. One of them was rising seven years old, and as he failed in the heat, when working some fallow ground this summer, he was laid off, fed up, and then sold. At the end of harvest his place was filled by a big young ox with immense horns, a cross of some kind, but a great tall fellow, who had been only broken to labour so far as being learned to drag a log of wood along. I was told he had never been wrought in plough gear, and I had to learn him to plough, and on Hornie's first lesson there hangs the tale of a tail!

The trained ox which remained of my original team was a nice, quiet, little thick-set chap, quite a jewel of the four-footed kind, and named Colin. It seemed to me that on being introduced to his new yoke-fellow, Colin took stock of the big-horned chap, and from the pawky side glance he gave, I now think he winked the other eye, and might have said, as the decent old wife critic said of the big minister, " Aye, we hae bulk there, but we'll sune see it a'!". We were not long in having a peep at Hornie's ideas of obedience, and of how he would conduct himself if he got his own way. He went the land-length down hill all right, but I found he had no idea of stopping when we reached the lower end, and so firmly was he persuaded he had to go straight on, that he leapt a pretty wide dry ditch, and dragged the iron plough with him, leaving that implement in the bottom of the ditch, and Colin and me on the side he had leapt from! The big ox being still entangled in the plough-gear, my action on the rein attached to the branks (or bridle) brought him round. The picture then presented by the two oxen standing looking at each other from opposite sides of the ditch, the plough sticking at the bottom thereof, with your humble servant, the team driver, looking on, the general mix-up made such a scene of confusion on a small scale as a clever artist might have pourtrayed on canvas, and named the picture "Flumixed!" For a little I scarcely saw how the situation stood, till the ludicrously comic side of the business struck me, and I said to myself, "I wonder what my freend Sandy, the smith, at hame, wid say if he saw me 'e noo?" Oh, how he would have enjoyed the sight. However, I got the two beasts extricated from the entangled gearing, lifted the plough from the ditch, reyoked Colin, and made him draw the plough round to the end of the return furrow, then went for the big ox, whose leap over the ditch seemed to have taken all the spring out of him, as he refused to leap back the way he came, and I had to lead him round by a bridge.

Then, as I thought he, in his own bovine perception or instinct, knew he had done wrong, I gave him a sound beating with the end of the rein, while he galloped round and round. Unlike the horse, one cannot hold an ox still while he is being chastised. I then drew Hornie alongside his neighbour, and re-yoked him to the plough. The most remarkable thing about this ox fracas was the quiet, actually thoughtful-like attitude preserved by wee Colin the whole time. That paragon of ox propriety looked so calm and dignified and chewed his cud the whole time, as if nothing had happened, only giving a look round now and again as I thought to see how his big foolish new mate was faring at my hands. I think if Colin could have spoken he would have told Hornie I had served him right, and I am not sure that Colin did not tell him so in ox lingo, or double Dutch, for when I got everything in working trim, and seized the plough stilts, or handles, giving them the word to move on, Colin shook his head, blew his nose, and lent Hornie several digs in the neck with his head, which I think meant in ox lingo on Colin's part to say, "Noo, ye great big-horned fule, ye maun behave yersel' or I'll gie ye anither lickin'!" I am glad to say that after this Hornie became a fine working obedient ox, and never during my time required another beating.

Martinmas, 1852, soon came round, and I returned to my beloved Strathmore valley, and on the 24th of November I was again at the old-time hiring fair in Letham. I had been but two hours on the ground when I was hired for the following year at about £4 more than I had in the North for the previous year. This was to a fine large and highly-cultivated farm, whose well-tilled fields overlooked the German Ocean, near where the already-described winding streamlet, the Lunan, loses itself in Red Castle's white sandy bay.

It was bothy life at this new place, and so similar to what I have described in previous chapters that I need not repeat the sketch. Although I had engaged for a year, my new master and I broke up the engagement by mutual consent at Whitsunday, and on the term day he drove me with him in his gig to the same fair in which we met. I remember when he drove round by the bothy to pick me up, I had a bag with two large volumes of Rollins' Ancient History, and he inquired what the books were? When I told him he seemed astonished, and said, "Aye, dae ye read Rollins' History?" I replied that I spent all my leisure time reading such books if I could get them, and that I had now finished eight out of the eleven volumes which the Parish Library at Rescobie contained. He said it was a pity he did not know sooner of my love for reading, as he had a well-stocked library, from which he would have been glad to have lent me such books as I liked.

He seemed a little disappointed now that we were parting, but did not express his regret, as I think he knew I was leaving on account of the uncongenial social environment of his place. His farm was one of two large holdings, where the farm buildings were only separated by the breadth of a road, and at each farm there was a male and female bothy, the latter being occupied in each case by the female field hands, who belonged principally to the Highlands.

But whether Highland or Lowland, with no supervision, and very little if any moral restraint put on either sex's conduct in their leisure hours, to put it mildly, any of the studious habits, with even an ordinary taste for the most rudimentary of life's proprieties, would have found, as I did, the associations simply intolerable. As stated, I cleared out, and after another half-year in the neighbourhood of Forfar, I got engaged to a place on the estate of Carsegray, where the proprietor was the refugee who took sanctuary and died within Holyrood, as recorded in a previous chapter.

This gentleman, as holding the entail of the estate, had let nearly all the farms on his lands at almost nominal rents, and on long leases, to punish his persecuting creditors, as he could not get but a debtor's subsistence from the revenues, and among the fine farms thus disposed of was the one I had now, in 1853, got engaged at.

A younger son of the proprietor referred to was lessee, but

as he held a commission in the East India Company's branch of the British Army, and had been ordered back to his regiment almost immediately after taking possession of the lease, he had to assign the management of those fertile fields to another life-renter of his father. The Major either died or fell in action in the East, and during my term of service this farm-lease went into the market, and was let to the highest bidder for nineteen years, at about £5 per acre of rent per annum.

A merchant from Arbroath took it for entrance at Martinmas, but during the summer the Major's displenishing sale took place, and I got paid my full year's wages when but three-fourths of the time had expired. I engaged for the remaining quarter of a year to the new farmer, for nearly as much as I had just been paid for the whole half-year on the previous engagement.

Before beginning this autumn contract I took a week's holiday, and re-visited the north, where I met, for the first time since our parting in 1852, my own girl I left behind me. I had a much longer journey to make this time, and passed beyond Gordon's Land. I remember being very anxious beforehand about that unknown district, and one night I had a remarkable dream. This was about a week before the date on which I commenced this love-inspired trip!

I had several years before heard of a certain parsonage connected with a Scotch Episcopal Church near where I thought I should pass, whose pastor of bye-gone days was the author of "Tullochgorum," and who also composed the quaint allegorical song of "The Ewie wi' the crookit horn." In my dream I thought I was walking along by the whin hedge protected roads of the "Doon-throu'" district, as the natives of Gordon's Land called

Reminiscences of an Old Boy.

it, and after passing through a pretty village near-by a riv(
also saw in this night vision a church and parsonage, and I n
specially in my dream that the church was undergoing repai:
the roof! Now comes the fulfilment! When about a week a
on a fine harvest morning, after passing through a nice vi]
near the home of my heart's delight, behold! there was
parsonage, and the church, both before me, and specially
spicuous were the slaters' and joiners' scaffolding on the rool
as I saw them in my dream, and the whole of the night vis:
surroundings were there in identical reality! I was infor
that I was actually looking on the spot where once lived
gifted song-writer I have referred to.

I had never been within fourteen miles of the place be:
and I dreamed this dream at an hundred miles distance.
was my first notable sleep vision, the memory of which I l
retained, and where the reality coincided so completely with
dream. I have had several dreams since then which have tu1
out true, warnings of the death of friends or relations.

The warning dreams came much later in life, and will
related in their proper place.

Chapter XXXIV.

"Through knowledge we behold the world's creation,
　How in her cradle first she fostered was ;
And judge of nature's cunning operation,
　How things she formed of a formless mass ;
By knowledge we do learn ourselves to know,
　And what to man, and what to God we owe !"

　　　　　　　　　　　　　　—SPENSER.

1852-53.—I return to Strathmore Valley, and in '53-54 am engaged at Newtonhall, near Laurencekirk. —A model farmhouse and steading of the time, but a bothy not a model. —A sleeping apartment for five without space enough for three sparrows to reel on the floor.—A Mutual Improvement Association in Laurencekirk.—I become a member.—General account of the winter work of this Association.—The impending war with Russia, and a subject for debate found in anticipating that terrible event.—A course of Lectures on behalf of the Association.—All Newtonhall unmarried servants sent adrift at Whitsunday, 1854.

At the Martinmas of 1853 I went to a place near the small market town of Laurencekirk, in the Mearns. The name of the farm was Newtonhall, occupying five pairs of horses. Its fields lie along both sides of that well-kept level highway which traverses the Strathmore and Mearns Valley, and along that beautifully diversified and fertile tract the traveller has the range of the blue Grampians in view the whole distance. The tenant and occupier of Newtonhall at this time was a solicitor in Montrose. He was unmarried, and we saw very little of him, the whole farming business being carried on by an overseer, or bailiff, who was a native of Forfarshire.

The unmarried ploughmen, all but one, were from the same district, the five of us being inmates of a bothy where we cooked our own food, and were meant to spend our evenings, a place through whose tiled roof the light of heaven played, and through the same openings the snow, hail, and rains of this specially stormy winter came in, and at the break of each storm a stream of melted snow passed in at the door and crossed the clay floor of this wretched sitting-room.

There was a large handsome dwelling-house on this farm, standing in the midst of a considerable space of ornamental ground, which reached to the public highway; and, with the fine-looking farm buildings, behind which our den, I had almost said kennel, was hidden from the public view, the outward appearance of this mansion and farm steading gave no indication that such a hovel as the one wherein we cooked and took our meals, existed. The horses and the stalled cattle were better housed than we were.

Our bedroom was in an attic over one end of the stables, where were three beds occupied by the five horsemen. The space here was so limited that there would not have been room, as the saying is, for three sparrows to reel on the floor. We had the whole breadth of the farm steading, a distance of over two hundred yards, to walk from the bothy to this attic crib, and in bad weather, after the day's labour, we had to spend the evening in this bunk.

Some of my mates never changed their wet clothes for dry. So after dressing, cleaning, and suppering their horses, they would return to the bothy fire in their damp garments, and afterwards go to sleep in the close overcrowded attic I have described. Was it much wonder that Jock or Geordie became prematurely old and decrepit? As it was in Burns' time, so it was with the farmers and proprietors of farms in my time of service, and the apathy and carelessness of our superiors in that respect, just emphasised what our National Bard so truly said was the sentiment of those in place and power towards their servants in his time—

"They, and be d——nd : what richt hae they
To meat, or drink, or licht o' day !"

This carelessness and indifference apparent in our employers just begot the same or worse carelessness in the majority of men so housed, and so neglected. I often tried to arouse their attention to the need of some reasonable self-assertion, and self-respect, by holding forth, in season and out of season, on the dignity and importance of our calling, insisting that husbandry, or land cultivation, was the most ancient of human occupations, and one which included all the other trades or pursuits, and the only trade which represented real wealth, because our occupation was the only one which could produce a surplus of the things essential for man's sustenance.

I also told the histories of men who had been taken from the plough to fill some of the greatest and most honourable places which the Sovereign of their country, or the popular will, could bestow. I am sorry to say my enthusiasm in the amelioration of their lot and my own, met with but very feeble response, and when I joined a Young Men's Mutual Improvement Association in Laurencekirk, and got my four unmarried mates, and one of the married cottars, to go with me to hear the papers read and the discussions entered into on the debatable subjects which took place at our meetings, I never got a man of them to join our membership, or take any part in the useful and entertaining proceedings. I told them on our way going and returning, when they were wont to argue, and argue very well too, that they should stand up in the meetings and state their opinions, as they did on the road, in their own broad Scotch. I really found some of them had as good if not a better grasp and perception of the subjects discussed as I had.

I remember the Eastern Political question, and the impending war with Russia were the chief topics in farm-cottage, bothy, or laird's or farmer's mansion, and among the members of this Association at this time.

We did not at this time discuss the nature or merits of the quarrel, for we did not know them, but when almost immediately after the destruction of the Turkish fleet, in the Harbour of Sinope, war was declared by Britain and her allies in the spring, we debated the following questions propounded by me, as to which of the following descriptions of the armies were the most likely to be the victors in the strife:—1st, would victory rest with the highly-disciplined, but badly-led troops, in a bad cause? or 2nd, would it be with the less-disciplined, but braver and better-led troops, in a good cause?

I took the less-disciplined, but better-led, and good cause side, and after three nights' very keen and determined debate I gained, or proved my case.

The experience and information I received at those meetings, and the benefit derived from a public lecture delivered to us monthly, in the Town Hall, by gentlemen selected by our president and vice-president, has been of much service to me ever since.

We got the use of the hall free, only paying for the gas, the public being admitted at 3d per head, and the free proceeds were spent in the purchase of books to form a library we wished to establish for the use of our members.

I remember very well who each of the five lecturers were, as also the subjects on which they so kindly and gratuitously tried to enlighten us. The first was a fine description of the River Jordan, by the Established Church minister. The second was an account of a summer tour in Germany, by an advanced leading farmer in the vicinity. His delivery was poor, but his matter was good. The third, which I considered the best, was on the political consequences of celebrated battles, beginning with Marathon, and ending with Waterloo. This was delivered by the Rector, or Headmaster, of a high-class seminary in Montrose. The fourth was on Reading, and given by a young Established Church student, and was his first appearance before the public, to speak on a secular subject, after leaving college. That lecturer is, and has been for many years past, a D.D. and minister of the first charge of a large parish at the ancient seaport which is the ocean outlet of the Scottish capital. The fifth was a chemical dessertation on the science of heat, with experiments in that element, and in electric energy. This was the first time I saw a galvanic battery. The lecture and experiments were delivered and conducted by our vice-president, an M.D. of the town.

I was the only farm servant member of this Association, and when we were discussing ways and means for raising the needful for our library, a motion was made and carried at one of the business confabs, which was that we should, or rather the presidents and secretary should, approach the merchants and the better class of farmers for subscriptions towards our object. The president said he would go with a good reason to the farmer of Newtonhall, and kick hard for a substantial sum for our purpose, telling him he was honoured by having in his employment the only farm servant who was a member of such an Association, which he, the president, was aware of, and he complimented me on the part I had taken in their whole winter's proceedings.

But Whitsunday was again approaching, and the overseer was warned off by the solicitor, although he had been engaged for three years, and was paid a year's salary by agreement to leave, he having undersold some fat cattle at a local market. This unexpected change of overseer put all of us adrift, whose engagements expired at the term. But before that time came I had an indication that the president of our Association had seen the learned gentleman on whose farm I served. I had the charge of, and worked a very fine pair of horses, regular beauties, great big, jet-black fellows, brothers too, with only two years between their ages. And one fine day in spring, as the solicitor was walking around his fields, he came along where I was raising drills on a long, fine-lying land length, and when he saw the pair of noble animals coming around and keeping step with each other in all the stateliness which those intelligent animals displayed when kindly treated and carefully trained, the owner's words to me were—" You have a very fine pair of horses, my man." I answered " Yes, sir, and they are as guid as they are bonnie, and they and I are great friends." " That's right," says he, " and you are making fine drills." I said " I ought to do that, for," I continued, " the horses are guid, the plough is guid, the day is fine, and the land in fine order." Then he walked off laughing.

The overseer and the other field workers seemed astonished to see the gentleman speaking to me, and when Mr Barnes (the farmer) was out of sight, the overseer came in great anxiety to learn what had been the nature of our conversation. He seemed much relieved when I told him we had been only speaking of the horses and the fine day. This overseer and the others declared that I ought to feel proud and honoured, as Mr Barnes had never been known by any of them to speak to a man about the place, but his overseer.

However, the term came, and I had to bid good-bye to my handsome equine friends, and although to some it may appear silly, it is nevertheless true, I have felt as much regret, aye, and real sorrow, at parting with a fine, intelligent, and well-trained pair of horses as ever I did in parting with neighbours and friends of the human race, for, did time and space permit, I could tell of incidents and adventures in the histories of horses I had charge of, and whom I rode or drove in saddle and harness, of various kinds, where the sagacity and apparent calculation on the animal's part, were so remarkable as to amount to almost reasoning power.

We are now hearing a lot about horseless carriages, and of horses being superseded by the auto-car, but I hope I shall not be here to see our roads and streets void of beautiful horses!

Chapter XXXV.

*" Pleasures are like poppies spread,
You seize the flower, its bloom is shed."*
—BURNS.

*" It was a vast and venerable pile;
So old it seemed only not to fall,
Yet strength was pillar'd in each massy aisle."*
—BYRON.

I return to good old Forfar. — Meet my teacher, Mr Roostycrank.—Attend his Summer Evening School and improve and add to my arithmetical knowledge.—Old Baigrie, my new master—his two walking-sticks and his deftness in the use of these weapons in locomotion or defence.—Baigrie's grandson, a precocious and cheeky youth, but forced to yield at the persuasion of his grandfather's stick. — The Land Measuring Lesson which was never given.—The Crimean War.—The Battle of Alma.—Effect of the news of victory on the inhabitants of Forfar.—The spirit and patriotism displayed all over the country at this time.

Whitsunday, 1854, saw me moved westwards again, to a smaller farm near the Priory of Restenneth, the burial place of honest George Dempster, the great reformer and farm servants' friend. The tenant here had his affairs managed by several trustees, as he had dissipated the income of the farm, and had thus to arrange for behoof of his creditors. He had lived a fast, if not a wicked, life, and was now reaping the reward of his sins and folly in the breakdown of what had been a fine system, so that he could now only walk by the aid of two

RESTENNETH PRIORY.

short stout staves. But he was very active when even thus crippled, and the best at using one of the said staves as a means of persuading either man or beast to go the way he wished them to go! Aye! and he could use the weapon here mentioned at close quarters, or throw it with almost unerring precision, and never miss an object at a very considerable distance.

He had a grandson who lived with him, and his wife and one daughter. The boy was about thirteen, and rather tricky and disobedient. When he had disobeyed some of the old man's orders, and was trying to shirk explanations by running off from his grandpa, how suddenly he was brought up, and his flight stopped, when the right-hand walking-stick whizzed through the air and hit the boy on the back crosswise, dropping him on the ground sometimes. I am astonished yet that some permanent injury was not the result of old Baigrie's boomerang practices. Yet it was a scientific feat, the throwing of the stick, and one I have never seen equalled, or even imitated for any but juggling purposes. This same boy was rather a precocious child, in fact he seemed to me very likely to walk in the ways of his yet visible ancestor, and sometimes made remarks which I thought rather advanced.

I remember one fine mid-day meal-hour the lad was standing in the door of the room where I had my bed and all my belongings, and when the old grandfather paddled across the farmyard at a little distance, that young rascal remarked aloud, but as if speaking to himself, "Na, na, auld age disna come its lane," then with a sigh like a very experienced old person, he added, " I assure ye no', for there's a guid lick o' laziness comes wi' it."

The cheeky young beggar's outcome so tickled me that I burst out laughing, but warned him that if his grandfather heard what he had just said, stick No. 1 would be sent for him. This grievous old man was an example of those who grow old in sin, being hardened therein, as on the last morning I was at the place he called out to me to go and look for his two crutch staves on the road between the farm and the town, he having been in Forfar the night previous, and meeting his old boon companions, he got "miraculous," as he phrased it, and parted company with his sticks, and must have crawled home the remaining distance on his hands and knees, as he could not walk without the staves.

When I took service at this place I met with what I had been looking for for some time past. This was an evening school, and although it was the summer season I found one established in Forfar, only about half-a-mile distant from the farm. The teacher of this evening school for grown-up pupils was none other than my old acquaintance, Mr Roostycrank, M.A., of Lunanhead, my old schoolmaster. That poor mortal was much reduced in circumstances by this time, as fifteen years had come and gone since last he and I met. He had the use of an up-stair room, where he also taught a day-school. Other two grown-up young men attended, but our teacher did not attend very regularly. However, when I did get his attention, I profited by his tuition. I commenced about the 30th May, and by the first week of August I had mastered Gray's Arithmetic from the " rule of reduction," onward to " vulgar fractions," and " mensuration." I used to fill my slate with the wrought exercises, and carry it home every night, and reaching the farm generally after ten o'clock, I turned in at once, and I considerably astonished the foreman, who was a married man, and lived in a house on the farm, when he called me the first morning after my first evening at school, when at half-past five he found me sitting on my knees, and using the top of my clothes chest for a desk, busy copying all the arithmetical exercises into a book, at which endeavour I had been employed since three o'clock.

This was continued till the commencement of harvest, or about five mornings per week for nine weeks. When nearing the close of those lessons I tried to get Mr Roostycrank, who was a skilled land measurer and surveyor, to come out to the farm with his chain and borrowing rods, to give me a practical lesson in mensuration, and the finding of the areas of square surfaces by square measure, and also by triangles. My teacher promised often, but never kept his word. At last he very distinctly arranged that he would certainly visit the farm on the annual fair holiday, and I arranged to stay at home to meet him to get this practical example shown me, although it was the only day we got during the six months for a holiday. After waiting till long after the appointed hour, I started along the road to the town, expecting to meet my tutor, but after reaching midway I came on this precious M.A. hanging over the roadside fence with his feet on the footpath, and his head near the ground on the inside. He was busy soliloquising, or telling some imaginary hearer that he was very sublime! His sublimity, and my disappointment at not getting the long-promised lesson in land measuring, so riled me that I did not disturb my besotted teacher's exoteric drunken reverie, but I left him where I found him, and went and saw the evening fair.

The annual fair at Forfar was a gay and busy scene! There I met with a number of my old mates, with whom I had worked in past years. We were glad to see each other again, and could not part, as the saying is, "dry-mou'd," so we adjourned to Peter Adamson's public-house, a house where the very best of everything of a drinkable kind was to be got. This famous little house of entertainment was situated near the Cross in Forfar, in the quaint-looking side street, rejoicing in the name of the "Osnaburg Pend."

By this time the Crimean war was a stern and undoubted fact, and the allied armies were disembarked on the shores of the Euxine or Black Sea, and when about six weeks thereafter, the news of the victory on the Heights of Alma arrived in Forfar, it proved how intensely popular the war was, for in proportion to the population of that ancient burgh, it had a heavy stake in the

OSNABURG PEND, FORFAR.

success or failure of the terrible conflict, and of the issues of the dreadful arbitrament, which the allies and their ruthless northern foe had appealed to. Forfar's interest in all the progress of this war will be better understood when I state the fact that eighteen young men, out of her population of under 12,000, were engaged in the battle of the Alma. And when the news of victory reached the home of those young men's nativity, the joy and rejoicing of their townsmen and relatives were boundless! I had occasion to be in the town on the forenoon of the Saturday when the joyful tidings arrived, and the light of patriotic pride and pleasure were visible on every countenance!

Even the women, young and old, were enthusiastic in their patriotic joy on this memorable day. I had occasion to call at an old furnishing tailor's establishment in town on the forenoon of that joyful day, but not finding the man in his workshop, I made my way to the kitchen door, and on looking in I saw the man's wife, a woman past middle age, at a washing tub. She on looking round withdrew her hands, and wiping the soapsuds from her bare arms, exclaimed, " Eh, Lord, man, there's been a richt fecht noo." " So it's said," I replied. " Aye," she adds, " and, by g—d, we've licket the Rooshians as clean's a bead!" This truly Grecian mother accompanied her brave assertion with a clap of her wet hands, which sounded like a loud report from a pistol. I thought to myself, when such is the spirit of the mothers of the North Briton, we need never fear but their sons will uphold the honour of our country on sea or land, through danger's dark career, even against the world in arms!

Of all the eighteen Forfarians who went into action at the battle of Alma, only one fell. He was " the only son of his mother, and she was a widow." Although I heard both sympathy and pity expressed on behalf of the bereaved mother, on this day of rejoicing over the victory, it was more like to that expressed in Mrs Hemans' beautiful song, which she puts in the mouths of the Greeks in regard to the fallen heroes of that warlike race, where the singer says:—

> " Breathe not those names to-day,
>   They shall have their praise ere long,
> And a power all hearts to sway
>   In ever burning song."

The power which sways all brave people's hearts was very well exemplified, when a few Sundays after the memorable battle a gifted son of the Free Church in Forfar preached a sermon in aid of the fund which was being raised for the assistance of the widows, orphans, and others who had lost, and were likely yet to lose, their life's maintenance in the cruel war. The sermon referred to was a masterpiece of graphic description, pathos, and eloquent oratory, which, it was said for the time being, made all hearts its own, and I heard it often spoken of as the only sermon, worthy of the name, that was preached on this war.

The rev. gentleman took his text from part of two verses among the old Hebrew prophecies. The words were "Thou hast heard, oh my soul, the sound of the trumpet, the alarm of war, and seen garments rolled in blood." The effect on the great crowd of hearers assembled, was a scene never to be forgotten! When the talented speaker told with such thrilling pathos, of which he was such a master, how their eighteen townsmen met the night before they went into battle, as all expected to be engaged in the coming struggle, and how each gave to each, in case of their death on to-morrow's field, some last message or small token. They who survived were thus solemnly commissioned to deliver to those whom each loved best at home, should any of their number ever return, or again taste the pleasures and friendships of their native Strathmore. It is on record that the effect of this eloquent sermon and its appeal turned out a very fair financial success, and helped to swell the sum of the patriotic fund.

I have mentioned that we usually had in this district one holiday during the summer half-year; but during the month of August, before harvest, a large number of farm servants in the counties of Angus and Mearns got the opportunity of another this year, when, by arrangements made with the railway company, through the large-hearted and advanced farmer near Laurencekirk, he whom I have mentioned in the preceding chapter as giving us a lecture descriptive of a summer tour in Germany. This gentleman got the railway company to agree to carry about seven hundred male farm servants from the two counties mentioned to Aberdeen and back, on the first Saturday of August. One train started from Laurencekirk station, and another from Forfar, and they were timed to reach the terminus within half-an-hour of each other. The fares were very moderate indeed, and included lunch in a large hall. We paid only three and sixpence for return tickets. The distance we were conveyed was $57\frac{1}{2}$ miles between the farthest points, or 115 miles on the double journey.

It was a bright sunny day, and the fine fertile, sylvan and mountain scenery, through which we passed at about twenty-eight to thirty miles an hour, for as often as I have seen it since, it never looked better than it did on that day of glorious sunshine and bounty-blest fields of yellow grain!

On arrival at Aberdeen, the whole, between six and seven hundred men, were marshalled, four abreast, and the fine brass band, from Forfar, struck up "O, gin I were where Gadie rins." We commenced the march up Market Street, and through the fine Market Hall balconies, and out and along Union Street, through the spacious rooms of the Mechanics' Institute. Our leader was warmly welcomed by the directors of that institution, who threw all their rooms open for our entertainment. In these beautiful apartments many splendid paintings adorned the walls. We passed into the hall in one file, and out in another, one up and one down stairs at the same time, making no halt, as it took a considerable time for such a number to pass. Then we marched to the Gordon Schools, and walked through them in the same order, thence to one of the Colleges, and repeated the same process of sight-seeing, admiring some very ancient painted portraits of famous men and women of byegone days. After lunch, still led by the band, we were shown over one of the largest and almost the only granite-polishing and stone monumental works in that city at the time. The rise and progress of Aberdeen was related to us by one of the speakers in the hall where we lunched. In the afternoon we were taken through the shipbuilding yards, and finished this magnificent day's experiences in a march round the Docks, being accompanied along the route by quite a crowd. Indeed, it looked as if all the inhabitants had turned out to see the rustic excursionists! I heard the leader complimenting the processionists on their orderly behaviour and good marching, declaring that the Aberdonians would think he had been training us to keep step for months past.

We left the city of strawberries and cream at about six o'clock p.m. in thirty-two carriages, drawn by three locomotives of the old light type; but so were the carriages then. No train with the same number of laden passenger carriages of the present day pattern would be allowed to leave any terminus now. However, that was the number returning that evening, and I remember the scene! Lovely as it was going, it was more beautiful returning, for what with the beauty of the weather, and the great crowds of the townsfolk outside the station gates, and the strains of "Auld Langsyne," and "The girl I left behind me," made an hour's enjoyment which lives and comes back, and with it a tinge of regret. This regret is more keenly felt, as nearly all the officials at that railway terminus, with whom I became in after years very well acquainted, have departed this life, and when I ever visit Aberdeen Joint Station now, I feel myself a complete stranger.

But to finish my account of this great special trip for ploughmen. The return to Forfar, from where we started in the morning, had a very tragic and sorrowful ending, caused by the accidental instantaneous death of one of our number, an old man of nearly seventy years of age, who had served one master about three miles from Forfar for over thirty years.

The accident occurred at the second station east of the town where our journey was to end. There is an overhead bridge there, which carries the public road over the line, and at the time the up platform extended a little to the east, and under that bridge westward also. The unfortunate man had a seat in one of two open carriages provided for the band. His seat was the one nearest the engine, and when the train halted he got to his feet on the seat, and was waving a red handkerchief for a flag while the band played. A large crowd of country folks were at the station, meeting friends on their return. In about a minute after stopping it was seen that the train was not drawn up far enough ahead on the platform, and the only two engines now in front were started forward with a jerk.

At that instant the old man toppled over, and fell between the couplings of the carriages, and the whole after-part of the train passed over him, cutting him in pieces. It was all the work of less than three minutes. I had a seat in one of the open carriages, and although I saw the man standing on the seat and waving a red handkerchief from the end of his umbrella, I did

EDZELL CASTLE.

not see him fall over, and none seemed to be aware that such a dreadful thing had happened until someone came to the leader of the band, and told him to stop the music as a man had been killed. It was a most melancholy ending to such a happy day, and a startling proof of the stern truth that in the midst of life we are in death!

Shortly after, I spent a six months' engagement working a pair of fine horses on the Home Farm of Mains of Edzell, about six miles north from the ancient city of Brechin. I have nothing of any great moment to record about my stay at this place. The pay was good, the work heavy, but we were well treated in regard to lodging and food. I mention my short time at this place because just about a quarter of a mile from the farm-house stands Edzell Castle.

In this fine old ruin I spent many a happy time, for every spare hour I had from my work I wandered about the old place, and in my fancy re-built and re-peopled the ancient structure. I felt great delight in pondering and speculating over the former greatness of the baronial pile. This is my excuse for introducing here a short sketch of its history.

Edzell Castle stands just at the foot of the Grampians, on the left bank of the West Water, and about half-a-mile to the west of the fine little village of Slateford, or Edzell. The ruin has been described as the most magnificent of any in the shires of Angus and Mearns, except those of Dunnottar, near Stonehaven.

The most remarkable feature of the ruins of Edzell is the donjin, sixty feet high, a beautiful piece of workmanship. It is called the "Stirling Tower." The origin of the name may be gathered from the fact that Alexander de Lindsay, youngest son of Sir David de Lindsay de Crawford, married the daughter and sole heiress of John Stryveline of Stirling, Glenesk. It may be presumed that the grand tower was named after the lady.

Until about a generation ago it was possible to get to the top of the tower, the stair being then entire, but it is now broken down, and the fine view that could formerly be got from the top is not now accessable, unless to very adventurous spirits.

Much has been written by antiquarians and others about the history of Edzell Castle, of its beautiful flower garden, of the quaint figures cut in the stone on the walls thereof, personifications of

Truth, Justice, Charity, Music, Astronomy, etc., etc. Our two illustrations are from the south wall of the flower garden, and are emblematic of "Geometria," and "Musica," and the other will give a good conception of Edzell Castle as it not stands.

Mr Andrew Jorvise, who wrote the history of the "Lands of the Lindsays," speaking of the old-fashioned baronial hospitality,

says—"From the magnificent style in which cooking was conducted at Edzell Castle, and the liberality of its owners to the poor, it was familiarly known by the enviable title of the 'Kitchen of Angus!' Oxen were roasted whole, and everything conducted in a correspondingly sumptuous style; and daily, after the family dined, the poor of the parish congregated in the court-yard, and taking their seats on the stout benches (which still remain) on both sides of the entrance passage, they received their quota of beef and beer from the fair hands of the lady, or daughters of the proud home of Edzell."

This half-year at the Mains of Edzell was my last place in connection with farm life in Scotland, but I followed the plough for yet another year in the north-east corner of England. My experience and adventures there will be found in the following chapters of this true history.

Chapter XXXVI.

*"The saying that the world must end in smoke,
Seems true in these last days for steam and coke,
Homeless, and counting home a dream,
From land to land we pass in clouds of steam."*
—From the German.

Martinmas, 1854.—Off to England per the paddle steamer "Britannia."—A sea voyage by night and scenes on board the stout old boat.—The Farne Isles.—The dawn at sea—My first sight of the English Coast.—Landed in the Tyne.—I see the ruins and debris left by a terrible explosion of chemicals.—Staying to read the Mayor's Proclamation thereon, my companions go off without me, and I am lost in Newcastle.—Get set on the road to my destination, and at length arrive at my journey's end.

At Martinmas, 1854, while at the term hiring fair in Arbroath, I, along with another four who followed the same calling, met a representative of a Scotch farmer, who rented and occupied two large farms situated between the rivers Tyne and Wear, near the centre of the English north-eastern coal district. With this agent we engaged to serve for the following year, at one or other of the places referred to.

Then our party was added to by another half-dozen who were hired to serve a brother of my new employer, in a neighbouring county, in the same region. We met by arrangement on the third day after the hiring fair, at the southern railway terminus in Arbroath, and took train southwards. After crossing the river

Tay, we were carried along through the "kingdom of Fife," and thence over the Firth of Forth, and reached Leith, the sea-port of Edinburgh, our Scottish metropolis.

At mid-night following we set sail for Newcastle, on board what is now known in steamboat history, as the stout old paddle-wheel steamer "Britannia," which then plied weekly with goods and passengers between the two ports indicated. This was my first night at sea on a coasting steamer, although not by many a night my last. The recollection of this trip yet remains very fresh with me, as the rather large complement of passengers was made up of all sorts and conditions, of both sexes, belonging to various nationalities, and occupations, and some of very doubtful occupation, I thought, when ashore!

I could notice that numbers of both sexes had reached various stages of inebrity before coming aboard. After we cleared the Firth, and were fairly at sea, the good old boat began to jump and swing! In less than an hour came mal-de-mere, that republican despot of over-charged stomachs, who knows no distinction of worldly rank, and on the swelling billow is no respecter of persons.

Soon the appearance of "the steerage," and also the deck, but especially "the steerage," presented such a spectacle of helpless and confused humanity that beggars description. The effluvia coming up the companion, and along the all-ways, sent our party on deck in great haste, and there we remained for the rest of the passage.

The night was calm, and not very cold, with a long heavy swell on the sea. Only one or two at most of our party were squeamish for a short time, but got better very soon, and with the steady onward speed of the "Britannia," we made good progress. As we passed the Longstone Rock, and the Farne Isles, made famous by the heroism of Grace Darling, in the never-to-be-forgotten rescue of the crew and passengers of the ill-fated steamer "Forfarshire," it was with straining vision and interested minds we tried to see through the mist, so as to get a peep at the now historic isles.

As morning advanced we saw all or most of the by-past night revellers, and late sea-sick passengers, now sound asleep! Aye, even the stout lady, a steerage passenger, who last night required four other ladies to keep her from jumping overboard, when in her drunken frenzy. She was now all serene! Morpheus had her ladyship fast in his balmy spell! Yes, sleep, the restorer of human health, was all around, and had led the motley throng to that paradise of rest, the sweet Elysium of forgetfulness!

I was too much engrossed in the novelty of my surroundings to think of sleep, and I walked the deck, or leant over the bulwark at the vessel's bow all night, enjoying my surroundings immensely. I had no companion on this my truly enjoyable night-watch.

When the grey dawn of the coming morning showed a streak of light on our port side, at first low on the south-eastern horizon, I saw the coast line on the right, I guessed we were nearing "our desired haven" on the shores of "the Land of Roses!" As the celestial night-lamps paled their light, and the monarch of day's beams struck the far northern mountain-tops, I knew by the sight of the great windmill towers, some of them with their great arms in motion on the morning breeze, that I was now in view of some of "the stately homes of England!"

The smoke issuing from coal pit-heads, and the hundreds of

coke ovens, also indicated that we were close to the home of the black diamond, and nearing the dwellings of the vaunted " hearts of oak!"

At length the good steamship crossed Shields bar, and began the ascent of the famous coal-begrimed and busy river Tyne. When passing up this renowned waterway, the seemingly endless lines of shipping, moored or anchored, tier upon tier, as far as we could see, gave us quite a new idea of the vastness of England's maritime commerce, as on this one river alone I saw more shipping than I had previously beheld at all the seaports where I had been. There were very few steamers; in fact, I cannot remember seeing any among the fleet, and quite a number of the sailing craft along the river were not of very large dimensions, but their numbers were legion.

After passing most of the shipping, and reaching the lower end of the built quay, we were brought up at the steamer's berth, and were met there by a man from the home farm who had been sent with a horse and cart to take us and our luggage to the farm, some miles distant, where we were to start work. On getting ashore, and after passing some sheds and warehouses on the south quay, we came on a large space covered with great mounds of bricks, broken and twisted roofing materials, and debris, looking like the wrecks of a very extensive range of buildings, which had faced the quay. Our guide told us we were looking on the ruin caused by an explosion of chemicals, ignited by a great fire, which originated in a factory on the other side of the river, and he told us that the same shock had wrecked the houses on the north side.

This was the greatest and most dreadful calamity which had ever happened to this town, in modern times. A large number of lives were lost through the victims being in bed when the explosion took place. Some idea may be gained of the terrific force of the shock, when it is recorded that the vibration was felt fully seven miles distant, as a night fireman at a fixed engine of a colliery, at the distance mentioned, felt the ground suddenly shaken. At the same instant the red fire sparks were shot out of the top of the smoke-stalk, to the height of nearly a hundred feet.

We had dinner in what would now be called by a longer, but which looks to me only a spoiled name, a "restaurant," but which rejoiced then in the name of the "North of England Dining Rooms." This was the first time I ever saw victuals ordered in by the plateful, or by separate dishes, and paid for on the principle of so much per dish. I thought it a very mean-looking yet expensive way, as it appeared to me as supplying the stomach's requirements by contract! All my previous experiences had been, when dining or supping from home, or at friends' tables, the good old hearty Scotch style of ordering a meal, and paying for the same at the regulation price, according to the class of house I chose to patronise, and only paying for liquor accompaniments separate. We got the inner man replenished, bit by bit, and I think the cost was something like two shillings per head, and we had no alcoholic liquors.

We started for our new homes, some going by road one way, and some by rail in an opposite direction. The cart was to bring our chests from the steamer to the Victoria or Central Station, at the south end of the wonderful High Level Bridge. That station had only been opened the year before, and was then named Victoria Station. While on our way to this station I stopped to read a proclamation by the Mayor, calling a public meeting to devise means for the relief of those unfortunate poor people suffering from the loss of relatives killed by the late calamitous fire and explosion, as also to help small shopkeepers who had lost their stock and means of subsistence through the same cause.

When I had finished perusal of the big sheet I found all my companions had gone on, and were now out of sight. I made off to follow their track, as I thought, to the foresaid station, but after a time I came on a monument to some Earl or other, and on crossing the square where this figure stands, I found myself at the corner of a main street which I guessed from the name led to the north, or in the exact opposite direction to where I wished to go.

I turned round, rather alarmed now, as the winter afternoon was fast wearing away, for here I was adrift in a strange town! There was a thick drizzling rain falling too. Walking back the way I had come I accosted a gentleman in a glazed waterproof, and inquired my way to the Victoria Station, and was much surprised and pleased when that real gentleman turned round and bade me follow him and he would show me the place. I therefore followed the gentleman, and after passing a few crossings he let me see the station, which was only a little distance off the main street I was in. I had actually passed the entrance street several times in my running about, after I had lost sight of my companions.

On going inside I made inquiry regarding a company of Scotsmen with a horse and cart, and a number of chests, but my friends had been and gone, some of the party with a train westwards, while those of my companions bound for where I had to go, had left by road, going eastwards. It was now nearly three o'clock afternoon, and I found I could not get a train to take me near my destination till half-past five, and that that train would only land me on the south side of the river Wear, at a point from which I would have to cross on a ferry-boat.

As one of the porters who knew the district said the distance by road was only about eight and a half miles, by the way the horse and cart had gone, and that by going that way I would arrive before the train mentioned would start, I set off, and left the town of coal by the fixed stone bridge over the Tyne, and passed out through Gateshead, and along the highway to Sunderland, at a rate of speed I could not reach now by at least two miles per hour.

The sun had been set about half-an-hour when I reached a line of railway running north-east. At this point of the line there was a level crossing, and I inquired at the gate-keeper for the castle for which I was bound. "Ah," he replied, "thee'st too far on a'ready," but he showed me the top of the great old oak woods surrounding the old baronial pile I wished to reach.

I had to cross a piece of moorland, and keeping the woods on a line between me and the south-west evening horizon, I at length reached the farm buildings, which were within the castle park, but separate from the castle a little distance. I knew it was bothy-life here, and I accordingly called there first, and was very much surprised to learn that my chest, with two of "the halflin's" boxes, had been left at the High Farm, two miles further west, so that I had already come about three miles out of my way. If I would reach my destination that night I had another two miles to trudge before I slept.

This was what my inquisitive love of reading the Newcastle Mayor's big proclamation had cost me in the present instance. However, to have my real destination decided the foreman took me to the castle, where we saw my new master, who confirmed my place as being really at the High Farm, but the master said there was no need for me to go there that night. He ordered the mistress to give me food, and said I could lodge with the castle men, and find my way to my place next morning; but after getting food I preferred seeing the end of my journey the same night, and set out for Hylton Moor Farm about seven o'clock, revolving in my mind the lines of Montgomery in his "Aspirations of Youth," where he says—

"Oh, they wander wide who roam
For the joys of life from home!"

Chapter XXXVII.

" England ! Thy beauties are tame and domestic,
To one who has roved o'er the mountains afar,
Oh for the crags that are wild and majestic,
The steep frowning glories of dark Lochnagar."
—BYRON.

My new employer, a good Scotsman and an excellent master.—Description of his farm.—Farming as it was then in that district.—A holiday trip across England in July, 1855, and incidents going and returning--The Midland Railway as it was then.—Thirteen hours, less an hour and a half at Derby, on the journey from Dudleyport, South Stafford, to within eight miles of Newcastle-on-Tyne.—What I saw in Derby.—What I ate there and the price thereof.

My English engagement turned out not a bad venture. Our master at the castle was an excellent man, and one who wished to make his servants comfortable. His farming had not up to this been successful. The soil was a very stiff, retentive clay, and farming had been very much neglected in this district, the mineral resources having been the principal industry for many years. It was a grand wheat-growing soil, when properly wrought, and with flour at three shillings per imperial stone, the price of wheat at this time was high.

Our master farmed over three hundred acres at £1 per acre, employing six pairs of horses, or three pairs for each farm. He had been unfortunate in his herd of cattle some two years before, and an epidemic of some kind had carried off all his dairy cows, so that he had to re-stock, and did so with the small-sized Ayrshire variety, and now worked the Castle Farm as partly dairy and partly grain.

Some of the fields on the High Farm had been lying in grass for thirty years, in the old crooked-ridge form, rounded up in the middle, to which all the soil had been gathered, while the deep crooked furrows, in the shape of the letter S, were thus left devoid of soil, and no attempt durst be made to straighten such ridges, as the moisture stood in the long crooked howe furs, and the ploughing of such old-time cultivation in straight ridges threw the deep soil into what were pools of water, where any kind of seeds just got drowned; but when the crooked hollows were drained, and the surface water let down to sand, or what was called a drawing bottom, then the upper soil, well wrought and manured, and made friable by lime, the case was won, and the moss-grown or withered white grass fields were made fertile, and all kinds of grain or green crops flourished and gave ample harvests.

The winter of 1855 was both wet and stormy, and with such a subject as this long-neglected farm, our work was often hard and disagreeable. The country around had little natural beauty, and was quite undiversified by hill, fell, or mountain range, and therefore to me it appeared tame and devoid of the appearances which give that look of romantic grandeur seen in north and south Wales, Devon, and Dorset, or in Cornwall and the north-west English lake districts.

Yet withal the district was very interesting, even under its ever over-shadowing canopy of coal smoke from the coke ovens and pit-head engine smoke-stalks, and its incessant roll of mineral, goods, and passenger trains. These supplied food for the mind, and kept the thinking powers active.

The manners and customs of our English neighbours are widely different from those of Scotland. This made them an endless source of interest, and gave us much amusement at times, especially the barbarous-sounding and extraordinary dialect of the natives. This curious "English jargon," I was much disappointed to note, my countrymen around me seemed all very anxious to imitate. Many a set-to they and I had about it, and when conversing with an uneducated English clodhopper, I argued that as they could not be expected to understand our County Canmore Scotch, and as none of us could successfully or intelligibly use their coal-country lingo, but could all speak plain English, that, I held, should be our means of verbal intercourse.

We were five miles from Sunderland on the south-east, and nine from Newcastle on the north-west. Sunderland was therefore our nearest market-town. During the winter I went to Sunderland on two Saturday evenings, when the great crowds and night-market and streets scenes were in full swing; but I never felt any pleasure in witnessing the Saturday night scenes of big towns or cities. Along with all the gaiety and apparent light-hearted pleasure going forward, as J. L. Robertson says in his poem,

> "Underneath all the apparent joy,
> I aye hear the tone of something sad
> Amid the great crowd wailing."

On one of my Saturday evening visits I met with a very pleasing incident, which I thought reflected credit on a business man's conscience. I had exhausted all my reading matter, and had nothing but a weekly paper. So I walked to the town this evening to replenish my library with something new. Entering a large book-shop I inquired for Mrs H. B. Stowe's "Sunny memoirs of foreign lands." The bookseller said he had it, yet after a considerable search he could not find it, and he came back and said so.

Said he, looking closely at me, "You are a working man," adding, "You will have read 'Uncle Tom's Cabin'?" I replied "Yes, I have the book."

"Well," continued this honest man, "after such a book the 'Sunny Memoirs' are simply latent gossip." He continued, "I can supply the book, yet as a working man I do not think you should spend your money on it, for it is the most disappointing book of the time."

I thanked him and bade him show me something more suitable, and I bought three books, one of which was "Emerson's Essays," I forget what the other two were.

At length this wet and gloomy Winter passed away, and although Spring did not really bring bright blue skies anything like the clear-vaulted arch which I often saw in fancy, over-canopying my well-remembered native valley, yet even the smoke-laden air of coal Durham's dark district, became more rarified and endurable.

The only memorable local event which occurred the following summer was the return of Captain McLintock from his Arctic expedition in search of the often-sought north-west passage, and also from his successful search for some vestige of the long missing Sir John Franklin expedition. The gallant McLintock's home was near our place, and there were great rejoicings, and free public-houses, for a day in the village nearest the Captain's home.

I got four holidays in July, and enjoyed them in a trip across England, almost from sea to sea, about the broadest way I could have gone. I have gone over the most of the ground often within the last twelve years. These frequent journeys commenced exactly thirty years after this trip in 1855; but the first one is the best remembered, and although the beauty of grand old England never palls on my sense of enjoyment, every recurring season is to me, as to most people, a new and ever living joy!

As the young and virgin spring is an emblem of all being renewed, and is a general harbinger of all that is good, so my first extensive sight of the fair homes of England, under a clear sky, and my progress through large tracts of the most luxuriant field culture, with so many rich wooded lawns and parks gracing the lordly-looking mansions, was delightful. That first summer trip of mine has remained a picture on my brain, for—

"A thing of beauty is a joy for ever."

On that first English holiday journey, both going and returning, I saw several phases of manners which amused me, notably the vivid touches of humour displayed by some of the passages verbal between my fellow travellers. For instance, on my way south, when a big Yorkshire cattle-drover, on stepping into the carriage at a small roadside station, and looking around for a seat, was directed by a stout well-dressed man seated near the door by which the rough-looking new-comer had entered, to go up to the other end, where he would get a seat. The carriage was one of the old style, seated lengthwise, and open from end to end. On hearing this quite civil and obliging direction, the big drover looked to his informant, and in pure Yorkshire told him to go to an unmentionable place, adding with another ugly name beginning with a big B, that he, and such as he, occupied two ordinary passengers' room, and ought to be charged first-class!

I could not but admire the restraint the big lot of passengers showed, for they all heard this ruffianly tirade. Yet no one took any notice of it, and as no one moved to make room for this uncomfortably outspoken individual, he had to make his way to the place indicated by the gentleman he had insulted, and he sat him down near the seat I occupied. He was no sooner seated than he drew out a big hunk of cold pork, with bread and cheese, and with the assistance of a long-bladed clasp-knife, he commenced an attack on the victuals in true unsophisticated English style. He very soon got outside the lot!

Then, unfortunately, a young man on his right asked him if he had got fed, to which the big drover replied by asking his questioner " If he had anything more to give him?" On the first questioner saying "No," the drover squared the inquiry off by asking "What the blanketty-blank was this youngster's business, whether he had got fed or not?"

The younger man did not reply, but a lady with inflamed-looking eyes made some mild well-meant remonstrance with the wild drover against swearing. Then the rough looked across and bawled out "Hiloa, there, old burnt-eyes, what have you got to say about it?" This remark raised a howl of execration from nearly all the passengers, as the poor old lady began to cry.

The gentleman whom this rascal had first insulted when he entered the carriage, took speech in hand, and told him to "hold at the men as much as he liked, but that he was not to be allowed to insult the women." I do not now remember what the drover said in reply, but the gentleman who rebuked him said that the stationmaster at Darlington would be appealed to when the train arrived there, and that a joint request would be made to have this disagreeable man removed from the carriage.

The rough reply to this resolution was about the coolest part of the episode, for the irrepressible rascal drew himself up, and said quite calmly, " Yes, and when we get to Darlington I will have some remarks to make too." We reached Darlington in due course, but before the train left that busy station our obstreperous passenger had disappeared, and no one saw him leave the carriage or marked the way he went.

I passed through York and via Normanton, which was then the northernmost point of the now great Midland Railway system. I reached Derby some time about half-past three o'clock in the afternoon, and left there at half-past four, via Burton and Tamworth, by the same Company's trains, even the present Midland Company. That was my first ride on an express train, as the Midland Railway Company took forward through passengers then with third-class tickets by any train.

There were only first and second-class carriages on that flying train, bound for Birmingham, and we only stopped at Burton and Tamworth, and at a station next to Birmingham, where the tickets were lifted. We arrived at half-past four o'clock, and I met my father, whom I had only seen twice in my life before, that I had any recollection of. That meeting is described at length in chapter iv.

My journey ended for this day in the centre of the " Black Country " of South Staffordshire. It was night, and a very hot night too, when we left Birmingham for Dudley Port, in a very crowded train. The distance is only a few miles, but the number of stations we stopped at was many, and the country appeared like one vast funnel of flame and smoke, filling the whole space between earth and overhead, as far as our vision could stretch, there being a far greater number of iron works then than there is now.

On the following day (a Saturday) we walked to within four miles of Bridge-North, and after leaving the black country we passed through a very fertile district, with big fine farms, cultivated in large fields, which looked more like those in Scotland than any I had seen while in the English districts. This was in the county Salop, or Shropshire, and near the banks of the Severn.

We returned on foot on Sunday the same way we went the day before, there being no railway then, as there is now, between the G. W. Railway to Kidderminster, and the single line which runs along the banks of the Severn to Bridge-North. I was amazed at the great Sunday traffic on the L. and N. W. Railway between Dudley, via Dudley Port, to and from Birmingham, because though there were numerous trains on Sunday in the North of England I had never been near them except when I got to Sunderland to church.

My father lodged in the house of a shoemaker in Dudley Port, who pretended to be a devout Wesleyan. The landlord and his wife got me induced to attend a chapel of which they were members. Here a much greater surprise awaited me than the great Sunday afternoon passenger traffic on the railways. That was a choir assisted by instrumental musicians, made up of two small and a big bass fiddle! There was a fix-up for a young Scot of the most pronounced Sabbatarian and anti-sacred instrumental music type!

One who had about three years before walked out of the quoadsacra Church at Forfar, in the face of the whole congregation, when the church choir with their leader sang a paraphrase to some ultra-variorum of a tune, where they repeated the second last line of each verse three times, in a tune where the uninitiated among the worshippers could not join! My father had, during his sojourn in this English country, got over his distaste for the instruments in church service, and he said not a word about how we would be treated to the tunes on no less than three fiddles!

However, there they were, and I did feel very queer when they struck up the first tune. Of course, to rush out of the place was out of the question, so I stood them, and before the end of the second song of praise, I really liked the effect, and found the singing was very heartily joined in by the whole audience. From that day to this (over forty years) I have been an advocate for instrumental accompaniments with sacred song.

There was another kind of accompaniment very freely indulged in by numbers in this Wesleyan audience, that was groanings and "amens." I have never been able to appreciate that kind of religious demonstration. The landlord and his wife, either one or both of them, gave way to these utterances, and although they have both joined the majority long ago, ever since I heard that that particular shoemaker embezzled the funds of a Workmen's Club, of which he was treasurer, I am suspicious of people who make such audible responses during prayer in public. I have found such folks often " pray without ceasing " in private, with the difference, which alters the sense, as in the latter case, the word " pray " is spelled with an " e " instead of an " a!"

But to finish the record of my long holiday journey across England and back. I returned by the way I went on the Monday, only I came back via Lichfield to Derby, instead of by the Trent Valley line. When I reached Derby I found I had over an hour to wait for what was known as the Government, or "parliamentary" train, and I went out to have a sight of the ancient town, where the first silk mill in England was erected, and whose big water-wheel had furnished one of the puzzling questions in calculation, which Grey's arithmetic used to present to the tyros in school exercises. I met with several strange incidents in this street perambulation, which I will never forget.

First, I came on what seemed the preliminaries of a street riot. I saw a crowd gathered at the entrance gate of an enclosure surrounding a fine church. There were several police constables in their square-cut dark coats and tall glazed-crowned hats, with their drawn batons, keeping the crowd from entering that gate, and evidently waiting to keep a free entrance for some important party. In a short time about twenty young and beautiful girls, arrayed in white garments, came down the street in procession, and way was made for them by the police, while hisses were raised by the crowd who had been waiting for them.

I asked a bystander who the white-robed young beauties were, and he told me they were going to play a part at a "Puseyite" marriage which was to take place in the church, and he added that the ritualistic mummeries which were now gaining ground through the teaching and tendencies of Dr Pusey's doctrines were arousing popular indignation to such a pitch that it was quite dangerous to persist openly in following what the people then looked on as subversive of true religion.

I did not wait to see the rest of the bridal party go in to that church, as it appeared quite certain the crowd at the gate would not be admitted. So I passed on and came to a dark sluggish river, which I was told was the Trent. There was a terrace of good brick-built houses and shops, and I observed in the window of one shop—it was one of the best class of grocery stores—a nicely got-up coloured package, about the bulk of a two-lb. package of corn flour, on which was printed the words, "Genuine Scotch Oatmeal, 8d per lb." I stood and looked at this remarkable package, and its more remarkable title and price, and I have often regretted that I did not go in and buy a two-lb. package to bring to Scotland as a keepsake! It might now have found a place in a museum of antiquities, to let the present oatmeal millers, and oatmeal sellers, see what they have lost through not being in the trade in Derby in 1855, when "the chief of Scotia's food" was there sold at four pounds fourteen and fourpence the boll of one hundred and forty lbs.!

My next strange experience was on entering a place, on the same terrace, rejoicing in the name of "Coffee rooms," but which looked almost like a private house. I ordered a cup of coffee and a slice of bread and butter, which was served to me very promptly, and were of excellent quality. Most people who may read this will allow that the two viands should have really been rather more than excellent, when I say that I paid one shilling for them!

I said nothing when the demand was made, but paid before I began to discuss the victuals. Finding them so good, yet thinking the middle-aged respectable-looking lady who served me had made a mistake, I ordered the same again, and the same price was sought and paid over without remark on either side.

Others who may read this may be ready to repeat the proverb,

"Fools and their money are soon parted!" I was a little inclined to think so myself, but I have a quite clear recollection that I have never tasted coffee like that before or since. It was served in large breakfast cups, and both bread and butter were apparently home-made, and of the same superb excellence. I had no other solids or fluids during the whole journey north, which, with the stoppage at Derby, and about half-an-hour at York, occupied thirteen hours.

When I got back to the station after my Derby sight-seeing, I found the train was in and crowded. The old passenger booking office was closed, and as I had to take out a ticket, I was directed to a side door. A porter who directed me, seeing I was a stranger, came to my help very smartly, took my money and brought me a ticket for my destination. I gave him a sixpence and my L. L. ticket, and he brought my bag from the luggage-room in a twinkling and got me a seat.

There was an apparent scarcity of seats, and the train being behind time, a scramble got up among the intending passengers on the platform, and there was a good deal of "deil take the hinmost" shown. I saw a very fine passage of arms between an old and a young lady passenger, the weapons used being the usual feminine blades of sharp, sarcastic repartee and retort. Those were the days of low platforms, when the passengers had to take hold of carriage-door brackets, especially elderly folks, and pull themselves up to reach their seats. Also, when all third-class carriages were cross-seated and open throughout, that is, the back divisions between the compartments were only carried up to about the height of the passengers' shoulders. The old lady I have referred to was accompanied by an old gentleman and a little girl, whom I took to be the old couple's grandchild. The gentleman was a fat, podgy, clerical-looking figure in a white neckcloth. His old lady, and the pretty little girl, got seated in the compartment where the porter had seated me. Nine passengers filled the compartment, and when the clerical-looking gentleman laid his hand on the side rod, and his foot on the foot-board to get up into this compartment, a young good-looking buxom lass put out her hand and shoved his reverence back, saying, "Don't you see, my good man, this compartment is full." However, the old man persisted, and was thrust back two or three times with the same remonstrance, the young lady laughing, and rather enjoying the old man's irritation. At the third repulse I was startled by the old party, who I took to be " in holy orders," breaking out with such a volley of oaths as completely astounded me and knocked my idea of him being a minister into a cocked hat!

However, the exploded clergyman got seated in the next compartment; but in sight of his stout and lovely spouse, who went for the mischief-making and laughter-loving young lady, who had by her fun prevented us from being over-crowded. The remarks which then passed between those two females made the most severely polite exchange notes of admiration. I never heard before such indulgence in quick retort between two of the same sex.

The old lady said first, she "did not like to see people so selfish," and the young one replied that she "did so hate selfishness too," and hinted that she had just concluded a desperate struggle against it! I did not catch what the old lady replied to that neat sarcasm, but the young one remarked that the old one " was surely going from home," and the old lady, as quick as thought, and so very politely, told her youthful opponent that she thought "she (the young lady) was already from home."

The next shot was a settler for the old lady! Her antagonist exclaimed, "Dear, bless me, cannot you live about an hour-and-a-half separate from your precious old man? There he is," and pointing to my once supposed minister, she added, "Why don't thee get over the back of the seat, and alongside of 'im?" This was like adding insult to injury, as the old man's darling weighed at least fourteen stones avordupois, and it would have taken at least two of us to have lifted her over.

This last shot silenced the verbal artillery, and there followed a great calm. I wondered much that the carriage-load of passengers did not show signs of being amused, not to say nearly choked with laughter, during the progress of this funny but well-bred contest, and I can only account for their stolid demeanour as a proof that if Scotchmen are subject to a want of perception of humour, the average Englishman is still denser.

We got started from Derby, and the long summer afternoon wore away, and the train north of that town being an ordinary one, was stopped at every station. Night fell on us a little after we left York, and when we reached the cloudy land of Durham it was quite dark, and I think few of my fellow-passengers, any more than me, knew where we were, while outside the barbarous-sounding guttral of the porters, calling out the names of the stations as the train slowed up, did not enlighten us!

There were no lamps in the carriages, and the whole crowd expressed their impatience and disgust at the poor accommodation and slowness of trains in general on this, then the "York and Newcastle line."

Since 1855 all the service has been improved and changed over the whole great system, but on this hot and smoke-beclouded July night, as we crossed the Wear valley, when we could not see each other in the old crowded carriage, I said aloud, in my very broadest Forfar doric," Hech, man, bit this is dreich wark!" and some one who I think must have been Scotch too, burst out laughing, and said to his neighbour, " There's Sandy growling in his corner too!"

At length the tedious journey came to an end, and I landed at the small station from where I set out four days previous, and reached my home at the High Farm at nine o'clock p.m. The account of my wonderful outing occupied my descriptive faculty for a long time, as I faithfully reported it in black and white, and sent it to my friends in Scotland.

Summer waned, and Autumn touched and ripened the products of both garden and field!

Chapter XXXVIII.

*" Thou,
Whom soft-eyed pity once led down from heaven
To bleed for man, to teach him how to live,
And O, still harder lesson how to die;
Disdain not Thou to smooth the restless bed
Of sickness and of pain."*
— BISHOP PORTEOUS.

Harvest ended and Autumn seed-time began.—I am taken ill—laid up and sent to an hospital.—Scarcely expect to see home again.—Much depressed at the thought.—Remarkable dream and partial recovery.—Leave the hospital.—Suffer a relapse.—Cured by an old Scotch doctor.—A night sea voyage home during a heavy sea, and how the small screw steamer behaved.—Conclusion of farm service life, and closing reflections.

When the ingathering and securing of the whole harvest was finished, as George Macdonald sings—

" Came the evenings clear, the mornings cool
Which foretells no wintry wars;
When the day of dying leaves was full,
And night was full of stars."

With this season also came the wheat seed-time for winter growth, and the preparation of summer fallows, as also the stubble-tilled ridges were finished, and only now awaited the rains of the Equinox to make the soil damp enough for successful sowing. The rains at length came in great abundance, and the precious seeds were literally baked or puddled into the soil, as this was held in that quarter as the only plan to prevent dry-rot in the wheat kernal, and thus ensure germination.

During the latter end of October also came the joyful tidings of how the Russians had evacuated their Crimean stronghold, and left that long and bitterly-contested fortress in the hands of the allied armies. I remember very well seeing the "fires of joy" blazing brightly, and illuminating the heights overlooking the Wear valley, on the same night

"When a horseman rode through the Forest-fields of Mar!"
and delivered at Her Majesty's Highland home, at midnight, the message telling of the long-prayed-for downfall, which was the happy harbinger of peace to Europe, and the end of a war which succeeding years have shown to have been worse than wicked, and wasteful, and so far as the improvement of the unspeakable Turk is concerned, has turned out absolutely useless.

As Autumn advanced the rains came down in a constant drizzle, as steadily as the sun came, but unlike the "Scotch mist," which, it is said, will wet an Englishman to the skin. In my experience, the "moisture" of the Wear valley, impregnated and over-laden with coal soot and smoke, penetrated farther than my skin. A day came, after a severe drenching, when I was found to be so sick that I could not turn out to my work. There had been a case of typhus fever at the Castle, where one of the servants had lain until the fever ran its course, our master's wife attending the case herself, and giving much kind care and nursing.

After this it had been resolved that if any more of the servants or family fell victims to this fell complaint, they would be sent to Sunderland Public Hospital. So on the second or third day of my illness a doctor was called in, and when he made his appearance I was struck with his boyish looks, for he was the youngest looking medical practitioner I ever saw. However, he appeared to be quite mature in his own conceit, for he at once pronounced my case one of the dreaded fever, and prescribed treatment and medicine accordingly, at the same time hinting that I could not be properly attended where I was.

Then on the morning of the fourth day, a hired carriage came from Sunderland, and I had to get up, ill as I was, and was driven the five miles to the hospital. The day was cold, damp, and raw, but I stood the drive pretty well.

When we arrived at the institution for human physical repair, I was shown into the hall, which in England simply means an entrance, or lobby, and there, seated on a wooden form, I waited my turn among a crowd of maimed and disordered beings, young and old, while the cold November winds whistled and howled through this common corridor.

I was set down there about half-past eleven in the forenoon, and it was fully three o'clock in the afternoon when I was called to the examining room. By that time I was so benumbed with cold that I could scarcely speak in reply to the rough old doctor, a practitioner of the town, who examined me. He was very deaf, and shouted at me in tones like that in which some rough men speak to a horse.

He alarmed me not a little when, after I had replied to one of his loud commands for me to speak up, he roared out, that " it was all nonsense to say I was suffering from typhus," and he declared that I was attacked with ague, lumbago, and rheumatism. Then he ordered me in the same tone to get up-stairs and go to bed at once, and remain there until I was told to rise. Cheerful, wasn't it? after being doctored for typhus.

The examining-room attendant showed me the way up-stairs,

and into a room labelled " Non-infectious Diseases Ward." There were only four open iron beds here, and three were apparently in use, but the occupants were not lying down, but sitting about the room, when I was ushered in among them. I was directed to a bed at a window overlooking the busy town, at the furthest side from the fire-place. I there lay down in such a state of pain, illness, and depression of spirit, that I did not seem to care what became of me now.

As I thought of all my dreams of overseerships! all my vain glory of preferment seemed very small to me now! Consumed with thirst and pain I would have given all I ever had for a draught of the pure spring water from the " Lady's Well " at Merlin Brae. During the long sleepless first night, and my wakeful nights after, as I lay tossing, and sometimes half dozing, the longing for home and friends I might never see again, gave shape to my half-waking dreams, and brought crowds of vision faces of those I loved and longed for!

At last one of these night visions or dreams, call them what you will, awakened hopes of happiness, and spoke of joys to come! For, on one of these wakeful nights I had dozed off, I dreamed that I was looking from a window out on what seemed a wintry scene! and my thoughts were, I felt in my dream, of the girl I left behind me in what was considered then the Far North, and I concluded if I did not recover, and that if I found a grave beside the Wear, neither my friends nor she would ever learn my fate, as I had had no opportunity to advise either her or them of my illness, and now was unable to write. I saw in my dream that as those sad forebodings passed through my mind, snow began to fall in light fleecy flakes, and the whole space I was looking on became very radiant with silvery moon-beams shining through the snow screen!

As I gazed in rapture on this beautiful appearance, whose glory was not like anything I have ever seen on sea or land, because of its indescribable splendour, which yet did not dazzle or overpower my dreaming sight, and as I looked I saw, still in my dream, the face and figure of her on whom had been centred my sad waking thoughts! This appearance seemed to float earthwards through the beautiful snowy fleecy shower, in white flowing garments, such as angels wear!

This may appear very fanciful to some persons' minds, but it is a true description of a beautiful dream, and when I had seen who the dream-figure represented, the vision fled, but its impression remained, and I think did me more good than all the doses of medicine I got in that hospital, as I did not despair of recovery after this, for hope revived within me, and whispered to me we should meet again. I left the hospital after being there three weeks, but before a week was gone thereafter I had a severe relapse, and had it not been for the help of a good English Samaritan, who introduced a famous Scotch doctor named Spence, I should not have been alive to tell this tale. This doctor was a sadly-dissipated, drunken old soul, but a complete master of his profession, for he, with three visits, bleeding with leeches, steam bathing, and administering the contents of three bottles of some herbal preparation, made by himself, set me on my feet so far.

In the course of ten days I was able to find my way per train to Newcastle, and from there took passage on a small screw steamer to Arbroath. This was the first screw-propelled boat I ever saw, and the passage across from the Tyne was a caution to me never to venture on board such a small crank craft as a passenger again. I believe the wee boat would not be more than eighty or ninety tons burden, and how such a plunging, tumbling-about toy lived through that heavy sea, and reached port in safety, astonished us all. We were only four passengers, three grown-up persons and a boy. We were all four of us sick the most of the time, after crossing Shields bar. While coming down the Tyne, where the water was smooth, we were congratulating ourselves on the prospect of a fine pleasant voyage; but when we got to the bar at the river's mouth, the boat made a sudden plunge, and lurched so far to port, as overthrew the cabin table, and sent all that was on it, including the lamp, to the floor, also throwing over the small stove, and making a general mix-up, which the captain or mate came and straightened out again, fixing the table, stove, and lamp so as to prevent similar mishaps on the passage. The steamer was quite new, and the fittings of the cabin had not previously been secured to withstand the kind of sea running this night, so on we went, the boat being tossed about like a cork, with the screw every now and again thrown out of the water, and the engine racing at a great rate.

Of course none of us knew what the noise of the engine running off meant, but after the sickness left us, and when again and again the wicked wee boat lay over, and threw her stern up, one of us would sing out to the others, "Hing in there, there she goes! They are winding her up again!" we really believing there was some clock-work arrangement about the staggering little craft. However, the long-looked for dawn broke, and we saw the distant range of the Grampians lighted up soon after by the wintry morning sun, and about nine o'clock in the morning, casting anchor, we rode there until the tide flowed high enough over the harbour bar to allow our small boat to enter the miserable harbour as it then was, for a manufacturing town such as Arbroath. We got ashore, and procured some food and refreshment. Then each went his separate way, and although our several homes were all in the same county, I have never once met one of those fellow-travellers since.

When I reached Merlin Brae my mother was much astonished, and looked rather alarmed at my appearance, as the previous illness, and the tossing about, and want of sleep the night before, made me look very bad. Indeed, I had a slight relapse of the old complaint, and the New Year of 1856 was a week begun before I was completely convalescent.

Thus ended the period of my life spent in country farm service, an occupation which is, or ought to be, the healthiest and happiest of all human callings, an occupation in which there is the greatest variety of food for the contemplative mind, where the procession of the seasons on their never-ceasing annual round are an endless joy to the seeing eye, and the heart which adores and loves all that God has set before it in the marvellous arrangement of this beautiful world.

Yet, as with all things which frail and imperfect man has set his hand to, farm service had many drawbacks—drawbacks which need never be in that or any other occupation. I hope that during the forty years that have come and gone since I last whistled at the plough, many improvements have been effected to sweeten the lot of the sons of the soil!

I have now completed the reminiscences on my life up to 1856; as that date ended my personal connection with rural life, but the "Old Boy," in the year of grace 1901, is still in the body. For the long period of forty-four years he has been actively engaged in city life, first for many years in the service of railway companies, and latterly as a steamboat agent. In these vocations he has travelled many times over the length and breadth of Bonnie Scotland and Merry England, and has also visited, as a commercial traveller and steamboat agent, the Green Isle, which the natives thereof rejoice in calling "The gem of the sea!"

He likewise wishes to inform his many kind friends, who have so very handsomely supported him by so liberally becoming subscribers to this volume, that should they like the present sample of his experiences, and ask, like poor Oliver Twist, "for more," he will gladly respond by publishing, at no distant date, the second volume of the "Reminiscences of an Old Boy," being autobiographic sketches of railway and commercial life from 1856 to 1901.

Finis.

Poems and Lyrics.

From time to time, during a long life, I have amused myself by (as Burns said) "stringin' blethers up in rhyme." The following verses have graced the Poet's corner in many newspapers both in Scotland and England. "Grigg's Studdy," and one or two other pieces in the collection, now appear for the first time in "guid black print":—

> "Some rhyme a neebor's name to lash;
> Some rhyme (vain thought) for needfu' cash;
> Some rhyme to court the country clash,
>   And raise a din.
> For me, an aim I never fash—
>   I rhyme for fun."

POEMS AND LYRICS.

Grigg's Studdy; or, the Tailor's Dream.

A TEAPOT TRAGEDY.

Grigg's studdy, tak' note an' tent weel fa't I mean,
It wisna a room, but a big yird-fast steen,
The name spell'd wi' twa d's means tae plain countra folk,
A smith's workin' anvil, or big hammer block;
An' the hauf o' Grigg's studdy lang stude to be seen
Near the Aul' Road 'at crosses the burn Reekit Leen.

Fan a youngster I've listened tae legend an' story,
O' ghaists, wraiths, an' spectres, in a' their grim glory!
The sichts whilom seen, dancin' roond that whin steen
Wer' a caution tae a'body late oot at e'en!
The tailor an' 'prentice wi' lay-brod an' guse,
Wha aft "whuppit the cat" in ilk big farm-hoose,
Aften swarfit an' swat as they passed by the place,
At the mirk midnicht 'oor, fan the unearthly race
Wer' believed tae be oot an' stravagin' abroad!
Atween Grigg's studdy green an' the knowe o' the road!

A'e day Tailor Rob o' the Heich Winkle Burn,
Had been "whuppin' the cat" i' Greyrigg for a turn,
Had laid by his steel bar, as the clock chappit aucht,
An' hied him ower tae the cheenge-hoose o' Wat Wabblestraucht.
Meetin' there wi' some cronies in a twa-handit crack,
Social joy it grew bricht, as the nicht turned black,
But Time winna wait for tailors nor nane,
An' the 'oor sune cam' roond fan Rob had tae be gane.

Settin' oot fizzin' fu', as ye may easy guess,
He maun pass the weird studdy, be he fu', be he fresh,
Rob forgot o' the ghaist, bein' three sheets i' the wind,
But he sune had tae rue sic a lapse o' the mind,
Wi' his back tae the breeze, blawin' fair frae the wast,
Fan the dreid howm wis reached, he met sic a blast
O' blue brumstane reek, did his stoot hert appal
As Lang Strang o' Lochroyal struck the deid 'oor o' twal!
The puir tailor stude, nail'd tae the uncanny spot,

A' his hair stude on end, like the horns o' a goat!
Hauf Rob's vision seen there, I'm no' fit tae declare,
His after-tale bein' as wild as his ain touzled hair.

He said ower the Howm spread a glamour that grew
Ilka moment mair fearsome for mortal tae view!
It wisna sunlicht, nor the mune's siller ray,
But like deid caun'le-licht warnin' man's deein' day!
A halo owerarchin' that bonnie green howe,
Wis nae bow o' promise tae Rob's vision now.
It wis biggit o' serpents an' satyrs sair mix't,
A' girnin' at Robin 'tween this warld an' the next,
Their cruel-luikin' een, an' their fire-forkit fangs,
Boded nocht but despair on an ill warld's wrangs!
As Rob stude sair stricken, dumfoondert, aghast!
Fa't a' this wid mean in his mind he owercast,
A voice thro' the lift soondit eldreich an' eerie,
It said, "Robin McRory, this nicht ye'll no' weary!"

At a smith's blazin' forge i' the background wis seen,
Wi' his haund on the bellows stood Grigg o' the steen,
Rob's picter o' Grigg mak's a wonnerfu' sicht,
As he kythed to his vision that wanchancy nicht;
He said Grigg's tow'rin' hicht wis twa ell an' a hauf,
(Ca' canny noo' Rob, or ye'll e'en mak' me lauch!)
Grigg wis braid in proportion, so continued Rob's story,
Wi' ilka limb strong as an aiken tree hoary.
But, O, for Grigg's face, 'twas a blank in Rob's tale,
It wis a' covered ower wi' some weird magic veil!
Big, broon toom e'e pieces, like burnt holes in a blanket,
Gied gleams o' fire flaucht aye as Grigg's hammer clankit.

Roond this ruifless smiddy hung sae mony queer things,
Their rehearsal by Rob my short memory dings,
In Rob's dream the masked smith seemed a keen antiquarra,
For a pattern hed he o' Auld Adam's first barra;
He'd a bit o' the cudgel gied Abel's death-clour,
Fan his ill brither, Cain, yon day dang him ower;
The strong leather apron at Grigg ca'd his ain,
Wis ance worn daily by auld Tubal Cain;
'Tis said this auld apron was gi'en tae Grigg gratis,
As the hide of a watter bull caught in Euphrates.

Balaam's cuddie's branks hang up on a cleek,
Fa't thae branks cud hae tauld, had they ha'en pooer tae speak!
Micht hae sattled the hash 'mang the ministers noo,
An' 'greed the savants 'boot the auld cuddie's moo.
Frae twa-legg'd cuddies' chatter some respite micht hae gien's
An' stapt the din-deavin' clatter o' toom-speakin' machines;
Grigg's auld-warld list wad tak' ower muckle time
For me tae complete it, in prose or in rhyme.

It appears that a getherin' o' goblin an' ghaist,
Broonies, witches, an' warlocks, that nicht held a feast,
At Grigg's inveetation the ghaist o' the steen,
Tae clear up some dark subject—whate'er that micht mean.

First o' the inveetit cam' a kelpie frae Noran,
Wi' a ghaist on his back, he cam' doon the glen roarin';
An' Grigg o' the steen, wi' a gowl an' a gape,
Himsel' gied a walcome tae auld Thrummy Cape.

The Birkenbuss spectre, sae dreary an' dreich,
 Cam' sune linkin' up wi' the ghaist Bonnybreich,
Neist wis heard far besooth soondin' through Lownie Slack,
The Dickmont-Law Piper frae "durance" come back.
Syne a hill-wanderin' spunkie wi' lowin' caun'le an' ruff,
Trotted in wi' the fiddler frae the back o' Be'fuff,
An' Bell o' Baderdie, that auld-warld witch,
On a brume-stick rade in through this nicht black as pitch,
A witch frae Lochroyal cam' wi' Madge o' the Muir,
Three carlins far-famed for dark deeds be ye shure.

Then neist cam a broonie, baith gruesome an' grim,
Yet baith guid an' yusefu' tho' I canna name him,
He brocht a freend wi' him, garr't e'en Robin smile,
'Twas a daur-deevil cat frae the banks o' the Nile,
Nae dummy, nor mummy, noo juist mind ye that,
But a livin', ance sacred, Egyptian cat.
A cat! Dae ye speir fat wis't tae dae there?
Noo, haud ye a wee, gin ye've patience tae spare;
It wis weel believed then, that tae lay the foul thief,
An' fair fley him hame! fling a cat in his teeth!

This weel-meanin' broonie hearin' o' this nicht's splore
Had hied him awa' tae the far Levant shore,
Meetin' auld Pharaoh's shade near the Great Pyramid,
Broonie borrowed this cat. Imphm! Aye, so he did!
Jalousin' 'at Robin micht land in a fix,
Broonie meant wi' the cat tae stop Beelzebub's tricks,
In a winged palanquin they had flown ower the faem,
This wis lang ere the era o' motors or steam.
So the cat's stowed awa' oot o' ilk bogle's sicht,
Wi' the broonie tae witness the ploys o' the nicht.

Auld Clootie cam' hindmost, an' awesome like tyke,
An' wi' ten younger deils took his seat on the dyke,
Syne Grigg o' the steen, rackle handit an' stark,
Ca'd oot, "Noo, ma freends, lat huz a' get tae wark."
Black Bell said, "Hear, hear!" the young deils cried "Hurrah!"
Ilk ghaist gied a grane like a sair roupit craw,
Clootie up on the dyke, being the chairman-elect,
Cock'd his tail in a curl, on his huifs got erect,
Gied a hoast an' spat fire, then quo' he—"Lat me see,
Oor first question noo is the subject o' 'T!'
A complaint has come doon tae my regions below,
Hoo that foreign yerb it'll sune work me woe.
"Tea-drinkin', forsuith, gin it spread ower the worl',
Then fareweel tae the power I haud fast by the barrel,
Fiercely ettled, I'll yet fecht for my whisky," said Nick,
"For o' a' the aids tae perdition 'tis the wale an' the pick."
Hornie added—"There's a knicht o' the needle an' sheers
Gets through twa unce o' tea i' the week, it appears;
The stuff's said tae cost three hauf-croons the pun',
Sic a slap tae my whisky, ye'll grant it's nae fun."
"Guid trogs!" cried Auld Thrummy, "an' that is nae lee!"
Wi' a screich bawls Hornie "Did ye say that tae me?"
"I beg yer heichness's pardon," cried Thrummy in fear,
Wha'd forgat 'at the father o' leears wis there!
Syne the hill-wanderin' spunkie spak up wi' some vim,
"The tea-drinkin' tailor! I'll sune show ye him."
Noo, Grigg, wi' his hammer gied the studdy a bang,
The rebound o' that lick roond a' the hills rang!
Believ't if ye like, or deny't gin ye can,
That whin-steen gied a soond like a white iron pan!
"Megstie me!" shouted Nick, "wha's this noo I see?"
Quo, Bell, "That's the tailor, whase wife drinks the tea."

Syne the Deil's advocate, wi' Rob's case in hand,
Nigh the great blazin' forge took his loon-luikin' stand.
He questioned Rob close, tryin' tae get him tae tell
If ony ane he kent, but Rob's wife an' himsel',
E'er meddle't wi' tea, that abominable stuff,
Rob near lost his temper, aye, an' near took the huff.

Syne Hornie himsel' ance mair took command,
He conjured Rob tae answer, at ance an' aff-hand,
Cloot threatened an' scoldit wi' muckle deil's snash,
Ilka wink frae his e'en wis a fire-fizzin' flash;
Syne the Dickmont-Law Piper, wi' chanter and drone,
He raised sic a skirl as thrilled Rob tae the bone.
Fan ance the din ceased, Hornie heckled Rob sair,
His ettlin' it seemed tae get Robin tae swear—
Tae forego his tea-drinkin' an' smash the tea pigs,
Or expect never mair tae be seen on earth's riggs.
Puir Rob, sair bemang'd i' the cluiks o' that crew,
Had tae promise compliance—what else could he do?

Roond an' roond him danced witches, warlock, and ghaist,
But the unholy music was ney tae Rob's taste,
Tae the Deil's "Delvin Side" frae the fiddler Be'fuff,
It was ill keepin' time tae the faur-travell'd stuff.
The big blazin' forge, and Grigg's pincers reid het
Garr'd this dreamer think sair o' the scaums he micht get;
They micht mak' the puir man rue the day he wis born,
An' leave his auld Eppie a widow forlorn,
Rob, near his hin'most gasp, noo bethocht him tae pray,
But his tongue missed the words he ettled to say!

But juist at the moment Rob thocht wis his last,
The Hirple-Howe cock gied his first mornin' blast;
Oh, sic a stramash syne took place on the green,
An' the black cat played lick Clootie's horns atween—
In a sicht-blindin' flash o' blue fire an' het ase,
Witches, warlocks, and ghaists, disappeared frae the place;
An undergrund thud shook the muir wi' a crack,
Black Catterthun rair'd, an' grey Turin rair'd back,
Some tods 'at were harryin' a ruist i' the glen,
They gat sic a gliff—ilka tod tint his hen,
Wi' their tails oot o' curl, an' a fear yelpin' whine,
They scoored hame tae their holes, an' were sune merry hyne.

So puir Robin won free, but hoo he got hame
He never could tell, this pairt o' this dream;
Fan the wan winter sun o' neist mornin' luik't in,
Through Rob's wee cot-hoose window, the sicht wis a sin!
For there on the flure-heid lay the tailor outspread,
O' the wife's cheeney tea-set he had just made his bed.

Sad, sair, an' disgruntled, puir Eppie cam' ben,
Yet speirin' fu' kind for this warst o' wild men—
"Oh, Robin," said Eppie, "ye've gien me sic a fricht,
Oh, I think I'll ne'er c'ower this terrible nicht;
Ye've shurely been dreamin' o' some awfu' like things
I' yer visions, when sleep gie's the waukin' sowl wings."

Fan Robin luik't up, his e'en blinkit an bleared,
Syne a sicht he'd sair socht tae his vision appeared,
It wis nae mair nor less than the cheeney tea-pot,
Ance a braw bridal present his guidwife had got.
The sicht raised Rob's dander, as red rags dis a bull,
He jumpit bauk hicht, an' lat oot a lood yowl!

"Ha! ha!" shouted Rob, "ye pooch-reivin' pest,
Come doon, dagon, ye beggar, an' share wi' the rest,"
So a clip wi' the laybrod Rob gied the braw pot,
A' in flinders it fell 'mang the previous lot!
Syne a proverb became the impartial condition,
When objects o' hate gae tae hale crokonition;
Gin the chief o' the lot hisna come tae the test,
Syne doon maun come dagon tae share wi' the rest.

Nigh twice forty towmonds an' twenty hae gane,
Since Robin an' Eppie lived up i' the Glen,
Their like's never seen noo the hale country roond,
An' tea costs raither less than three hauf-croons the pund;
Atween whisky an' tea there's a lang-standin' quarrel,
It's ill guessin' whilk's upmost—the tea-pot or barrel!

But we've a' a guid guess which herb it sud be,
We'll ne'er dream o' deils gin we only drink tea,
Lat tailor Rob's dream an' his actions that morning,
Be to a' Bacchanalians a terrible warning.

The Child's Warning.

"Out of the mouths of babes and sucklings thou hast perfected grace and praise."—Matthew xxi, 16.

A handsome, merry, dark-haired boy,
His mother's love, his father's joy,
Played in a room where stately grace
With cultured taste adorned the place.

While I sat waiting the boy played on,
He seemed quite happy though all alone;
On looking up he saw me there—
Stepping softly round he sat by my chair.

Then turning on me his lovely eyes,
He gazed through his curls in mild surprise;
In dulcet tones, as from bells of gold,
Looking straight in my face he said, "You are old!"

"Oh, not very old, dear boy," said I;
"When very old," quoth he, "you will die."

O! reply so stern! I paused for breath,
Hearing one so young speak of time and death;
But I oftimes think since that evening mild
That a prophet may speak through a little child.

May it not be? When so lately come;
From God's fountain of life, the spirit's home;
So sweet, so pure, and so undefiled,
Is the fearless faith of a little child.

In Memoriam.—Lord Airlie.

"Who battled for the true, the just,
  Be blown about the desert dust!
Or seal'd within the iron hills!"—Tennyson.

A deathless fame to Airlie's name,
  Our stricken hearts beat high;
Old Scotland gains another wreath
  Of flowers that cannot die.

The noblest knight of chivalry,
  Chief of an ancient name,
Upheld on Afric's distant veldt
  Old Scotland's deathless fame.

So here upon this grey old hill,
  Beside his fair domain,
We build this shrine, sacred to love,
  To immortalise his name.

The rambler 'midst the sweet spring flowers,
  Where Esk's fair waters stray,
May linger here in pensive hours,
  As falls the evening grey.

While snow wreaths bind the Grampian range,
  While stars beam from the sky,
While time rolls on, and seasons change,
  His name shall never die.

Though marble waste, though bronze will rust,
  And granite sure decay,
Men will revere his honoured dust,
  Till time's last dying day!

Sandy M'Sleek,

THE AULD CLOCK DOCTOR.

A COUNTRY PARISH SCREED.

A cobbler of clocks he lived in yon wud,
In an auld-warld hoose that for ages had stude,
The quaintest auld figure e'er seen in thae pairts,
Playin' mony queer cantrips in life's game o' cairts.

His lang solemn phiz had a look sour and grim,
Ane wad thocht desolation had settled wi' him.
He wore a white neck-cloth and blue wincey coat;
His weskit an' knee-breeks were o' the same lot,
Blue leg an' fur hose—aye, an' clear-buckled shoon,
While a red-tappit bonnet aye happit his croon.

He mendit time-keepers—or pretendit to dae,
Surely thae things were stauncher at that time o' day,
Or 'tis perfectly clear, Sandy's roch handy wark
Wid hae sent them agee, far mair frae the mark,
Some fouk thocht him daft, but bide ye a wee,
O! nae fule was Sandy, tho' pawky was he.

'Tis no' his clock-cleanin' I care to repeat,
But the record he made as a sham and a cheat.
In the auld kirk laft he sat—no' very far doon,
But he aye left the seat ere the ladle cam' roon',
'Tis no' easy guessin' what aye gard him rin
Ere the elder got near him to gather his tin.

But Sandy M'Sleek had a dainty bit plan,
For self-glorifyin' the cunnin' auld man;
He clinkit his pennies a' in a wee pock,
And at times toddled doon to the manse wi' his troke,
Gin he met wi' the parson, he posed as a saunt,
Fu' o' lang-nebbit phrases and hypocrite cant.

To recount half his antics, were ower lang to tell,
But for tricks and conceit he carried the bell,
Sic a twa-faced auld sinner was there never seen,
O' an ill speck for youth or for onything clean.
He lived at a time when, it noo seems to me,
The morals o' auld Scotland had slippit agee,
When he and sic like, and a coarse upper ten,
Were the warst o' examples for maidens and men.

I ance got a fricht wi' the weird-looking bloke,
My hert it dunts yet when I mind o' the shock,
On yon hillhead we met, near the iron-yett swing,
As I crossed to the skule on a morning in spring;
There the emerald tassels hung frae a larch tree,
Made a sun-dazzled curtain 'tween Sandy an' me.

I got but a glisk o' the lang scranky neck,
'Neath the red-tappit bonnet maist stannin' erect,
A'e look did for me, as so weel dae I mind,
I took tae my heels and I ran like the wind.
Syne I met a broon, a big hairy baiste,
He looked as if speirin' the cause o' my haste,
Then trotted awa' at his ain canny shog,
At the time I thocht him some man's collie dog.

That mornin' hoo aften I've mindit it weel,
When I met wi' the tod as I ran frae the deil;
The day is lang past, years fifty and fower
Have circled aroond wi' their sunshine and shower.
That tod's likely deid, and Sandy's at hame,
Afar yont the reach o' oor praise or oor blame;
I houp he socht mercy, and was freely forge'in;
May his like never mair in this warld be seen.

Lines composed in Fitz Park, Keswick.

Once more by Gretna's crystal stream,
   I charmed and silent stand,
Enchain'd as in a Heavenly dream,
   Within this mountain land.

Ten years bygone, I saw the place
   When hill and dale were gay,
All bathed in summer's golden sheen,
   And nature's rich array.

The years have passed, their fates have flown
   On time's swift-hastening hours—
Their seasons come, their seasons gone,
   With all their floods and flowers.

This day on Derwentwater deep,
   The misty hills look down;
From Skiddaw's height a storm doth sweep,
   O'er mountain, vale, and town.

Yet wheresoe'er my footsteps stray,
   Is nature's brilliant guise;
Though flowers may bloom but for a day,
   Here beauty never dies.

Earth's floral mantle, far outspread,
   In crimson, blue, and gold—
Each tint and shade a jewel made,
   The loveliest forms unfold.

Within those arbours of delight,
   And shade of stately trees,
Serenely falls the ambient light,
   Mid songs of birds and bees.

Heart-thrill'd, with sylvan music here,
   A bard may sing or pray,
When sunset gilds yon azure sphere,
   Or dawns the newborn day.

Exalted on the muses' wings,
   Here fancy takes her flight,
And higher than yon hill top sings
   Up to the gates of light.

This earth-created paradise,
   This beauteous, calm retreat
Presages fairer worlds than this
   Beyond the mercy seat.

Farewell, sweet Gretna's winding stream,
   With Derwentwater clear;
Your charms aye form an endless theme
   For pilgrims wandering here.

Through wooded vale by hill and dale,
   Ye sing as on you go,
Till on yon endless ocean's swell
   Thy mingling waters flow.

So let us pray, when on life's breast
   Flows our last tide of time,
Borne on that wave to reach a rest,
   Eternal and sublime!

That Four-Legged Stule.

The stule is auld-farrant, a queer-lookin' relic,
Its seat being made o' a mountain-ash stick,
Wi' its legs a variety, an' no a' a'e length,
It has no claim to beauty, but I wat it has strength.

A'e leg is o' aik, and twa made o' ash;
The fourth is a brume-stick; the stule never cost cash.
Oor great grand-da made it, a hunner year gane,
An' gin that stule cud speak o' the times it has haen,
Sic a leal hamely story that auld thing cud tell;
When by weans in their glory it was ridden pell-mell,
Ower and ower the flure-heid when in their daft glee,
The stule was oor horse, or oor dog, dae ye see?

To mony a thing handy we cud it convert,
Trailed alang on its face, we aft made it oor cairt;
When well load wi' toy traffic, sae earnest we'd plod,
Just like the auld carriers wha then held the road,
And hoo mony wee lassies, auld-fashioned and droll,
Hae buskit that creepie and made it their doll;
Wi' a leg by ilk, twa wad learn it to walk,
And fu' kind cox'd it on wi' their ain baby talk.

Ay, four generations hae used that auld stule,
Pairt fifth now sits on it, and he is nae fule;
Fu' o' queer vagarie, he licks a' that's ga'en,
An' he fair dings them a' as a mimic o' men;
In antics prolific, ilk purpose to gain,
The stule is a steam-boat, his tram-car, or train.
And wheesht, speak laich, an' listen wi' grace,
Juist tak' ye a keek at that three-year-auld face.
In big wonner's name, noo, what's wee Charlie at?
But haudin' a prayer meetin' wi' the stule an' the cat!

In the very neist meenit he's on a steam-boat,
Wi' the stule for the bridge, he's noo fairly afloat;
And he the bold skipper, sae jolly and free,
Wi' his hand on the rail keeps a bricht weather e'e.

He can ease her, and stop her, go astern, or ahead,
A' his signal's been learned by his ain Buird o' Trade,
For, like the prayer meetin', it's a pantomime,
Yet tae his infant mind it is simply sublime.

To you it seems silly, douce elderly man,
Yet ye ance was a laddie, mind that, gin ye can;
And if ye canna mind it, I pity your case,
Sair hardened and squeezed ye've been in the race.
If ye dinna see, aye, as weel's understan',
That the wee laddie aye is the dad o' the man;
Frae the far fount o' life wee lassies and them
Come tae play oot the drama in this warld's game—
A gey ravell'd hesp, to man's finite mind,
Is the queer complications we hear ever find;
But he'en faith, like wee toddlers, we a' may win thro',
Whaur a guid endless life waits for baith me an' you.

The Barber's Opinion.

"A prophet is not without honour save in his own country, and in his own house."—Matthew xiii. 57.

The saying is true as first uttered by one,
Wha kenn'd a' our failin's, and what is in man,
By the Galilean Lake, though uttered langsyne,
And often repeated its truth winna tyne.

In men's jealous natures, their pride and conceit,
Be they Jew or Gentile, the sma' or the great!—
Right often the truth o' this maxim I've proved,
By casual acquaintance and friends I have loved.

A'e instance, I mind o', to me seemed so queer,
I hae thought o' its drollery for mony a year;
A'e nicht after gloamin', I had sitten doon
In a sma' barber's shop in a Scots borough toon,
There waitin' my turn, I got on the crack,
Wi' that man o' soap-suds there thrang at my back.

Among ither questions, I happened to speir,
If he kenn'd so and so, and I named a friend dear—
Ou, aye! he kenn'd him, and I added then,
Is he not a credit and king among men;
With bright penman skill, wit, and genius seen,
Writes wi' pathos and power, you ken what I mean?

The barber looked up, gie'd his razor a grip,
Cock'd his heid to a'e side wi' a curl on his lip—
I canna weel tell or describe how he did it,
"Humph!" says he, "him, he's a bletherin' ediot."

O! that answer transfixed and doubled me up,
I sat sair dumfoondered, and felt like to drop;
Then a councillor came in, to him I referred,
The barber's queer answer, I newly had heard.

That councillor laughed loud when he heard it explained,
And said I should ken that no honour was gain'd
By genius or merit within a man's hame,
Save wi' siller, or some other warl-worthy name—
Get siller! mair siller, by hook or by crook,
Then no barber nor weaver will gie the doonlook.

Possess gowden guineas, or even get the name,
O' earth's fadin' treasures, 'tis a' quite the same,
Though your heid be as hollow's a meal-girnal toom,
And your sowl could be held in a hen's steekit thoom,
Though false as old Satan, and fu' o' deceit,
At kirk or prayer meetin' gae take the chief seat—
If never found out, you are baith guid and clever,
And you may get a saint's place on this side the river.

But, "I rede ye tak' tent," on life's far winter side,
All your schemes are seen through, for they winna there hide,
In the clear licht o' Heaven is laid bare every sin,
If you live by deceit, then ye winna get in.

Tibbie:

AN OLD VILLAGE WORTHY.

O! Tibbie was a rare ane, of that there ne'er was doot,
When she gaed hence she didna leave her marrow hereaboot;
In life she wore her winceys sans gaudy tinsel braws,
Her thick-soled shoon were weather proof frae a' the winter snaws.

No queer fantastic headgear did Tibbie's broo adorn,
The fearfu' hat vagaries noo wad hae roosed her bitter scorn.
For many a year, wi' eident cheer, she speiled Pitscandly's braes;
Kept her wee cot-house a' by hersel' through lonely widow days.

At three score an' ten she held her ain, and aye was steeve an' stark;
At morn or eve could tramp a mile, an' aye fit for the wark.
No fuss nor freaks had Tibbie, sae fearless, frank, and free;
A' ane to laird or beggar man wad Tibbie's answer be;

Yet neither rude nor insolent, for modest was her mein;
Her crisp replies straucht to the point, a' said what she did mean.
A sterling type of womanhood, best of the peasant band;
High-soul'd, of independent mind, pride o' our native land.

When garrulous gossips' slanders did reputations kill,
The envenomed spite o' leein' tongues, our auld friend like't ill.
Her a'e short answer, aye the same, to defamation's tale,
Was Gude grant that story binna true, just keep it tae yersel'.

In this weary warld four-score years, puir Tibbie wachled through,
Twice forty summer suns she saw licht up yon Grampians blue.
Then at length the ca' that comes to a', fell on her watchfu' ear,
She hail'd the message welcome, for faith had cast out fear.

When autumn winds were soochin' lown, on a lovely sunset eve,
And the wan leaves were drappin' doon, was Tibbie called to leave.
Her body, low on Lemly's bank, now rests in yon kirkyaird;
There rests the dust o' a' her kin, below the rank green swaird.

Her record's clear from any blot, and free from every taint,
But friends and neighbours miss'd her, who Tibbie's worth weel kent.
Her faithfu' life, her peacefu' end, the annals of her time,
Shed a halo round her lowly cot, her deathbed made sublime.

The Commercial Traveller of all Ages.

Let me mention a trade of a class in particular,
They are rife on each road and conveyance vehicular,
Their trade is ancient as Adam—aye, some weeks before that;
It was known in Nod's land where Cain his wife gat.

When men began barter, or to buy or to sell,
The travelling commercial was know there quite well;
So down through the ages, to reach our own day,
Come the sellers by sample, commercials are they.

The pedlar and hawker in far eastern lands,
Old records declare, were the Ishmalite bands.
From pedestrian and packman to the stage with six horse,
The aristocratic bagman held on his high course.

No small drink was he in his own estimation;
There's none left like him now in our Democratic nation.
'Midst my wanderings so wide o'er the fair British Isles,
I oft meet those trade agents and bask in their smiles;

In special enjoyment I laugh at their fun,
When the leisure hour comes, and the day's business done;
When deep words of wisdom some sage member speaks,
I oft get the answer my barren soul seeks.

Their beliefs are as various as the goods that they sell;
Sometimes samples unfiltered from Truth's crystal well;
But oh! for their politics—mention them not—
They are mixed of all sorts, like a Heilan' kail pot.

Yet all hail the commercial, his true enterprise
Is the great civiliser, progressive and wise;
Many men, many minds, yet true brothers all,
By commerce all empires must aye stand or fall.

Toast our British commercials—the kings o' their kind,
Where true progress is made by the conquests of mind;
While Britain's broad standard floats o'er the broad sea,
There the British commercial forever will be.

When wild war's dread tumult in all lands shall cease,
And the whole world bends to the blessings of peace,
Then commerce and freedom universal shall reign,
And the world's federation unbroken remain.

K

Flowing Years—And Whither.

"Deal gently with us, O ye flowing years,
  Let frosted locks and failing breath be long
Before they chill us by prophetic fears
  Of that dread moment which shall end our song."
—J. W. Nicoll.

Let me say amen to that poet's prayer,
  When returns my natal day,
May cheerful hope my youth declare,
  Though my locks bloom like the May.
Now time seems short which in youth seemed long,
When my aim was high, and my arm was strong,
Then my world rang sweet with life's siren song,
  And joy came with each new day.

From a cradle cot to an old man's chair,
The mutations of time cross here and there,
And seventy years with their toil and care,
  Bring nigher the hour all dread.

Were this world all there is to share,
With no thought beyond this life to spare,
No wonder, if joy with us were rare,
  In the flight of the silent years.

Yet a better, a brighter, a purer life we may gain
When for us hath ended all things mundane,
  We may join an immortal sphere,

There live true life in a fairer clime,
Unclogged by the trammels of earth or time,
Where no sorrows e'er sadden the joys sublime,
  Of the denizens dwelling there.

In that blest home of pure delight,
Where no circling sun disperses night,
To endless day, and in garments white,
  The redeemed from this world awake—

Awake to the joys awaiting there,
The fulfilment of hope, of faith, and prayer,
Though of service and sorrow here all had a share,
  Whate'er this life's lot has been.

While the swift-moving cycles of time roll on,
When of friends bereft, and we feel alone,
While mere earthly hopes perish one by one,
  Or fade in the ambient air;

May each spirit mount up as on eagle's wing,
To join in the new song which seraphs sing—
That song of love to our Saviour King,
  With the hosts of the ransom'd there.

Then farewell earth, and all things sad,
In the Master's home we shall be glad,
A certain reward for all labour we've had,
  Is the heritage waiting there.

A Summer Morning.

There's a mantle of mist round the mountain top,
  Bright glints o' the sun in the glen,
With a scud o' storm on the green fell's slope,
  And the sang o' the burn i' the den.

There's a glisk o' sweet wind in the June-green tree,
  And health in the balmy air;
There's a Heavenly grace in the morning free,
  That calls for men's praise and prayer.

There's the mystery of life in commercial strife,
  For victims fall thickly there;
'Mid the city's din, shouting who shall win,
  With howls of hope and despair.

Thus from day to day, as time passes away,
  While the millions are born and die;
The enigma of life unanswered for aye,
  Will be ever the wherefore and why?

A Summer Evening by Loch Ryan.

When fields and flowers are fresh and fair,
Good is the balmy summer air,
  Culhorn's woods among;
Where blackbirds and the mavis note,
With love tones from the stock-dove's throat,
  Pour forth the grand bird song.

The umbrageous glade, the sylvan shade,
By oak and ash and fir-tree made,
  To shield earth's floral gems.
These jewels stud the wild-bird hames,
Those screen the sun o'erhead.

That orb hangs low o'er Coreswell's side,
His amber gilds Lochryan's tide;
  And from the glowing west
The light serene of closing day
Now glorifies yon upland way,
  And crowns the eastern breast.

A gloamin' mist Glen-Ap has kist,
That dew-drop mantle swathes its breast;
  And fair o'er bank and brae,
In loveliest twilight charm is drest,
  This land o' laigh skies grey.

And wandering near those waters clear,
  This glorious night in June,
When sea and sky as one appear,
  Bright fancy seeks yon farther sphere
  Beyond yon stars and moon;
While birds and flowers are sleeping here
  Through summer's midnight noon.

Yon light for lonely mariner,
On ocean far his guiding star
To mark the line where breakers are,
  Or, land upon the lea,
In this hour shows no wintry war,
  Upon the slumbering sea.

But changeful is the restless tide,
And calm for aye will ne'er abide,
  So like the life of man;
Incessant troubles, strife and pride,
  Mar life's mysterious plan.

Yet beacons bright, with Heaven's own light,
  Are radiant on life's shore,
To guide men's steps to wisdom's height,
  And bless them evermore;
While faith gives courage in the fight,
  We conquer o'er and o'er.

An Easter Song, 1894.

There is cheer in the thought for hearts worn and weary,
  Nearly whelm'd in life's turmoil and sorrow,
To hope from each day, though its vista be dreary,
  May arise a better to-morrow.

Afar, by the valley of doubt and despair,
Stands the covenant-angel, who aye watches there—
  He's our guide to the river of life—
On its evergreen banks shine the bright goal of prayer,
  There ends all the heart's weary strife.

May God freely grant, when at life's closing hour
  Our hearts feel their last faint emotion,
Strong faith to sustain, and hope-giving power,
  To embark upon death's lonely ocean.

No call shall surprise the soul strong in faith
That follows the Man who first conquered death,
  And escaped from the bonds of the grave.
Let a loud Easter hymn resound through all time
  To the only One mighty to save.

When death of the body is life's jubilee,
And the unfettered spirit from bondage set free
  Hath the undefiled heritage found,
With the palm, and the laurel of faith's victory,
  All the loved and the ransomed are crown'd.

A Summer Evening by the Almond.

How good was the eve of that July day,
   As I walked 'neath yon stately trees;
Light clouds were afloat on the twilight grey,
   And soft was the moorland breeze.

There the golden gleam of the star of love
   Arose in the east, as I moved along;
It's beam shone faint through a leafy grove,
   But hushed was that hall of the warblers' song.

The night closed around, as it ever comes,
   To rest the weary and soothe the sad,
When the children of toil, in their wretched homes,
   May sleep and dream, and in dreams be glad.

All glorious night! o'er this mighty zone
   The angels pass on their journeys far,
Our dark night dwellings they oft wait on,
   And are first to greet our morning star.

Yes! bright angels may come to homes of sin,
   On their errands of love to the sons of earth,
And oft, 'mid this world's confusion and din
   Speak comfort and peace at a troubled hearth.

Re-awakening good in a smitten soul,
   When crossed and tossed on life's tempest rude,
Who of passion strong may have lost control,
   Till they almost question if God is good.

May each lovely night and morning clear,
   Ever bring like joy to all hearts of men,
As moves in me as I wander here,
   By Almond's winding, bosky glen.

English Lakeland.

By hill and dale, by lake and vale
  Of this romantic land,
Doth tender grace and beauty dwell,
  Enshrined on every hand.

Fair Windermere and Kendale vale
  Half circles Morecambe Bay,
Their verdure fann'd by soft sea gale,
  As falls the closing day.

Rare beauty lures the wandering feet
  Of him who lingers here;
And new-found glories ever greet
  The stranger's eye and ear.

All tempest torn, time worn, and grey,
  Yon solemn mountains stand,
Where Wordsworth wreath'd the poet's bay,
  To grace his native land.

By Rydal Mount and Grassmere Lake,
  Hark! how his echoes swell!
For purity and manhood's sake
  They ring o'er flood and fell.

Afar, by Derwent's winding sheet,
  Laid low in death's alloy,
The dust rests of that poet sweet,
  Who sang the Farmer's Boy.

His robe of song adorns yet
  Those mountains evermore,
And tell in stanza fitly set
  Of cascades of Lodore!

Then see where Scott with wizard pen,
  Tells his enthralling tales,
He adds a grandeur to the glen,
  And charms yon fairy dells.

Coniston vale we may not miss,
   No! no! that shall not be;
This world-fam'd spot of loveliness
   Nurs'd kings of minstrelsy!

Here Coleridge lived, and poesy's themes
   He penn'd, both terse and clear;
Expressing more than mortal dreams
   To poet-hearts so dear.

Here also walked that king of song,
   Chief in Apollo's train,
Late Laureate, in a courtly throng,
   In our lov'd monarch's reign.

Those giant minds immortal stand
   Beyond the ridge of time;
Their songs thrill hearts in every land,
   Like Seraph strains sublime.

How sweetly bright this evening light,
   Illumes the lone lake lands;
And limpid streams from rock-bound height
   Roll on to Morecambe sands.

Soon midnight pale in dewy veil
   Shall wrap the sleeping flower,
And I must fly this bonnie vale
   When springs to-morrow's hour.

To mingle 'mid the haunts of men,
   Where worrying care and strife
Harass the mind and fog the brain,
   And blight men's business life.

But sunbeams bright I've gathered here
   Shall light my winter through—
Blest sights and sounds in mem'ry clear
   Keep fresh as morning dew!

Among the Hills and Isles.

How good it is to feel the grace,
 The secret, soothing powers—
While we, with Nature face to face,
 May scan the opening flowers!
When, far from towns and tumults,
 We spend some peaceful hours.

What joy supreme! when heart-care free,
 'Neath sunlight in full glow;
When summer beams dance on the sea,
 Or autumn's soft winds blow.
Oh! blissful time! Joy pure and free!
 Which poets only know.

To see the grandeur o' the isles
 Round Scotland's ancient shore;
Where surging seas cause saline breeze,
 Health-giving treasures pour;
And birds' and bees' sweet melody
 Add music to the hour.

Or, cradled deep 'mid lofty hills,
 Where fair Loch Lomond smiles;
See water nymphs by mountain rills,
 Green banks, and lovely isles,
With Alpine range and mountain swell,
 Fair glens, and dark defiles.

Here chieftains bold in ruder time
 Strove hard for pride or fame;
And reived or fought, nor counted crime,
 To win a warrior's name;
While cruel revenge took wider range,
 Where'er their watch-words came.

A nobler sight now meets the light
 In this our modern day,
When every tribe and clan unite
 By loch and mountain grey,
And bonds of peace and concord bright
 Tie down the deadly fray.

The Grahame's pale ghost, M'Gregor's shade,
 In silent wonder stand,
For wild Colquhoun in peace lies down,
 MacLean has dropped his brand;
And other clans their peace have made,
 And joined the loyal band.

Now white-robed peace o'er all the hills
  Bless days of busy men,
As Nature's charms by wars sad ills
  Are ne'er destroyed again;
No slogan calls the clan to arms
  From clachans in the glen.

Here, fairer now may morning spring,
  And grander fall the night;
Here, sweeter music birds may sing,
  And men have more delight;
Here God and Nature's worship bring
  From great to greater height.

Cissie, V.R.
A BANFFSHIRE POST MESSENGER.

At the thought I now utter the derisive may laugh,
And the scoffer may flout my word-photograph;
A' ane to me is their censure or blame,
As my sang speaks in praise o' a canty auld dame.

Although Cissie be auld, sunburnt, and broon,
Most sensible head-gear she wears on her croon;
No' a thing like a riddle, fantastic wi' flooers,
But a gaucy protection frae sunsheen or shooers.

In Her Majesty's service she does her pairt weel,
Baith sturdy and hardy, like steel to the heel;
No humbug wi' Cissie, but fair hornie oot,
Though her oot-rig be no' quite the fashion I doot.

I kenna her story, nor I carena to ken,
Her quaint, striking figure my fancy has taen—
It kyths like Humility, Patience, and Faith,
So calm and content like for life or for death.
O! a famous auld buddy, I think, weel I wat,
Is the Longmanhill post in her Corean hat!

Ye braw lasses, sae uppish an' daintily drest,
Wi' the figments o' fashion so sorely opprest,
Tak' a pattern frae Cissie, an' dinna deride
An example like hers, free o' a' empty pride.

'Tis far better than braws, or bloom o' the skin,
When the hale figure tells o' contentment within;
And the goal o' life's purpose we a' may win at,
Though we trudge ower the leys in a Corean hat!

Thanksgiving.

Thou God of love and God of grace,
  Thou friend of youth and age,
Hast blest my lot in every place,
  My life at every stage.

Sustained by Thine unfailing arm
  Through helpless infancy,
By strangers nursed, kept still from harm—
  Supported aye by Thee.

In boyhood's free and careless hour,
  Ye sent a faithful guide
To shield me from temptation's power,
  While flowed youth's rising tide.

In manhood's proud and vaunting day,
  When sin sought to beguile,
Thy precepts proved my strength and stay,
  When pressed by Satan's wile.

Now past for me time's noontide,
  With life's eve drawing nigh,
Still let me in Thy faith abide,
  To cheerful live or die.

Death's harbinger is failing breath,
  It whispers numbered days;
Oh, what is life bereft of faith,
  In all God's wondrous ways.

The wealth men seek to win or keep,
  Through sore exertion strained,
With mind harrassed and banished sleep,
  Is nought but sorrow gained.

The hero's prize, a laurel leaf,
  Or rousing poet's lay,
Yet poet's bays and world-wide fame,
  Will quickly pass away.

But joy may be securely stored
  For the soul if so inclined,
And riches hid in Heaven adored,
  Await the immortal mind.

All glory give our God of grace,
  Our Friend from youth to age,
His presence fills all time and space,
  All life in every

GLOSSARY

OF

SCOTTISH WORDS AND PHRASES,

With their English Meanings.

Aft, after.
Antiquarra, antiquary.
Ane, one.
Awesome, frightful-looking.
Ance, once.
Ain, one's own.
Auld, old.
'At, that.
Atween, between, or betwixt.
A'e, one.
Acht, eight.
Aiken, oaken—an oak tree.
Awfu' awful.

Bauk hicht, high as the rafters or bauks, or cross roof beams.
Blawin' blowing.
Branks, a kind of wooden or iron bridle.
Brume-stick, broom-stick.
Brunstane, brimstone.
Burn, a small stream or brook.
Barra, barrow.
Bemazed, overpowered.
Broonies, brownies—fabled, supernatural; beings not generally malvolent.
Bogle, bogie, or ghost.
Besooth, to southward.
'Boot, about.
Canmily, cautiously.
Chappit, struck the hour.
Chaumer (Aberdeenshire), chamber, farm-servants' sleeping room.
Cheeny, china-ware.
Cronie, boon companion.
Crockonition, complete smash.
Crack—twa-handed, a conversation between two.
Caun'le licht, candle-light.

Clankit, a metallic sound.
Catterthun, two hills or fells some miles north of the scene of "The Tailor's Dream."
Cheenge-house, licensed public-house
Carlins, old witches.
Clootie, Satan in person.

Dancin', dancing.
Dang 'im ower, knocked him over.
Deid, dead.
Dyke, the fence of a field or stream.
Deein' day, dying day.
Disgruntled, out of temper and distressed.
Dumfoonder'd, dumfounded.
Dings, beats.
Dreid, dread or fear.
Death-clour, death-blow.
Daur-deevil, dare-devil.
Doonlook, frowned on.
Dickmont-Law piper, a man who played the Scotch bag-pipes, and whose ghost figured in "The Tailor's Dream."
Delvin-side, the name of an old Scotch dance tune.
Dagon, an allusion by the Tailor to the god of the Philistines.
Doon, down.

Eldreich, wild or unearthly sound.
Ell, an old Scotch measure, nearly corresponding to a yard.
Eerie, dismal or frightsome.
Ettled, intended.
Ettlin' intending.
E'en, eyes.

Fan, when,
Faem, sea foam.
Fat, what (Aberdeenshire Scotch).
Fizzin' a noise as of cooling hot iron.
Fire-flaught, sheet, or white lightning
Fley, to frighten.
Fleg, to frighten.
Freend, friend.
Frae, from.
Forsuith, forsooth.
Fecht, fight.
Fiddler befuff, a worthy who frequented merrymakings, and played the violin.
Forgat, forgot.
Forket, forked.
Flure-heid, the floor of a room.

Gaucie, sagacious-looking, or graceful.
Guse or goose, the Tailor' flat iron.
Ghaists, ghosts, spectres, or spooks.
Gane, gone.
Gied, gave.
Gilravish, waste, unthrift.
'Greed, agreed.
Gien, given.
Getherin' gathering.
Granes, Groans.
Gruesome, Shuddering.
Guid, good.
Garr'd, compelled.
Gin, if.
Ging, to go on, or going.
Gliff, a moment startled.
Grey Turin, a mountain near the scene of "The Tailor's Dream."

Hauf, half.
Heich, high.
Himsel' himself.
Haud ye, hold, or wait.
Huifs, hoofs of horses or cattle.
Heid head.
Huz, us.
Hoo, how.
Hoast, to cough.
Heichness, highness, as your highness' pardon.
Hirple Howe, a farm near the scene of the dream, from where the cock crew at dawn, which dispersed the midnight spirits.

Hin'most, the last, or in the rear.
Het ase, hot ashes, or pulverised cinders.
Harryin' robbing.
Hame, home.

I'mphm, aye or yes, sarcastic.
Ilk, each.
Ilka, every one.
Inveetation, invitation.
Inveeted, invited.

Jalousin' imagining.

Kyth, to appear.
Kythed, appeared, or came in sight.
Kenna, know not.
Knowe, a bank or brow in England.
Kelpie, a fabled water-spirit in the form of a horse.

Lat, let.
Lay-brod, lay-board carried by tailors whereon they ironed or smoothed new-made garments.
Loon luikin', guilty or thief-looking (loon meaning really in original Scotch, a thief. In Buchan or lower Aberdeenshire, the word is applied to indicate young boys only).
Leevin' living.
Lee, a lie.
Lift, the heavens.
Leears, liars.
Lang Strang, the bell of Lochroyal (Forfar) gifted to the burgh by a benefactor of the name of Strang.

Mirk, dark.
Megsty me! an ejaculation of surprise.
Merry-hyne, fled afar, and out of sight.
Mune, moon.
Moo, mouth.

Neist, next.
Neive, fist.
Noran, a mountain stream in the vicinity of the Dream scene.
Noo, now; the present time or moment.
Nocht, nought.

Ooncanny, dangerous.
Oot, out.
Oor, hour.
Oot-by, out of doors.
Oondergrund, underground.

Prentice, an apprentice learner.
Pooch-reivin' pocket robbing.

Quine, queen or young female.

Rackle-handed, strong, or iron-handed.
Riggs, ridges of land.
Rair'd made a roaring noise.
Ruifless, roofless.
Roond, round.
Reid het, red hot.
Ruist, Hen roost.
Ruff, neck frill.
Roupit, hoarse.
Ramfoozled, stupified.

Shuir, sure.
Stravaigin' wandering about.
Steel bar, the Tailor's needle.
Sillar, silver.
Studdy, a Scotch blacksmith's anvil.
Stricken, sore struck.
Spak' spoke.
Soondit, sounded.
Splore, an entertainment.
Snash, ill temper and harsh words.
Sune, soon.
Skirl, the scream or the skirl of bagpipes.
Speir, to ask.
Soond, sound.
Steen or stane, stone.
Stark, without fear.
Sair, sore.
Sichts, sights.

Scaums, Singeing deep, or scalds.
Scoor'd ran at a swift pace.
Screich, scream, or shriek.

Tauld, or in Aberdeenshire Scotch, taul', told.
Thud, a knock or blow.
Tods, hill foxes.
Tint, lost.
Towmond, a twelvemonth, or a year
Too'rin' hicht, towering height.
Twa, two.
Tea-pigs, a set of tea-ware.
Tent, to pay attention.
Three sheets i' the wind, more than half drunk.
Touzled, in confusion.
Toon, empty.
Tae, to.

Uncanny, dangerous-looking.
Unce, ounce.

Vim, vigour or energy.

Workin', working.
Whilom, sometimes.
Whin-steen, whin-stone—a water-worn, very hard boulder stone found where furze or whins are common.
Wer', short for were.
Winna, will not.
Wha'd, who had.
Whuppit, whipped.
Wid, would.
Wanchancy nicht, that ill-fated or unfortunate night.
Walcom', welcome.
Wark, work.
Warlocks, males corresponding to females or witches.
Wauken, to awaken.

Yird-fast, earth-fast.
Yird, earth.
Yerb, herb.
Yafu', old Aberdeen dialect, meaning awful.
Yusefu', useful.

SYNOPSIS

OF

THE FIRST TEN CHAPTERS

OF

Railway and Commercial Life:

BY THE AUTHOR

OF

"*REMINISCENCES OF AN OLD BOY.*"

Memorials of Railway Service, Railway Travel, and Business Life, in the Towns and Cities of the United Kingdom, and in Ireland, during the 42 Years ending Nineteenth Century.

CHAPTER I.—End of Crimean War.—Return of remnants of troops.—Supposed close of the Eastern Question, and some short reflections on the wicked uselessness of the War just ended.—Application for a situation on the Aberdeen and Scottish Midland Joint Companies' Lines of Railway.—First interview with the General Manager of a Railway.—Satisfactory nature of that meeting with a gentleman, truly one of Nature's mould, and with no nonsense about him.—His career and sterling character.—Description of the Lines now forming the northern portion of the Caledonian system, with part ownership by the North British Company.—Dubton Junction, and my turn of night watching.—Sleeping on a night watch, and how to keep awake.—A startling June night visitor.—Not certain at first sight whether of Celestial, Territorial, or Infernal origin.—The mystery cleared up before the night mail arrived.

CHAPTER II.—A train on fire, and how I fared at the extinguishing of same.—Description of staffing railways in the north in the fifties —Some instances where newly-appointed Guards and Stationmasters forgot their identity, and assumed airs and authority in the most ridiculous and droll manner.

CHAPTER III.—Opening the wrong points, and what came of the blunder.—I get shifted to another Station.—My new Superintendent, a disagreeable crank.—His Successor the very opposite.—More anecdotes.—The humorously-absurd expectations of some of the Public as to Railway Service and liability.—Electric Telegraphy and public inquisitiveness.

CHAPTER IV.—Man's inhumanity to man exemplified in the case of my third Chief, or Stationmaster, under whom I served.—Royal luncheoning, and perfervid loyalty on the occasions.—Donati's Comet, and the magnificent appearance thereof.—A big Railway Fight between our Company and the S. C. Coy. at Perth.

CHAPTER V.—The close of the difficulty between Scottish North-Eastern and Scottish Central Railways.—Amalgamation of Caledonian and Scottish Central Lines, also North British and E. and G. Lines.—The Winchburgh Accident, and its effect on the E. and G., then the joining of the Edinburgh, Perth, and Dundee and Fife Lines with the North British.—Narrative of my own experiences.—The General Manager's prediction, which has been only partially realised.—Offer of more pay at another Station.—Declined for various reasons.—A search for missing goods, and result.—The Volunteer Movement; its rise and progress described generally.

CHAPTER VI.—Memorials of Railway Service on the old S. N. E. from 1856 to 1860-61.—The great gale, 3rd October, 1859.

CHAPTER VII.—The Card-Sharpers on the Railway, and their victims. —Trial of the Gang at Aberdeen, and Conviction and Sentence.—The Snow-storms of 1860-61.—Closing days of Railway service at Stonehaven, and my departure for Peterhead as Agent for Pickford & Coy., of London.

CHAPTER VIII.—Landing at Mintlaw for Peterhead.—A short History of Pickford & Coy., my new Employers.—First impressions of Peterhead.—Opening of the Railway Extension.—A would-be popular Parish Minister.—His special sermon on the Opening of the Completed Line.—A would-be aristocratic lady wasted on a poor Stationmaster.

CHAPTER IX.—Business qualities of Peterhead traders as I found them in 1860.—Began my relations with them as I ended.—Satisfactory results.—My first experience of a Peterhead Hotel-keeper.—The landlady at the "Swan," a regular Tartar.—Close of Pickford & Company's contract.—My first and worst error in judgment, the loss of a first-class appointment in the south, a life-long regret.—Description of a night-march on foot of 31½ miles.

CHAPTER X.—First Literary Attempts and Successes.—Description of a Police Court case at Peterhead.—First year of Prizes by a Scotch Newspaper.—Reference to the Damios of Japan.—The American Rebellion.—Our Country's Influence, and breaches of the Laws of Neutrality.

FORFAR: PRINTED BY JOHN MACDONALD, "REVIEW" OFFICE.

Milton Keynes UK
Ingram Content Group UK Ltd.
UKHW050023070524
442290UK00012B/502